New Capitalism?

The Transformation of Work

Kevin Doogan

D0709313

polity

First published in 2009 by Polity Press

Polity Press
65 Bridge Street
Cambridge CB2 1UR, UK

Polity Press
350 Main Street
Malden, MA 02148, USA

ISBN-13: 978–0–7456–3324–4
ISBN-13: 978–0–7456–3325–1(pb)

A catalogue record for this book is available from the British Library.

Typeset in 10.5 on 12 pt Monotype Plantin
by Servis Filmsetting Ltd, Stockport, Cheshire
Printed and bound in Great Britain by MPG Books Ltd, Bodmin, Cornwall

The publisher has used its best endeavours to ensure that the URLs for external websites referred to in this book are correct and active at the time of going to press. However, the publisher has no responsibility for the websites and can make no guarantee that a site will remain live or that the content is or will remain appropriate.

For further information on Polity, visit our website: www.polity.co.uk

This work is dedicated to
Frank Doogan

Contents

Figures and Tables

Preface

It is more common to find a preface in the subsequent editions of a book which helps to update the discussion presented in earlier work. In this case the need to write a preface has arisen in the gap between submission of the manuscript and the printing of the edited copy. Truly the crash of 2008, that some have described a 'financial tsunami', marks an event of historical proportions and, in the short space before the printer puts the book to bed, a brief commentary on recent developments might be helpful. In the first instance it is necessary to answer the obvious question: to what extent does the present financial crash alter this analysis of new capitalism? There are several risks in this regard. At a time of market panic it is impossible to predict the extent of forthcoming global recession, or depression as the IMF suggests. One year after publication the world might look a very different place. The combined efforts of central governments and central banks, the 'global fire fighters' of the financial collapse, may have brought about some stability. Alternatively Margaret Thatcher's adage that 'you cannot buck the market' may, in the wake of billions of wasted dollars, yen, Euro and pounds, be proved on this occasion to be grimly prophetic.

While the form and consequence of financial collapse was not forecast by the analysis presented here I would suggest that the crisis is not some ghastly aberration in the normal running of the new economy. The financial crisis is a far deeper and more malevolent episode, but it can be situated in the recent history of financial speculation and over-production that is exemplified in the bursting of the dot.com bubble and most importantly the telecoms crash in the early years of this decade. Economists often refer to 'exogenous shocks' that upset the natural workings of the market, but to see the current crisis as some 'deus ex machina', a device to solve the narrative plot of the new economy, lacks credibility. A special report for *The Financial Times* on the 'World Economy 2008' has suggested that 'if the crisis can be contained, the outlook remains relatively bright. Benefiting from the forces of globalization, the world has enjoyed its most successful period for nearly forty years and abject poverty has been eliminated from swathes of the poorest regions, especially in Asia'.[1] The impression is given that if it were not for the excesses of the housing market, where commission-driven lenders created the sub-prime collapse which caused the international credit crunch, then the 'real economy' would have enjoyed continuous expansion and unprecedented wealth creation. Not only does this falsely portray the historical record of capitalism over the last four decades, airbrushing the return of mass unemployment, multiple economic recessions and growing global income inequality, it fails to get to grips with the structural weaknesses and imbalances at the heart of contemporary capitalism.

The present account of new capitalism stresses the growth, and until now, the triumph of neoliberal policy. Three factors are offered in the opening chapter to explain the rise of a more irrational and intensely ideological form of capitalism that emerged in the last quarter of the twentieth century, namely: deregulation, financialization and the reconfiguration of the ownership and control of corporations. With the events of 2008 these factors emerge with even greater explanatory significance. The collapse of Lehman Brothers is a particular case in which the greed of corporate executives provides eloquent testimony to the analysis offered here. In early October 2008 a US Congressional Committee called CEO Richard Fuld to account for the bankruptcy of the 158-year-old investment bank and also asked why he had earned $484 million in salary, bonuses and stock sales since 2000. A fairly unrepentant Fuld explained to the committee that it was company policy 'to align the interests of corporate executives and employees with company shareholders'. This speaks volumes about corporate leadership that has prioritized increasing share values over company profitability. In the midst of financial market collapse there is considerable interest in city bonuses, but there is little recognition that this practice cuts across Wall Street and Main Street. The corporate appropriation of wealth lies at the heart of what Robert Brenner has called 'the bubble economy' and suggests that the divisions between the so-called 'real economy' and finance are in this regard exaggerated.

Finally the analysis of new capitalism has emphasized the importance of ideology, and the way in which new capitalism is represented and understood. The debates considered in this book, whether in relation to pension reform, welfare restructuring, corporate mobility or labour market change, will only intensify. What is clear is that the current period portends a sea change in economic policy debate. Gideon Rachman of the *Financial Times* has suggested that the conservatism of economic ideas, evident since the early days of Reagan and Thatcher, has gone bust. He suggests a pendulum swing in economic thinking, ready to embrace state control, regulation and planning. If the utterances of world leaders are anything to go by, then he seems to understate the shift in the ideological landscape that has gripped policy makers. In this regard the prize for the greatest volte-face might well go to the French President Nicolas Sarkozy.

> A certain idea of globalization is drawing to a close with the end of a financial capitalism that imposed its logic on the whole economy and contributed to perverting it,' Sarkozy said. 'The idea that the markets are always right was a crazy idea.[2]

Hardly surprising in these days that several observers of the current scene have reminded us that 'those whom the gods wish to destroy they first make mad'. If we do not want to share the same fate it behoves those critical voices, who have long argued from the sidelines about a different set of economic priorities and the restoration of rationality in social affairs, to step up to the plate and come forward with alternatives.

Kevin Doogan
13 October 2008

[1] Chris Giles in *The Financial Times* Special Report, 10 October 2008 (www.ft.com/world-economy-2008)
[2] 'Sarkozy attempts to soothe the French on economy.' *International Herald Tribune*, 25 September 2008

Acknowledgements

It is usual to thank a large number of people who helped, encouraged or supported the author in the writing of the book. In this particular case I am struck by the fact that a number of people will probably be surprised to be included in the list of acknowledgements. But there are people who, out of sense of public service, collegiality or friendship, offered help, advice or data without fuss or favour, in ways that were more helpful than they would have expected. There are statisticians in Europe and North America who have greatly assisted in generating labour force survey data for the analysis of long-term employment. I was given access to data from the Bureau of Labor Statistics in the United States and I am especially grateful to Ryan Helwig, who supplied the Job Tenure Supplements to the Current Population Census, and Ray Mataloni, who supplied data from the Bureau of Economic Analysis on the operations of American multinational corporations. Jonny Johansen and staff at the European Labour Force Survey also supplied detailed statistics on long-term employment in the European Union.

There are a number of people with whom I have shared ideas or received help or encouragement. Special thanks are owed to Gary Bridge, Dick Bryan, Allan Cochrane, Brian Corrigan, Marcel Erlinhagen, Ray Forrest, Mike Gonzales, Alaister Hatchett, Matthius Knuth, Hilary Land, Ruth Levitas, John Lovering, Gregor MacLellan, Theo Nichols, Diane Perrons, Teresa Rees, David Shonfield, Gerry Stoker and Leah Vosko. I am greatly indebted to Peter Fairbrother, who read the whole work and provided extensive comments to guide its development. I was very pleased to take up the visiting scholarship at the School of Economics and Political Science at the University of Sydney where Australian colleagues listened with good grace while an outsider offered a different take on job stability and casualization in Australia. I am grateful to Emma Longstaff, the commissioning editor at Polity, for her patience, and to friends and colleagues in the School for Policy Studies at the University of Bristol, and research students on the Doctor of Social Science programme.

It is also commonplace to mention, finally, the nearest and dearest, and there is pressure to think of something appropriately grateful for the support that they have offered during the writing process. There is a risk that it turns out like a message to the backroom staff, who were heroic in their own way, and without whose help etc. etc. But it is probably best in this instance, simply to apologize. To say sorry for hogging the study, or for working late at night or early morning, but the biggest mea culpa is for the distraction. Sorry for the number of times that I have been asked a question and offered nothing other than a glazed expression as I chewed over the rise of the student labour market in Canada or casualization in Australia, while vaguely hearing background noise that requested me to pass the ketchup, clear the table or help with homework. With love and thanks to Alison, Michael and Liam.

Introduction

In the 1960s it was the young radicals who sang that 'the times they are a-changin'. Dylan's lyrics spoke to a range of protest movements concerned with the questions of the day, from civil rights to the Vietnam War, and to a radicalization that imbued the universities and workplaces with a sense of resistance and raised expectations of social and political possibilities. In subsequent decades 'the changing times' is a refrain that is taken up by preachers of a very different outlook. The proselytizers of change today are increasingly found amongst the sharp-suited government spokespeople, spin doctors, management consultants, business gurus, financial analysts and think tank experts, all flanked by an array of journalists and academic commentators.

In the 1960s Dylan sang of the aspiration for changes to be made by groups and movements while the current anthems present firms and workers as victims not as the agents of economic transformation. Today, the mantras of modern life depict change as the outcome of technological development and institutional restructuring that affects firms and employees, economies and governments. Competitive pressures are perceived to operate outside the realm of negotiation and regulation and they countenance only adaptability and flexibility of response. These are exogenous forces for change that are survived rather than harnessed. Survival is offered to those companies who can keep apace with the breakneck speed of technological innovation, who stay ahead of the competition and 'reengineer' to meet new market conditions. This is dehumanized progress, not the product of the great inventions of a second industrial revolution, but a seemingly alien transformation of society. Global forces, apparently outside the control of nation states, determine the pattern of industrial development and transform the fabric of society both nationally and internationally.

Over more than four decades it is possible to discern a narrative of social development that has evolved both politically and substantively and now embraces the idea of societal transformation. Earlier accounts of social change highlighted industrial restructuring within national economies. Daniel Bell's depiction of the rise of 'post-industrial society' in 1960s America was relatively modest in its ambition, pointing to a structural shift in the economy due to the growth of the service sector. Bell was reluctant to draw any wider sociological inferences and repeatedly warned against exaggerating the significance of technological change and the emergent notion of the 'knowledge economy'. Contemporary transformation is played out on a far broader canvas embracing global processes that transcend national boundaries, extending discussion from structural change to disruption of the life course, from institutional fragmentation to cultural practices and values and expectations. Many of today's commentators appear much less inclined to temper their accounts or to limit the significance of their observations. A world of change is presented increasingly devoid of any continuity with the past, in which the new is unprecedented rather than merely contemporary.

In recent times discussion of technological advancement and institutional adaptation has reached the point at which leading social scientists and high profile commentators have begun to entertain the idea of a 'new capitalism'. Richard Sennett's work on *The Culture of the New Capitalism* and *The Corrosion of Character: The Personal Consequences of Work in The New Capitalism* (Sennett 2006 and 1998) has been extensively cited in North America and Europe. In France Luc Boltanski and Eve Chiapello's account of the *New Spirit of Capitalism* has been hailed as a classic. The writings of Diana Coyle, on the *Paradoxes of Prosperity,* subtitled 'Why The New Capitalism Benefits All', has received the heavyweight endorsement of Paul Krugman. The term 'new capitalism' may have come into use because 'the new economy' is a neologism whose currency rose and fell with the dot.com boom-and-bust cycle of the 1990s. The 'knowledge economy' is widely used but is confined to particular sectors of the economy most associated with technological innovation, whereas new capitalism captures a broader sense of evolution within, and of, society. More importantly for present purposes, accounts of new capitalism stress particular transformative forces, mechanisms of adaptation and relational change.

It is suggested here that the mutation from the post-industrial narrative to new capitalism has been facilitated by a specific representation of the transformation of work. Adaptation in the world of work is the transmission belt linking institutional change and technological inno-vation, on the one hand, and the contemporary experience of moder-nity on the other. Given such explanatory significance, interest in new forms of employment and labour market restructuring is no longer confined to labour economists and industrial relations experts. Labour market transformation has moved to centre stage in all those accounts that suggest that developments in contemporary society are *qualitatively* different in character and significance from their antecedents. Thus David Harvey considered labour market flexibility as one of the key conditions of postmodernity. Richard Sennett's account of work on the new capitalism considered 'change in the modern institutional structure which has accompanied short-term, contract or episodic labor'. Manuel Castells' *Network Society* described a new mode of development in contemporary society based on the new informational technologies which lead him to conclude 'that we are witnessing the end of the salarisation of employment'. Ulrich Beck's account of *The Brave New World of Work* anticipated the 'Brazilianization of the West' which envisaged regression to some semi-feudal form of artisanal labour. Zygmunt Bauman described contemporary capitalism as pro-foundly individualized due to changes in the connections between capital and labour which globalization has frayed and rendered tenuous. In this way the post-industrial narrative has evolved to the point at which new relations between capital and labour are imagined. *The term 'new capitalism' thus covers a literature which considers societal shifts based on a more tenuous connection between employers and workers.* To bear witness to the end of salaried employment as Castells seeks to do, is to offer a prediction of truly Cassandran proportion, envisaging the meltdown of the contractual structures that underpin the wage system. Castells does not follow the logic of his position which could point to some post-capitalist labour process, as he remains committed to the idea of a new mode of development *within* capitalism. His idea of network society therefore sits easily in this new capitalist framework, even though he, and many others, do not specifically adopt the term.

There is a looser meaning of new capitalism and wider literature that transcends the post-industrial debate, which suggests that the contemporary transformation of work has given rise to *new employ-ment relations* characterized by a much greater sense of precariousness and insecurity. This perspective presents the decline of traditional industries which offered stable and secure jobs and their replacement in a new 'contingent economy' that offers temporary, part-time and casual work, much of which is based on flexible contracts. Writing about *The Disposable American* Louis Uchitelle (2006) suggests that until the 1970s 'the great majority of the nation's employees held long-term jobs'. Economic changes in subsequent decades have been characterized by mass layoffs in the US economy and endemic job insecurity. Where companies previously valued loyalty and rewarded long-term commitment, downsizing has swept across corporate America throwing large numbers out of work with radically different employment consequences. Uchitelle suggests that voluntary or involuntary job changing was previously associated with improvements in wages, while today's job changers experience a fall from grace into the lower reaches of the labour market with much poorer working conditions, wages and benefits. In considering Europe Bonoli argues that there are 'new social risks' of poverty and family instability, which express a new set of contingencies associated with the post-industrial labour market, although his account stresses that these are disproportionately experienced by new social groups such as lone parents, young people, the less educated and those with low skills or old skills (Bonoli 2007). Both accounts stress the qualitative shift in the experience of contemporary capitalism expressed through labour market change and the new relations of employment it generates, even if they will have different emphases on who will be the principal casualties of this process.

New Capitalism: A More than Sceptical Critique

The critique of new capitalism presented here challenges the ideological, methodological and empirical basis of the societal transformation thesis. Its case is partly based on the strength of the statistical evidence which points in the opposite direction to new capitalist narratives. Thus the labour force survey data from North America and Europe discussed here shows that job stability has *not declined* and that long-term employment *has increased* in many sectors of the advanced economies. Moreover it argues that certain forms of labour market flexibility which are said to portend the decline of traditional employment, such as part-time employment, have largely facilitated the integration and retention of labour, rather than leading to the labour market 'disaffiliation' that many have suggested. It is argued here that the institution at the heart of the vision of new capitalism, the labour market, is far less adaptable and responsive to change than many commentators imagine. The accounts of new capitalism therefore rely on a transformation mechanism which, if studied carefully, appears surprisingly resistant to adaptation and unable to substantiate relational change in society. Therefore the labour market is not the perfect medium through which technological and institutional processes can generate new employment relations. It serves as conductor of pressures for change, but also acts as an insulator against them. Consequently, if the labour market is not the medium through which all forms of insecurity and precariousness are generated, alternative explanations have to be provided.

In challenging these perceptions of new capitalism the following discussion is not confined to a critique of the positions advocated by the high profile public intellectuals mentioned above, or a questioning of those perspectives which suggest that new industries, which offer precarious employment, have replaced traditional employment and secure jobs. This critique recognizes that perceptions of a sea change in the relations between employers and workers are widely held by economic commentators and have come to receive broad public acceptance. Such views are reinforced in a variety of media from academic literature, to business journalism and the policy statements of governments and think tanks. Many of these views inform public perceptions which are expressed in everyday settings, from the pep talks of schools' careers advisers, the canteen discussions of newspapers, to the neighbourhood conversations of the work experience of families, friends and acquaintances. Therefore the critique offered here seeks to go further than a scepticism towards public perceptions and conventional wisdom. It attempts to explain how the situation has arrived in which a substantial gap has emerged between many public perceptions of changes in the world of work and a more objective assessment of change and continuity in the labour market and wider economy. Thus it will not only challenge the concepts but, by examining the rise of neoliberal managerial discourse, it will also seek to explain how the ideas have developed and spread internationally since the 1980s.

It is necessary to examine ideology and to some extent methodology in the new capitalist narratives because a distinct set of ideas about transformative changes in society are represented in particular ways. This is no small challenge because the evolution from post-industrialism to new capitalism is linked to a greater abstraction in the representation of change. 'Knowledge', 'innovation', 'informationalism' and 'networks' are nebulous concepts, difficult to pin down and resistant to close scrutiny, while globalization is a term whose usage is perhaps inversely proportional to the precision of its meaning. This new world is characterized by its ethereal qualities, its weightlessness and its virtuality. Transformative forces have a ghostly quality – all motion and no matter. Previous periods of capitalist development were powerfully symbolized by steam engines, aircraft and motor cars, and large factories where people had 'real jobs' because 'they made things'. The new capitalist Zeitgeist is captured in global processes, in the instantaneous transfer of capital, planetary flows of information and communication, interconnection and networks. Devoid of the materialist iconography of the past the current conjuncture lacks definition and lends itself to negative description – what it is not, rather than what it is. Thus the new period of development draws its distinction from antecedents in a retrospective characterization of the present, variously described as post-industrial, post-Fordist or post-modern. Therefore it is suggested, that the ideology of new capitalism rests upon an idealized representation of contemporary society. In leaving behind the concrete realities of industrial society the discussion of new capitalism is 'dematerialized'. Diana Coyle describes a 'weightless world', Charles Leadbetter describes the contemporary experience as 'living on thin air', while Bauman talks of a 'liquid modernity'. This is a mode of representation that eschews the 'static' world of structures and organizations for the dynamic turbulence of processes and flows which imbue social relations and identities with a sense of fragility and impermanence. It is a mode of representation that inclines discussants to specific ways of thinking about social development. It privileges discontinuity and it 'over determines' the role of technological change. In stressing the significance of global flows of finance, and the integration of capital beyond the national economy, it greatly exaggerates the mobility propensity of non-financial capital and neglects the continuing significance of the role of the state in the workings of market economy. These are not weaknesses or imbalances in approach but the inevitable consequences of a world view that is conceptually dematerialized.

Rematerializing Social Development

New capitalism cannot be usefully critiqued within its own terms, by offering an alternative set of abstractions. Idealized accounts of societal transformation are best challenged on more concrete empirical and methodological terrain. The present critique of new capitalism is driven by an attempt to *rematerialize* an understanding of social change, to substantiate the working of the economy and thus to reveal the 'machine in the ghost'. It will seek to regain the conceptual balance between the 'out there' and 'in here' dynamics of social development. The perception of markets and globalization as exogenous forces beyond government reach emphasizes the sense of powerlessness expressed by nation states and the greater exposure of companies and workforces to 'blind' market forces. The heightened impact of exogenous forces is tied to the sense of state withdrawal from economic life and the demise of public protection. In these neoliberal times, policy rhetoric takes as read the benefits of deregulation, privatization and liberalisation. New capitalism is as much post-Keynesian as it is post-industrial. Therefore the discussion presented here will seek to 'reinstitute' the market by identifying the critical role of social regulation and government intervention, which have effectively been airbrushed out of new capitalist surmising.

Furthermore, there is a second sense in which globalization and technological innovation are seen as 'out there' in that they are perceived as self-sustaining processes that run on their own momentum according to their own logic. Global economic integration feeds off itself, driven by the self-expansion of capital flows, while informationalism is driven by the higher pursuit of knowledge. *The transformativity of contemporary technological and institutional processes thus relies on the extent to which they are perceived as autonomous and 'disembedded'.* In the new capitalist narrative transnational companies are tenuously connected to localities, independent of government control and subsidy, self-reliant and self-sustaining. The new informational mode of development is driven by intellectual curiosity rather than government policy or even commercial interest. In the face of such abstraction the present work seeks to endogenize the internationalization of trade and production, and to assess critically the determinants of technological innovation and its impact on the world of work.

Methodology and ideology are linked in particular ways in accounts of new capitalism. In deriving relational change from the impact of new forces transforming the world of work the labour market is seen as the repository of technological change and corporate restructuring. However, one of the ironies inherent in the new capitalist approach is that a post-industrial view of the world is rooted in an industrial or 'productionist' understanding of labour market change. It would appear logically consistent for the post-industrialists to conceive a labour market largely determined by service provision, yet this is curiously absent in the literature. The discussion remains preoccupied with the corporate restructuring in manufacturing and this helps to explain the profile of concern with downsizing, outsourcing and corporate relocation. *If the salience of each and every sector was proportionate to its contribution to employment trends a very different picture of*

contemporary capitalism would emerge. For this reason alone the transformation of work considered here is not confined to manufacturing
and related industries, nor does it assume corporate restructuring in
manufacturing provides a template for others to follow. Schools are
not run like chemical plants and steel production finds little resonance
in the provision of hospital services. If the task is to consider societal
transformation based on new employment relations it seems necessary to have a similarly broad understanding of the transformative
impact across the spectrum of activities, including public and private
employers, covering production and service sectors. Therefore, given
this broad institutional framework, the present discussion is not situated *within* the workplace in the sense that it is not concerned with
production or labour process or micro level analysis of work organization. Given the analytical significance of the representation and
perception of change it will consider managerial discourse rather
than management practice as such. In taking a more comprehensive
overview of forces driving and constraining labour market change the
transformation of work is considered in relation to changes in employment patterns, casualization, contingency and job stability, dualism
and polarization in the workforce, occupational and compositional
adjustment and changes in welfare benefits, such as health benefits
and social security and pension provision. These are the factors that
are said to constitute the new patterns of engagement between
employers and workers and should therefore define the scope of the
transformation of work considered in the following chapter.

It is the contention of the work presented here that the labour
market responds to *two imperatives* and is determined by the requirements of both production and reproduction, broadly defined. Only a
minority of the labour force is engaged with the immediate needs
of production. In the advanced economies there are more people
employed in education and health services than in manufacturing.
Indeed, health services made the second largest contribution to job
creation during the so-called 'new economy boom' in the United
States in the 1990s. *Moreover, many of the compositional changes in the
workforce and adjustments in employment patterns are not explained by the
rise of 'the flexible firm', but by the growth of jobs in education, health, and
social service provision.* Since a large component of labour power is allo-
cated to 'its own' welfare and reproduction it seems remarkably blinkered to consider only the immediate requirements of production.
Labour power is itself a commodity whose value relates to the social
investment in its education and welfare, both in the present and for
the next generation of workers. Thus the labour market cannot be

reduced to some derivative status, passively responding to the changing needs of production, it is argued here that the labour market must be moved centre stage and theorized 'in its own right'. In putting labour market change under the spotlight different dynamics emerge which both drive and constrain adjustment in the level and form of employment. The reproductive requirements of the economy are less variable, evolve over a long time frame and engender job stability alongside changes in the form and composition of employment. Independent of both technological change and corporate restructuring, there are other factors at play which generate new employment patterns which require consideration in any account of the transformation of work.

In this attempt to rematerialize contemporary social development the role of the state is emphasized for several reasons. In the first instance it is necessary to reclaim the market as 'an instituted process', to use Polanyi's term, as it is commonly misrepresented as some stateless realm of economic interactions. As suggested above, the transformativity of technological and institutional processes is tied to the sense of the perception as autonomous or disembedded processes. Therefore the reinsertion of the role of the government in the contemporary capitalism is a necessary counterbalance to those perspectives whose statelessness serves to exaggerate the pace and scale of societal transformation. Secondly, independent of the corporate sector, the state is an agent of labour market transformation in its own right and has contributed to occupational and compositional change and to the rise of new patterns of employment. Thirdly, it is necessary to establish the significance of welfare regime change and the decline of public protection systems as a factor in the rise of social insecurity and precariousness. However, the state has a low profile in many contributions to the new capitalist literature. Where it does merit consideration it is perceived as the victim of corporate restructuring, powerless in the face of global market forces. Linda Weiss and others, in contrast, have considered 'the myth of the powerless state' and suggested that the transformative capacity of government is not confined to tax raising and public spending, but is evident in a range of direct and indirect interventions in the economy (Weiss 1998). Such an approach to governance is adopted here as it offers a better understanding of the expansion of welfare alongside changes in the form, provision and finance of welfare services.

The decision to cross the border between production and reproduction, taking in employment and welfare, has tactical and strategic dimensions. Since the mid 1990s intense concern has been raised by prospective changes in health provisions, non-wage benefits and pension schemes. These have major implications for the length of working lives, retirement income and insurance coverage for workers and their families. In the European Union the major focus of industrial unrest has been public spending reform, and changes in benefits and retirement provisions. More generally, in North America and Europe social provisions have been adjusted to achieve labour market outcomes, just as recruitment and employment practices have responded to alterations in public and private benefit provisions. In these circumstances to narrow inquiry to the 'productionist' concerns of technological change and corporate restructuring would ignore many of the determinants of labour market change as we move into the 21st century.

In recasting the discussion to include production and reproduction, not only is a better understanding of the factors that drive and constrain employment market change offered, such a breadth of perspective provides a better test of labour market and welfare outcomes. It is suggested here that job insecurity might be usefully reconceptualized as a broader social insecurity arising out of the representation of globalization and the restructuring of welfare regimes, rather than an outcome of technological innovation and job obsolescence. The role of government is thus highlighted and not sidelined. This is 'an age of insecurity', to quote the *Guardian* journalists Atkinson and Elliot, in which anxiety and uncertainty are to some extent 'manufactured' for both political ends and economic advantage. Pierre Bourdieu insisted that precariousness (précarité) is a new mode of domination in contemporary capitalism (Bourdieu 1998). It is suggested here that public perceptions have been distorted by the systematic exaggeration of the mobility propensity of capital, the impact of technological change, the decline of job stability and the rise of contingent and temporary employment. This may seem crude and to present the idea of systematic exaggeration is to risk the charge of conspiracy theory. Mindful of the damage inflicted by such an accusation the account of the narratives of post-industrial change, presented in the opening chapter and in the conclusion, has distinguished systematic exaggeration from conspiracy. Conspiracy reeks of plotters working behind the scene to hoodwink the masses. The discussion of new capitalism considered here suggests instead a 'confluence of narratives', as a set of ideas articulated in different milieux by a variety of commentators across a political spectrum of views. This spectrum of views ranges from neo-conservatives to libertarian anti-capitalists such as Michael Hardt and Tony Negri. Indeed one of the more controversial observations of the present discussion is *the presence of left wing harmonies in the neoliberal chorus*. Perhaps out of a sense of sympathy for the oppressed and downtrodden, or a loss of faith in their capacity of working people to defend or advance their interests, a pessimism about labour's prospects have inclined many to exaggerate trends towards individualization, impermanence and job instability. Thus a curiously sympathetic echo is added to the general neoliberal refrain of immutable change.

If the charge is not conspiracy there is a lesser indictment facing those who wish to challenge public perceptions and policy prescriptions, namely arrogance. It might appear that only someone with an overweening sense of their own importance and insight could possibly make such counter intuitive claims, appearing to stand above the fray and suggest that many public perceptions are wrong. The response offered here is that public perceptions are, on the one hand contradictory rather than wrong and, on the other, authentic and genuine even if their views lack a solid base in evidence. Contradictory or paradoxical perceptions are explored in the opening chapter, with the public both signing up to the view that 'there are no jobs for life' but also that 'they want you to work until you are seventy'. Many might also suggest that public perceptions are real, regardless of whether they are based on statistical fact or not, and to some extent this is arguable. However, because they are authentic and genuine it does not mean that these perceptions cannot, or should not, be questioned. Any recognition of the authenticity of public perceptions should also not leave unnoticed the political and economic interests that are served by an exaggerated sense of precariousness and powerlessness. It is not unreasonable to suggest that certain political and economic interests are reassured if there is widespread acceptance that modern jobs are now unstable and employment insecure, that the balance of power has fundamentally swung in favour of multinational capital and that governments can no longer guarantee social security from the cradle to the grave.

The Structure of the Book

New Capitalism is based on particular transformative forces, mechanisms of adaptation and relational change. It is expressed in a specific mode of representation, suggested here as an extended form of dematerialization. This projects autonomous and disembedded social processes that systematically exaggerate the mobility of capital, the

pace and significance of technological change and the retreat of the
state. The labour market is the transmission mechanism through
which new social relations and broader societal transformation is conducted. The critique presented challenges each element of this framework offering a critical assessment of the impact of technological
change, globalization and welfare retrenchment, each of which are
covered in separate chapters. This suggests a discussion over a broad
terrain, which together with the comparative focus on North America
and Europe, risks a range of topic coverage which is challenging. It is
certainly a wider canvas than that covered by familiar concerns of
industrial relations and the sociology of work. Moreover, the argument and the findings presented here are at odds with commonsense
understanding of the changing nature of work, and a significant
investment has been made in seeking to explain the gap between
rhetoric and statistical realities. The first three chapters are concerned
with the perception and representation of social change. Chapter 1
explores the evolution of 'the relational turn' in post-industrial narratives, which has increasingly focused on new forms of engagement
between capital and labour. It also charts a shift in the mode of representation of social change from the empirical to the experiential and
the articulation of a set of ideas of social transformation expressed in
business, policy and academic milieux. Together these accounts rein-
force the message of the unprecedented nature of technological and
institutional change. At the heart of these accounts is the emergence
of a management literature that eschews the idea of planning in favour
of managing uncertainty while stressing adaptability and flexibility.

Chapter 2 explores technological change as an autonomous social
process with its own momentum, logic and outcomes. As a consequence of the autonomization of social process the pace, scale and significance of change appear exaggerated, especially when tested against
the statistical evidence of the employment impact of information and
communication technologies and the transnational mobility of capital.
While globalization is a multi-dimensional concept, Chapter 3 focuses
specifically on capital mobility. New employment relations are said to
emerge as a result of looser connections between employers and
workers with disembedded, spatially indifferent capital, able to orbit
the globe in search of low-cost options. A clear distinction between
financial and non-financial capital is drawn, in which transnational
corporations appear to be extraordinarily immobile and attached to
their home economies. A further analysis of the transnationality of
mobile capital reveals remarkable stability in the balance between
domestic and foreign spheres of activity.

Chapter 4 examines the labour market as the mechanism or medium through which social processes can transmit new relations of employment. This warrants putting the labour market at the centre of theoretical endeavours. In order to theorize the labour market in its own right, it is necessary to establish a broad framework that can capture both productive and reproductive imperatives. A large part of the workforce is dedicated to the reproduction of labour power, and there are more people employed in education, health, and social services than in the production industries, so it is necessary to capture the dual functions of the labour market. The institution of the labour market is considered in the discussion of the commodification of labour power, using Britain as a case study, and adopts Marx and Polanyi as the theoretical frameworks.

Chapter 5 considers globalization, demographic change and social welfare. In exploring the transformation of work in relation to the requirements of reproduction this chapter explores welfare state restructuring as both the cause and consequence of labour market adjustment. Welfare retrenchment is said to be the principal outcome of corporate globalization, but this is considered as a one dimensional reading of the impact of globalization. Rather than a simple notion of state retreat, the discussion suggests the changing policy priorities and the recommodification of welfare. This has resulted in very large increases in employment in education, health and social services which are simply unacknowledged in 'productionist' accounts of the transformation of work. Demographic change is also considered as a driver of welfare reform and is the centre piece of the global reform of pension schemes. This has emerged as a critical issue for organized labour in Europe where the raising of retirement ages is high on the agenda, whereas in the United States the demographic pressures are presented in support of the privatization of social security. The challenge for analysis is to recognize that welfare retrenchment affects different constituencies and can be compatible with welfare expansion.

Chapter 6 explores the flexible labour market and the contingent economy. The casualization of employment and the significance of temporary work are considered and the discussion finds that they have been greatly overstated as a feature of new employment patterns. The case for new forms of engagement with employers rests substantially on the evidence of increasing contingency in employment which is marginal at best. In reality the evidence relies on the assumption that all forms of non-standard employment are precarious, which is simply untenable. The key to the argument is the treatment of part-time working, which is a feature of temporal flexibility that strengthens rather than weakens labour market attachment. Furthermore, the rise of labour market flexibility, in relation to non-standard forms of employment, owes more to changes in the welfare state than to the practices of 'the flexible firm'. Part-time employment has risen dramatically in education, health and retailing which expresses the increased availability of working women, but also, less spectacularly, the rise of the student labour market.

Chapter 7 challenges the case for new capitalist employment relations by analysing the statistical evidence of job stability and long-term employment. Contrary to widespread public perception, job stability has not declined, and even during a period of employment expansion in which average job tenures fall due to the arrival of new starters, the increase in the long-term workforce has been highly significant. In Europe the decrease in long-term employment occurs in 7% of the workforce and is largely concentrated in agriculture. The loss of long-term jobs in the United States occurs in a small number of sectors, accounting for 20% of the workforce. In North America and the European Union the story is similar, in that long-term employment rises in old and new industries, in public and private sectors and in high turnover and low turnover firms. Contrary to the new economy hype long-term employment is associated with increasing employment of professional and technical grades. In contrast to the perspective of new relations of employment giving rise to increasing temporariness, long-term employment expansion owes much to the rise of women's participation in the workforce and the increase in part-time working.

Given continuing job stability and rising long-term employment, Chapter 8 considers the significance of a phenomenon that is often called 'job insecurity'. The challenge in explaining the rise of job insecurity is made more difficult in that it seems to have little to do with the levels of unemployment and the rate of redundancy. Francis Green has pointed out that insecurity as a media topic was *not* mentioned during the 1970s and 1980s, when levels of mass unemployment returned to the advanced economies and appears to rise in the 1990s when employment prospects improved. Part of the explanations for this paradox is that job insecurity expresses an anxiety about the consequence rather than the likelihood of job loss. In the United States, for instance, loss of job can mean a loss of health insurance for the whole family, which is potentially disastrous for family finances. Another explanation is that the impact of the recession of the early 1990s was experienced by labour market groups that previously had high expectations of job insecurity. When earlier recessions were focused on manufacturing the loss of jobs fell on the service sector and on white collar workers who previously had a lower risk of job loss. Another element of the discussion is that job insecurity is too focused on the nature of the job and not the environment, the institutional context in which work takes place. This opens up the discussion of precarious employment as a consequence of the greater exposure of workers to the irrationality of market forces. In this sense it is possible to see job insecurity as 'manufactured uncertainty'.

The discussion presented here builds on research in the European Union and extends to North America. The Canadian material is given less prominence than the United States due to the relative size of the economy and the significance of the United States as the economic and political superpower. Mexico is not featured in the North American discussion, as this analysis focuses on developed economies. The European case is taken to cover the European Union, due to the availability of data, although there will be particular references to specific countries as and when appropriate. There is of course unevenness in the circumstances of the individual member states of the European Union, but the labour force data has been gathered from twelve states who were members of the Union in 1992, in which case the divergence of conditions will not be as pronounced.

1

From Post-Industrial Society to New Capitalism: The Evolution of a Narrative of Social Change

At the start of the film *Annie Hall* Woody Allen tells the joke about two women in a restaurant who complain about their meal.

> One woman says to her friend, 'The food in here is absolutely poisonous.'
>
> 'Yes,' says her dinner companion, 'and they give you such small helpings.'

The joke turns on the conjoining of two incompatible observations. Each perspective is reasonable in its own right but not in relation to the other. This apparently perverse logic presents an ironic complaint about quality and quantity which could be retold today and applied to the different perspectives that relate to the nature of the contemporary transformation of work. Thus while one person might lament the fact that 'there are no jobs for life anymore', another might well agree and add 'yes, and they want you to work until you are 70.'

Seemingly paradoxical observations abound. In America, Jeremy Rifkind, President of the Foundation for Economic Trends in Washington DC, writes about 'The End of Work' (Rifkind 1995), while Juliet Schor writes about 'The Overworked American: The Unexpected Decline of Leisure in America' (Schor 1992). The term 'downsizing' has captured the public mood in Europe and North America in the views of a variety of different commentators, from Michael Moore to Pat Buchannan. However, if the trends towards mergers and acquisitions in the private sector, and indeed in employment growth in many parts of the public sector, are to be discerned, many organizations would appear to be getting larger. In writing about the flexible labour market in the United States, commentators such as Will Hutton (2002) make much of the fact that 'Manpower', the temporary employment agency, is the largest private sector employer in the United States, conveying a huge expansion of temporary or contingent employment in recent times. Yet temporary employment accounts for less than 5% of the American workforce and is fairly modest compared to most countries in North America and Europe. More widely, across most of the advanced economies there is a pervasive sense that work has become more precarious and jobs more insecure. A study conducted by the OECD (1997) showed significant anxiety about the fear of job losses and redundancies among all advanced industrial economies. Yet, consistent with the paradoxes alluded to above, the statistical evidence points to stable job tenures for the most part and increasing long-term employment.

Indeed with certain issues there is not only a gap between public perceptions and empirical or material reality, they almost appear to have a wholly independent existence. In looking at job insecurity and demographic change public sensibilities and empirical realities seem to be moving in opposite directions. In relation to the former, Francis Green makes the point well that the concept of *job insecurity attained broad public currency when economic conditions improved in the 1990s*. In the early 1980s, when mass unemployment returned to levels not experienced since the great depression of the 1930s, there was no expressed concern with job insecurity as it is understood today. Mass unemployment, redundancies and poverty dominated public concerns, but not job insecurity or precarious employment as such. In short it became a topic of international concern in the following decade when labour market circumstances in many countries became more benign (Green 2005).

Demography will be considered in greater detail in Chapter 4, but for the present discussion of public perceptions it is worth noting the widespread belief that demographic pressures are said to be reaching some kind of tipping point. Across the advanced industrial world a 'demographic crisis' has been discovered due to increased longevity and falling birth rates. A story of 'ageing populations' has become so commonplace as to be unremarkable, but it has almost come out of the blue. Until recently discussions of the demographic crisis were concerned with unsustainable population growth and yet, within a few short years, the crisis has almost moved into reverse with population ageing and declining birth rates. This is a significant turnaround in perception, yet, in the absence of war, famine, disease and migration, populations are not subject to sudden change in structure. Birth and death rates are observed over decades and demographers have not radically changed their population projections well into the 21st century. The question therefore arises with both demographic ageing and job insecurity as to how and why these ideas have come into prominence, seemingly independent of population and employment trends.

The initial impetus for the present work arose from a desire to explain the prevalence of perceptions of job insecurity alongside the statistical evidence of continuing job stability. However, as later discussion shows, the gap between evidence and perception extends beyond the question of job tenure into other areas such as capital mobility, technological innovation, welfare retrenchment and demographic change. At times it appears as if the scale of the transformations that underpins the new capitalism is inversely proportional to the evidence to support such accounts. It is therefore necessary, in the first instance, to recognize that the case for societal change relies on transformative factors whose presence and impact are the subject of debate. However, the present discussion also acknowledges that the absence of supporting evidence does not seem to diminish a general sensibility that 'we live in a fast changing world' or that today's jobs are no longer associated with the sense of security and advancement that they previously conferred.

Accordingly there are basically three ways of addressing the gap between perception and reality. One position is to say that statistical measurement provides the only purchase on the real world and, if public opinions lack empirical evidence, they are simply false. In the face of paradoxical or groundless perceptions it is perhaps tempting for the more enlightened amongst us to retreat into the cloistered world of the academy, take comfort in the companionship of superior intellects and find solace in statistical evidence and rigorous scientific inquiry. This would be an easy, if perhaps arrogant response, except for the fact that these days the academic community seems less than impressed with statistical evidence as empirical inquiry has lost some of the kudos it once enjoyed. Moreover, academics not only share many of these perceptions with the public, universities often provide the expert commentators who articulate these ideas and help establish them as common sense.

In contrast, a second response is to assume that those accounts of societal transformation, based on technological advancement, global market forces and institutional restructuring, speak to a change in contemporary experience that is so profound that contemporary measurements cannot divine their existence nor calculate their impact. Any gap between evidence and societal transformation is thus understood as a limitation of the statistical methods employed and the obsolescence of data sets that they generate. This is essentially the line of explanation offered by Diana Coyle in her account of new capitalism. To her credit, Coyle is one of the few commentators who acknowledges the lack of evidence for the ground breaking claims she offers, and she is also prepared to consider the merits of the sceptics' critique. Her most detailed account of new capitalism acknowledges 'the measurement problem' and accepts that productivity growth is hard to connect with the implementation of new technologies (Coyle 2001). She acknowledges, 'that an important weapon in the armor of the New Capitalism advocates is therefore the likelihood that radical new technologies are implemented slowly, so that their effects can take many decades to emerge'. In this way the gap between evidence and the 'reality' of change is either irrelevant or statistically unavoidable. Whilst many reject 'crude empiricism' and recognize the challenges of classification, measurement and interpretation in statistical analysis, acceptance of the statistical mismatch that Coyle suggests is, to a large extent, an act of faith.

A third attempt to square the circle is offered by those who suggest that statistical evidence represents material reality, but public perceptions are also real in that they have real consequences. In relation to the globalization debate for instance, Colin Hay and Ben Rosamond (2002) have noted that sceptical counterclaims, supported by hard facts, have not dented the support for the globalization orthodoxy. Accordingly they suggest the existence of a material reality and a 'discursive reality', rooted in a mode of representation of social change and a public acceptance of its credibility. The present discussion takes this as a way of progressing, but also suggests that it is important to attempt to explain the emergence of the space between material and discursive realities. In some ways what is really new about new capitalism is this distance between rhetoric and reality which has no equivalence in previous decades. Therefore an important challenge for any analysis of new capitalism is to identify the well springs of a mode of representation that constitutes a discursive reality at variance with empirical or material reality. This may seem off-putting to many readers, raising the prospect of impenetrable textual deconstruction, but the reader should be assured that this author has no such inclination. However new capitalism is not just based on a description of actual developments, but increasingly on normative accounts of current trends and future possibilities, depicting a world, not as it is, but as some would wish it to be. Therefore the task is not confined to the analysis of change, but to understanding the ideology that underpins an increasingly powerful mode of representation of societal transformation.

It is suggested here that public perceptions of labour market change are part of a larger mosaic of contradiction and confusion, of seemingly opposing perspectives that serve to express and convey a broader representation of the world of work and wider society. These perspectives are rooted in narratives of societal change that imbue technological development and corporate restructuring, and institutional adaptation with a transformative capacity. These forces are expressed through labour market change in new forms of engagement between capital and labour, based on tenuous connection and transient engagement, which are said to engender insecurity and individualization. The term narrative is used here because of analytical significance of the representation of societal development and the meanings, understandings and assumptions that people have acquired of it. It is also useful to consider narratives in that they draw attention to form and content in public discussion, in media commentaries and in academic debate. To speak of narrative form and content also invites consideration of style and substance, of narrators and audiences, of the medium and the message. These narratives have emerged from the discussions of structural changes in advanced economies that preoccupied much of the earlier 'post-industrial society' debate initiated by Daniel Bell. Over some four decades post-industrial narratives have evolved from a concern with structural change within industries and macroeconomic outcomes, to accounts that stress technological innovation and organizational processes within firms, and latterly to suggest cultural and relational change. There is a contextual shift from considering changes within national economies to a new emphasis on global processes. The pace of change is said to increase exponentially and the unprecedented discontinuous nature of transformation is emphasized. It is argued here that the rise of a new managerial literature, signalled in the publication of a number of key business texts in the 1980s and 1990s, defined a new trajectory that came to embrace the idea of the 'new economy' and a 'knowledge economy', eventually consolidated the narratives of new capitalism. More recently there is a greater appreciation of ideational change in a 'new spirit of capitalism' that provides the ideological platform on which societal transformation is represented and understood.

Ideology is not a term that many people feel comfortable in using today as it invokes a variety of notions from false consciousness to state sponsored propaganda. The latter redolent of conspiracy and the former evoking intellectual hubris. However to ignore the ideological dimension in the representation of societal change is to impose severe limitations on the discussion of new capitalism and to deprive analysis of key developments since the beginning of the post-industrial debate. In the 1960s commentators sought to capture the nature of capitalism after 'les trente glorieuses' – the post-war boom in advanced capitalist societies. They looked at the industrial structure of economies that had reduced unemployment, produced high levels of growth, low inflation and especially in comparison with the depression of the interwar years asked *'Has Capitalism Changed?'* (Tsuru 1961). In contrast the last quarter of the twentieth century has been of a radically different experience punctuated by periods of high inflation, low growth, and the return of mass unemployment and periodic crises of profitability. There have been intense debates about the policy responses, which have featured on the role of the state, the virtues of corporate freedom and flexible labour markets, and the deleterious impact of punitive tax regimes and overly generous welfare systems. Discussants have been fully aware of ideological camps and the politics surrounding policy remedies. As will be seen later in this chapter enormous financial resources have been invested in naturalizing the workings of the market, in constructing a vision of a deregulated economy and in promoting the merits of flexibility. The debates are more concerned with change as a means than as an end, highlighting processes and possibilities rather than outcomes. Increasingly accounts of change are those people wish to happen rather than have, or necessarily will occur, and for that reason alone it seems extraordinarily self-limiting to deny the ideological construction of social transformation.

A Brief History of New Times

It is understandable that most readers of the new capitalist texts take at face value the claim that we are living in new times. If learned academics, government officials, consultants, journalists and business leaders say that society is witnessing the new dawn of technological change, a period of unprecedented social and economic transformation, then this idea will have widespread acceptance. If some are sceptical of such claims there is a tendency to portray the non-believers as lacking insight and imagination, locked in the past, unaware of current developments and unappreciative of the speed of change. When such scepticism is informed by historical comparisons the non-believers are deemed to be 'old fashioned'.

The tendency to render the contemporary as 'unprecedented', however, involves analytical distortion and ideological risks. In the first instance such accounts deny the audience the vantage of historical comparison against which their assessment of social change can be made. In order to stress the significance of their perspectives on the pace and consequence of social transformation it is very tempting to say that the processes observed and the technological possibilities predicted are of greater scale and import than anything that came before. Their claims are given a newsworthiness they might not have otherwise obtained which affords some degree of protection against charges of exaggeration and reckless imbalance. Yet it is a protection that only lasts for as long as the audience is willing to accept the unprecedented nature of the changes observed. If there has been some diremption in social development, the preoccupations of contemporary discussion should offer no retrospective connection with earlier perspectives of social change. If we live in a period of 'discontinuous change', as Charles Handy claimed in the 1990s, it follows that current themes should be entirely novel, a set of ideas without precedent, a debate without a past. Once these connections are established the credibility of new capitalist narratives are undermined in significant ways. Thus Charles Handy might have hoped that his readership had no knowledge of Peter Drucker (1969) who had previously written about the 1960s as 'the age of discontinuity'.

It is therefore suggested here that a genealogy of the new times is attempted that might identify any precedents for contemporary accounts. This is not only to provide some historical context but also to capture the contemporary character of today's version of new times and to identify the mode of representation specific to the narratives of new capitalism. The evolution of the post-industrial narrative into an account of societal transformation based on new employment relations has taken place over more than four decades. For present purposes it is possible to date the narratives of new capitalism from the late 1960s. The work of Daniel Bell, Peter Drucker and Alvin Toffler in America defined the contours of the post-industrial landscape, which continue to provide the reference points of contemporary transformation scenarios. In Europe, Alain Touraine and Andre Gorz tied the transformation of post-industrial society to questions of new and old social classes and movements. In *Farewell to the Working Class* (Gorz 1982) the focus was on the decline of the industrial proletariat, while Touraine (1971) considered the significance of the student movement. Thus the early American discussion seemed concerned with changing social and economic outcomes while the European debate seemed concerned with changing agency. In setting the scene for his own version of change in industrial society Daniel Bell cites the prevailing accounts of that time, with Dahrendorf (1959) writing about 'post-capitalist society', Lichtheim (1963) considering a new Europe as 'post-bourgeois', Etzioni (1968) writing about the 'postmodern', Boulding (1964) describing the 'post-civilized era', Eisenstadt (1972) the 'post-traditional' society, Kahn and Wiener (1967) 'post-economic' society, and Sjoberg and Hancock (1972) discussing 'the new individualism' in the 'post-welfare state'. A very strong impression of sailing in 'charted water' thus emerges from the themes discussed in the 1960s by American and European social scientists.

Daniel Bell's Post-Industrial Society

It is worth considering in some detail Daniel Bell's account of the coming of 'post-industrial society' and Alvin Toffler's *Future Shock*. The former was arguably the most influential account of its type, a precursor to Castells' analysis of the informational age and the rise of network society. The latter is chosen for its resonance with the experiential accounts of contemporary work transformation offered by Ulrich Beck and Zygmunt Bauman. It is not that Bell's account is the first of his kind, indeed he recognized that the term 'post-industrial society' was first coined by Arthur Penty in 1917. The power of Bell's account of the coming of post-industrial society is based on his analysis of changes in the industrial structure of the economy and occupational composition of the American labour market. The methodological superiority of Bell's case is also reinforced by historical comparison with pre-industrial and industrial society. He provides statistical evidence of occupational and sectoral change in America and offers international comparisons with Europe, Japan and the less developed world. Bell discusses 'the axial structures' of the American society in the 1960s. These include: the shift from a goods-producing economy to one based on the provision of services; occupational change with the pre-eminence of the professional and technical class; the centrality of theoretical knowledge; the planning and control of technology and decision making based on intellectual technology.

He adopts the tripartite division of the economy, devised almost 30 years earlier by Colin Clark (1957), and considers the shifting significance of the primary, secondary and tertiary sectors. Bell does not suggest that America is the template for other countries to follow, but the fact that this is the largest and most advanced economy in the world underpins the growing importance of 'services' as a proportion of Gross National Product and increasing percentage of the labour market. Thus the changes in social structure in post-industrial America rest in significant measure on the share of service sector employment at 61% compared to 34% in industry. This contrasts with less developed regions of the world economy, which were predominantly based in agriculture that employed more than industry and services combined. It contrasted much less sharply with the advanced European economies, where industry and service shares of employment were approximately equivalent at 45%. Occupational recomposition in Bell's account is based on the shift from blue to white collar employment. The declining significance of manual employment in lower socio-economic groups is matched by the growing importance of non-manual occupations particularly suggested by a projected increase between 1960 and 1975 in the professional and technical grades. During this period he forecast an increase of 4.6 million professional and technical jobs, which represented an increase from 12.2% of the workforce in 1960 to 14.9% in 1975.

Related to the shifts from blue-collar employment in industry to white collar employment in the services sector is the role of knowledge. The term 'knowledge industries' was first coined by the Princeton economist Fritz Machlup (1962) and later developed as 'the knowledge economy' by Peter Drucker (1969). In Bell's account of post-industrial society knowledge is organized for the purpose of social control and the directing of innovation and change. This is theoretical or scientific knowledge rather than experience and empiricism. In relation to the economy for example, he noted that, in the 1960s, there were more scientists practising their craft than had lived in the preceding 4,000 years, an argument that has been trotted out on many occasions since. With the growth of intellectual technology, rather than mechanical technology, knowledge became the strategic resource of post-industrial society. In this new technocracy the key social groups of scientists, engineers, mathematicians and economists, replace the industrialists and entrepreneurs of the old industrial society.

Post-industrial society in the hands of Daniel Bell contrasts with many contemporary accounts in that it is socio-economic, rather than societal, is historically retrospective rather than prospective and, despite other weaknesses, is a far more balanced assessment of social change than the more indulgent claims of epochal transformation currently on offer. The measured judgments over the nature and extent of social transformation are best observed in the discussion of technological change. When today's 'new agers' breathlessly describe a world in constant flux, an informational society of incomparable technological capacity, it is salutary to consider the circumspection and caution at the heart of Bell's judgment of historical change. He asks, for instance, how it is possible to measure the rate of technological change.

> What makes the problem all the more vexing is that we are repeatedly told that we are living in a time of 'constantly accelerating rate of technological change' which is creating new and 'explosive' social problems. Now, no one can deny that a good deal of technological change has taken place since World War II: atomic energy, electronic computers, jet engines are three of the more spectacular introductions of new products and processes. But the difficulty with the publicistic (and political) argument is that the word 'rate' implies a measurement, that somehow the changes that are being introduced now can be measured, say, against the introduction of the steam engine, the railroad, the telephone, the dynamo, and similar technological devices of the nineteenth century. How does one distinguish the change wrought by electricity from that created by atomic energy? We cannot. Both are 'revolutionary' innovations. But there is no way of matching their effects in a comparable way. (Bell 1974, p. 198)

He also seeks to curb the excesses of his contemporaries. Against the originator of the idea of 'knowledge industries' Franz Machlup, who argued that some 29% of US GNP in 1958 was spent on knowledge, Bell suggests that the figure should be much smaller and knowledge industries confined to research (but not development which was largely devoted to missiles and space), higher education and the production of new knowledge as intellectual property. Against the idea of accelerated social change popularized by Alvin Toffler's *Future Shock* he argues that, in terms of the daily lives of individuals, more change was experienced between 1850 and 1940 when railroads, steamships, telegraphs, electricity, telephone, automobile, motion picture, radio and aeroplanes were introduced than in the period since, when change is supposed to be accelerating (Bell 1974, p. 318).

Bell's work is more circumspect in tone and consciously more restricted in scope than Toffler's *Future Shock*. For Bell the axial structure of the economy does not provide the basis for a wider sociology. Political regimes and cultural change cannot be derived from economic or social structures. Social structures pose 'management problems' for the political order but do not determine their form and internal processes. A new technocratic society raises cultural questions, given the privileged position of knowledge, but post-industrial society is essentially a socio-economic phenomenon.

Alvin Toffler's *Future Shock*

Toffler's 'super-industrial society', by contrast, is much closer to those ahistorical perspectives of contemporary social transformation. *Future Shock* represents the stress and disorientation induced in people who are subjected to too much change. It encompasses moral and cultural dilemmas, changes in life style, consumption, work, careers, communities and social commitments. The qualities of street preacher ('the disease of change') and life style coach ('the human side of tomorrow') run through this work. It echoes with the corrosion of character described in the 'new capitalism' of Richard Sennett (1989) and the writings of Zygmunt Bauman (2001) on the 'individualized society'. Toffler very briefly considers historical change but only to set the tone and context for his more extravagant claims about future society. Thus he admits that the past 300 years have witnessed a 'firestorm of change', but in super-industrial society this is now accelerating.

> For what is occurring now is in all likelihood, bigger deeper, and more important than the industrial revolution. Indeed, a growing body of respectable opinion asserts that the present moment represents nothing less than the second great divide in human history, comparable in magnitude only with that first great break in historic continuity, the shift from barbarism to civilisation. (Toffler 1970, p. 14)

It might be suggested that this is hyperbole on such a scale as to be illogical. If society is in the throes of such extraordinary transformation, how can it be envisioned by anyone who had lived in such antediluvian ignorance? How could the nomadic tribes-people of hunter-gatherer society imagine Greek temples, Roman cities, the state, the family or private property? If Toffler is the modern equivalent of 'prehistoric man witnessing a world totally new', then is it not unreasonable to assume his observations, similarly, would be less than insightful?

Future Shock focuses on several key themes including novelty, diversity and adaptability, but central to Toffler's vision is the idea that we live in an 'Age of Transience'. Transience is a state of impermanence that penetrates our consciousness radically altering the way people relate to each other and the wider society around them. There is a new temporariness in everyday life. The disposability of diapers and plastic pens signify a 'throw away society'. The spread of 'rentalism' is a characteristic of societies 'rocketing towards super-industrialism'. Rentalism was manifest in the growth of apartment building in 1960s America which was taken to mean 'minimum involvement housing', in the expansion of car rentals and in the spread of hire services from building equipment and power tools to catering. Rentalism signifies the lack of commitment between people and the products and services they use.

The decline in 'durational expectancies' is reflected in the world of work as rentalism spreads into employment. Occupational change and employment turnover had increased to such an extent that job tenure in America declined during the 1960s from 4.6 years to 4.2 years. Toffler cites a Labor Department Survey of the time that seems very familiar to today's labour market commentators who write about the 'death of the career'.

> In the beginning of the 1960s 'the average twenty year old man in the workforce could be expected to change jobs six or seven times'. Thus instead of thinking in terms of a 'career' the citizen of super industrial society will think in terms of serial careers. (Toffler 1970, p. 99)

Through such changes social relationships in companies and in the community become more transitory. The rise in geographical mobility and occupational mobility makes social contact ever more precarious. Toffler witnesses the rise of 'modular', almost nomadic families increasingly unable to settle their children in school and establish long-terms relationships in local communities. The key word, characteristic of organized life in super industrial society is 'temporary'.

The work of Daniel Bell and Alvin Toffler provide the starting points for the contemporary representation of the societal development, not only in the sense that they are significant referents for today's debates, they also provide the contrasting end points on a spectrum of theoretical or methodological approaches. In short, Bell's work is scientific in that his evidence is systematically gathered and the conclusions are rooted in historical comparisons. Toffler's evidence appears anecdotal by comparison and his approach is ahistorical. The social transformation he anticipates is disconnected from previous economic and social developments. Modern technologies arrive out of the blue, like some alien intelligence. It is an act of faith that the pace of technological change and the social and economic consequences it portends have no parallels in human history. Once cut loose from the anchorage of meaningful historical perspective the author is free to indulge in prediction that lacks any semblance of proportion and balance. Ruled only by the need to impress his audience and to convey the significance of his own pronouncements the tendency towards hyperbole is irresistible.

New Capitalism – A Confluence of Narratives

Post-industrialism has developed over four decades but it is perhaps simplistic to imagine one story or manifesto for the new times that we live in. It is perhaps more accurate to refer to a set of overlapping and mutually reinforcing perspectives that operate at different levels, variously addressing expert, technical and policy audiences but also reaching the general public through the different mass media. New capitalism may be viewed as a confluence of narratives that, in combination, speak to new transformative forces, mechanisms of adaptation and the emergence of new social relations in society. There are few books that seek to offer a comprehensive coverage of the forces, mechanisms and outcomes of change. Manuel Castells' *The Rise of the Network Society* offers the most complete account of societal transformation, charting a new informational mode of development, the transformation of work and the end of salaried employment, but such a coverage is exceptional. Some, such as Antony Giddens, emphasize macro themes such as technological advancement or globalization and derive societal transformation without specifying the mechanisms by which this might occur (Giddens 2002). Others might take employment change as their starting point and extrapolate to broader developments in society, without discussing the determinants of labour market adjustment, as with Hutton (1998) and Harvey (1989). Some prefer to take as read the transformative character of institutional change and concentrate their energies on mapping the cultural expression of the new capitalism in the personal experiences of a more individualized society (Bauman 2005; Sennett 1998 and 2006). In his *Brave New World of Work* Ulrich Beck seeks out a 'political economy of insecurity' extrapolated from certain labour market trends and his projections of the future of work. Other additions to the new capitalism literature stress the impact of technological change, as with *The Weightless World* by Diane Coyle (1998, 1999), *Living on Thin Air* by Charles Leadbetter (2000) and *The New Rules for a New Economy* by Kevin Kelly, the 'technoecstatic' editor of *Wired*.

Cumulatively the evolution of the post-industrial narrative involves the shift from structural to relational change, the diminishing presence of agency and the increasing sense of exogenous forces. There is an exponential increase in the pace of change such that the current period is imbued with a transformativity that demands discussion of a 'new economy' or a 'knowledge economy'. This development of the new capitalist narratives is also increasingly associated with a restructuring of the world of work in which the labour market is the transmission mechanism between technological innovation or institutional adaptation, and different forms of engagement between capital and labour, which express a more precarious existence in a more individualized society. The discussion of new capitalism presented here attempts a broad coverage critiquing the transformativity of technological and institutional change, with a particular focus on the labour market and prospects for new employment relations that generate precariousness and insecurity.

In relation to ideology there is another feature of this confluence of narratives that reinforces the sense of a qualitative shift in societal development. Indeed one of the most intriguing aspects of the story of the new times that we live in is that it merges left wing and right wing perspectives and sympathies. Thus Michael Hardt and Antonio Negri and Slavoj Žižek, influential figures within the anti-capitalist movement, have accepted that the rise of 'immaterial labour', i.e. 'labour that produces immaterial products, such as information, knowledge, ideas, images relationships and affects', has become hegemonic in the sense

> that the contractual and material conditions of immaterial labour that tend to spread to the entire labour market are making the position of labor in general more precarious. (Hardt and Negri 2005, p. 66)

If neo-conservative think tanks, management consultants and libertarian anti-capitalists such as Antony Hardt and Tony Negri describe the decline of traditional forms of employment due to technological advancement and institutional change, the spread of political views represented must add to the credibility of these narratives. From very different standpoints, one perhaps lamenting the decline of labour, the other celebrating the demise of institutional resistance, a picture emerges that employment stability and job security have been left behind and now only recalled in a cloth cap nostalgia for the good (or bad depending on perspective) old days when unions were strong, when people had real jobs in manufacturing and when national economies were regulated by the state. Thus a left wing contribution, stressing the decline of unionized manufacturing jobs and their replacement by new service industries where people are offered non-unionized 'McJobs', can bolster a pro-business view of the advent of the flexible labour market. In similar vein the 'myth' of the end of jobs for life offered by Handy (1994) and Bridges (1996) is reinforced by left wing commentators such as Peck and Theodore (2001), who in this author's view, greatly overstate the significance of temporary employment trends.

In this confluence of narratives, both left and right positions are prone to some repositioning. To some extent what has happened is that the right has settled in the ground that used to be the preserve of the left. As mentioned in the introduction, to a degree the right has appropriated the rhetoric of change previously associated with radical or critical voices, but it is also evident in the rhetorics of 'crisis', 'security' and 'sustainability'. In some senses also the left has shifted the ground on which such discussion of societal change has taken place. In many respects the post-industrial literature can be regarded as a post-Marxist phenomenon, indebted to those ex- or post-Marxists who have made key contributions to the genre. This is evident in the early years with the work of Daniel Bell and Andre Gorz, later in the 1980s and 1990s with Martin Jacques and Charles Leadbetter, but arguably the mutation of the post-industrial narrative to New Capitalism owes a very large debt to the post-Marxists such as Manuel Castells, Richard Sennett, Zygmunt Bauman and Ulrich Beck, who have repositioned the debate about changes within capitalism along the political spectrum. They have elevated the discussion from industrial to societal restructuring, and not surprisingly, given their backgrounds, these authors have grounded their accounts of societal changes on increasingly transient forms of engagement between employers and workers.

The New Spirit of Capitalism

Insights into the evolution of the post-industrial narrative, from structural change in the economy highlighted by Daniel Bell to relational change in society, described by the likes of Sennett and Castells, are offered in the work of Luc Boltanski and Eve Chiapello. The former, a French sociologist and erstwhile colleague of Pierre Bourdieu, the latter a French management theorist, have attempted to describe 'the ideological changes that have accompanied recent transformations in capitalism'. These have been captured in the magnum opus *The New Spirit of Capitalism* which highlights the emergence of new representations of economic life. The spirit of capitalism 'is the set of beliefs associated with the capitalist order that helps to justify this order and, by legitimating them, to sustain the forms of action and predispositions compatible with it' (Boltanski and Chiapello 2007, p. 10). Building on Max Weber's work on the new ethos that attended the rise of capitalism, the authors describe a spirit of capitalism that conforms to three distinct phases of development.

The first spirit was associated with the end of the nineteenth century and arose with a familial form of capitalism. It is symbolized in the bourgeois entrepreneur, in bourgeois morality and values, familial or patriarchal relations with employees in relatively small firms, a strong belief in progress, the future, science, technology and the benefits of industry. The second spirit of capitalism held sway between the 1930s and the 1960s. The focus was less on the entrepreneur than on the organization, represented by the large bureaucratized firm whose heroic figure is the manager. The third spirit of capitalism is 'isomorphic' with a globalized capitalism which evokes a flexible world of multiple projects performed by autonomous people. Boltanski and Chiapello stress the importance of management literature to an understanding of the representation of social transformation, arguing that it allows the most direct access to the ideologies associated with the spirits of capitalism in the last century. The birth of this literature at the beginning of the 20th century coincides with the rise of a new social formation, of professional managers and administrators that rose to prominence with the growth of large firms. This occurred in tandem with the sidelining of the owners' position in the firm as they were consigned to a more passive role as shareholder.

The management literature of each successive embodiment of the spirit of capitalism targets the principal characteristics of the preceding phase of development. Thus the second spirit of capitalism legitimizes the manager or 'cadre' whilst simultaneously critiquing or delegitimating the traditional employers of familial capitalism. Specifically targeted are the small employers who abuse their property rights, place family interests above that of the firm and wider society, and who shun modern organizational and marketing techniques. The management literature of the 1990s, that expresses the third spirit of capitalism, similarly challenges key features of the preceding phase of development. 'The struggle conducted in the 1990s thus has its objective largely eliminating the models of firms constructed in the previous period . . . by deligitimating hierarchy, planning, formal authority, Taylorism, the grade of cadre and lifetime careers in the same firm' (p. 85).

A significant element of their analysis of the new ideological configuration of contemporary capitalism is the comparison of French and American management literature written in the 1960s and 1990s. Key targets for recent management authors are large bureaucratic organizations and the planning systems they sought to maintain. 'Anti-authoritarian' processes of control are celebrated as democratic and liberating as the non-bureaucratic virtues of flexibility and adaptability are championed. Significantly, Boltanski and Chiapello's analysis of the *new modalities of control* in modern industries emphasizes two dimensions, namely externalization and decentralization. The externalization of control is evident in a new model of the firm as a network. The network metaphor applies internally with the prominent role attributed to autonomous teams of workers, and in the greater sense of trust within the company that has replaced top down executive control and close monitoring of staff. Internal adaptation also includes the autonomization of units or sectors within large firms, which are treated as profit centres in which bureaucratic control is replaced by market control. Externally, networks of firms arise as a result of increased outsourcing and/or subcontracting of operations, networks of firms in industrial parks are cited, as is the model of the third Italy, although these are more commonly discussed by economic geographers and sociologists rather than management authors.

The externalization of control is manifest in the emphasis placed on customer satisfaction as the touchstone to guide corporate operations. Customer care dogma has two effects – in directing self control towards profit making and secondly in transferring the control exercised by superiors in the 1960s to control by the customer. In other words, unplanned markets determine the success and profitability of firms as long as there is sufficient internal adaptability and flexibility. Internal or executive control is transferred to the market and the management role is to lead the company to ride the waves of change in order to guarantee survival. Moreover internal decentralization amplifies the externalization of control in that the introduction of just-in-time stock control systems pass risk on to the supplier and on to the workers within the firm.

The New Spirit of Capitalism goes on to consider the dismantling of the world of work, and new forms of capitalist critique. The former will be considered in Chapter 5 alongside other accounts of labour market transformation. At this point it is worth suggesting the strengths and some of the weaknesses of Boltanski and Chiappello's work. The strength of Boltanski and Chiapello's account is that it examines the 'ideological platform' on which contemporary transformation of work is based. They highlight management literature as the most direct means of accessing this set of ideas and their comparison of management literatures in different periods assists the analysis of the evolution of post-industrialism to new capitalism. They usefully capture the emergence of new modes of control in contemporary capitalism, which is represented in the externalization of market dynamics.

The key weakness is that Boltanski and Chiapello have no practical concern to explain why one spirit came to replace another. The second and especially the third spirit appear almost out of the blue. The spread of these ideas is particularly associated with production industries, because Boltanski and Chiapello argue that the changes described by the literature are more obvious in those firms with the greatest use of Taylorist methods of production. There is thus a vague sense of causality, in that the third spirit is loosely connected with the restructuring of Fordist industries but this is not integrated into their discussion. The lack of attention to causality occurs perhaps because, at times, they appear ambivalent about whether they are dealing with the rhetoric of the management literature or the practical reality of change. Thus they stress the importance of the model of the firm emerging as network, with the rise of subcontracting and outsourcing, while at the same time acknowledging that the large firms have got larger.

The third spirit arises unannounced and unrelated to broader institutional changes in society with the changing role of the state conspicuously absent, and the wider consideration of neoliberalism missing. The discussion of the new management literature presented here suggests that this is not some spontaneous shift in managerial thinking and has to be understood as neoliberal managerial discourse. The third spirit appears after Reaganism and Thatcherism and is a consequence of a government policy change directed at the greater exposure of economies to market forces. Reagan is the political expression of a concerted corporate intervention in the political and policy fields intended to bring about a sea change in public expectations of the state's role in the economy, and the virtues of market freedoms. Although this is a French account, the absence of neoliberalism in the rise of new managerial discourse is a critical weakness. In order to gain an understanding of the ideological forces at work it is necessary to turn to Thomas Frank, David Harvey and Doug Henwood to situate the new managerial discourse within a neoliberal framework.

The Ideological Context of New Capitalism

To explore the specific form and the development of 'the new work order' it is necessary to consider the rise of neoliberalism since the late 1970s, and with particular reference to the United States and the United Kingdom specifically. In recent decades the ideological shifts within western capitalist societies emanate from the triumph of monetarism and the perceived change in role of the state in delivering social and economic policy objectives, and the reassertion of the superiority of markets as allocative mechanisms. This process later became labelled as 'neoliberalism' by its critics, but only with hindsight does the scale and significance of its ascendancy gain due recognition. Several key works on neoliberalism serve to highlight the changes that have unfolded in the corporate world since 1979 namely *Capital Resurgent* by Gérard Duménil and Dominique Lévy, and David Harvey's '*A Brief History of Neoliberalism*'. In both works the authors have demonstrated that neoliberalism represented more than a policy shift aimed at deregulation and liberalization, but constituted a reassertion of the interests of economic elites and a restoration of a more direct expression of class power.

Like other accounts of the rise of neoliberalism in the United States Harvey notes the importance of a memo written in 1971 by Lawrence Powell, Richard Nixon's nominee for the Supreme Court. His was a call to arms to corporate America to answer the ideological attack on the free enterprise system in the United States. It invited the National Chamber of Commerce to take up the leadership of this challenge and answer the chorus of criticism from the college campus, the pulpit, the media, intellectual journals, arts and sciences and politicians. Universities were seen as the key battle ground and Powell recommended the creation of an intellectual infrastructure capable of rolling back the liberal tide, taking on anti-business opponents ranging from Ralf Nader to Herbert Marcuse, but also seeking to address wider audiences through a major intervention in public relations and government affairs. Powell's memorandum is credited with inspiring the creation of The Heritage Foundation, the Manhattan Institute, Cato Institute, Citizens for a Sound Economy, Accuracy in Academe and other powerful institutions. Jerry Landay describes the origins of such foundations and think tanks and the corporate interests they serve.

> A highly integrated front of activist organizations has been generously funded by the banking and oil money, of the Mellon-Scaifes of

Pittsburgh, the manufacturing fortunes of Lynd and Harry Bradley of Milwaukee, the energy revenues of the Koch Family of Kansas, the chemical profits of John M. Olin of New York, the Vicks patent-medicine empire of Smith Richardson of Greensboro, and the brewing assets of the Coors dynasty of Colorado. Their grants have paid for a veritable constellation of think tanks, pressure groups, special interest foundations, litigation centres, scholarly research and funding endowments, publishing and TV production houses, media attack operations, political consultancies, polling mills and public relations operations. (Landay 2002)

Since the 1970s the United States has seen a prolonged period of corporate mobilization. The Business Roundtable, an organization of CEOs, 'committed to the aggressive pursuit of political power for the corporation' was founded in 1972, together with the US Chamber of Commerce, whose membership expanded from 60,000 firms in 1974 to a quarter of a million by 1984, were central to this mobilization (Brenner 2007; Harvey 2005). Brenner notes also that in 1974 labour was raising more in political funding than the corporate and trade association Political Action Committees, but by 1984 the PACs were raising two and a half to three times labour's contribution to political funding.

This mobilization of corporate interests was given heightened urgency in the changing economic climate of the 1970s and 1980s. In many parts of the advanced economies the 1970s saw a crisis of corporate profitability, of low growth and high levels of inflation. In October 1979 Paul Volker of the Federal Reserve hiked interest rates to squeeze inflation out of the economy and to restore profitability. This was more than an anti-inflation remedy. Duménil and Lévy argue that the 'The Volker shock' represented the assertion of a particular fraction of the dominant class in which financial interests were predominant. 'Finance reasserted its power and interests in relation to workers, company managers, those responsible for economic and social policies in government and public and semi public institutions both national and international' (Duménil and Lévy 2004). Thus, for most of the post-war period the share of national income for the top 1% of income earners in the United States was approximately 8% of the total. This was an acceptable slice of the cake during periods of prolonged expansion, but in the 1970s the crisis of corporate profitability and economic stagnation led to a wealth crash that was expressed in the precipitous decline in asset values of stocks, property and savings. By the end of the 1970s the situation became intolerable and called for decisive action. As a result of the monetary policies introduced by the Federal Reserve, the share of national income of the top 1% income earners was restored and later climbed to 15% of national income by the end of the century. The situation was similar in the United Kingdom where the top 1% of income earners saw their share of national income doubled from 6.5% to 13% over the same period. The reallocation of wealth was part of a rapid increase in wealth inequalities across the OECD countries while globally 'the income gap between the fifth of the world population living in the richest countries and the fifth in the poorest was 74 to 1 in 1997, up from 60 to 1 in 1990 and 30 to 1 in 1960' (Harvey 2005; UNDP 1999).

David Harvey suggests a number of elements in the rise of neoliberalism including: Financialization, Deregulation and Changes in Corporate Leadership.

(1) Financialization involves the rebalancing of the wealth between financial and non-financial corporations. During the 1970s the relative net worth of financial corporations to non-financial corporations slipped from 17% to 12% but had climbed to 23% by 1999 (Duménil and Lévy 2004). Production industries began to extend their activities into financial services, including credit and insurance operations, to speculating in currency and futures markets. Mergers began to diversify activities across production and financial services leading to a spectacular growth of investment in financial services. In 1952 the funds held by financial corporations were one tenth of that held by non-financial corporations, but by 1999 they were nearly twice as large (Duménil and Lévy 2004). Harvey's survey has concluded, not unreasonably, that 'neoliberalism has meant the financialisation of everything'. Finance's influence over other sectors of the economy tightened and the financial system gained a privileged position in the policy concerns of the world leading states. In any conflict of concern between Main Street and Wall Street, the latter would be favoured.

(2) Deregulation. The collapse of the Bretton Woods institutions in 1973 and the abandonment of exchange rate control and the acceptance of floating of rates signified the new monetary and financial order. Limits on capital movements were lifted in 1974 in the United States and 1979 in the UK, and then the rest of Europe with the Single European Act of 1986. After the Volker Shock of 1979 the Reagan administration provided the political backup with further deregulation, tax and budget cuts, and attacks on trades union power, most symbolically in the arrest and chaining of the leader of PATCO the air traffic controllers

union. Deregulation of telecommunications, airlines and finance also greatly reduced restrictions on corporate freedoms. Finally corporate taxes were slashed and the top rate of taxation reduced from 70% to 28%.

(3) Corporate Leadership. The vital connection between neoliberalism and changes in management thinking has been made by Thomas Frank, Doug Henwood and David Harvey. Frank (2003) is particularly convincing when he discusses the change in management thinking in America since the early 1980s which brought about two key adjustments in business leadership in terms of corporate structure and the incentive mechanisms for executives. Frank stresses that the new management thinking that emerged in the 1980s marked a decisive break with 'scientific management' that had prevailed for several decades until that time. The earlier 'managerial revolution' described by James Burnham (1941) rested on the idea of managerial authority and the functional separation of capital ownership and control. Scientific management underpinned the hierarchical control of all aspects of production and the professionalization of management. This idea rested uneasily with free market ideologues, for if company activities could be planned and controlled it did not require a huge leap of imagination to see that economic forces could be planned and controlled for the society as a whole.

With the rise of neoliberalism it was not long before such ideas were subjected to sustained attack. Thus, in 1982 a little-known management consultant from McKinsey, called Tom Peters, co-wrote *In Search of Excellence* which purported to identify the secrets of success of the most competitive American companies (Peters and Waterman 1982). Since that time Peters has been at the forefront of new management thinking based on the bureaucratic purging of corporations and their compliance with the will of the market. Delayering of management control, downsizing and outsourcing were the recurrent themes of organizational innovation as the winds of change swept through American companies. Corporate restructuring consciously exposed firms to the vagaries of (invisible) market forces. Irrationality was celebrated in the break with scientific management. Successful companies were those that 'thrived on chaos' (Peters 1987) provided they were close to the consumer and had the speed of responsiveness to changing demand. The sub-title of *Liberation Management* (Peters 1992) was 'necessary disorganisation for the nanosecond nineties'. If the previous managerial revolution separated managerial control from share ownership, the next managerial revolution involved a further dissociation of management from ideas of control or planning, which were then externalized as control by market forces.

Having established a new corporate mindset the second aspect of neoliberalism produced, in the 1990s, a realignment of interests between shareholders and corporate executives. Changes in incentive schemes occurred in which remuneration packages increasingly relied on share options to recruit and motivate senior executives. Not only did those account for the meteoric rise in personal fortunes of the top brass, but it has been suggested by Henwood (2003) and others that share price also came to dominate the evaluation of a company's current and future value and critically to influence corporate decision making. Corporate analysis was less concerned with balance sheet assessment of performance and earnings than with share values whose connections with reality grew ever more tenuous (Williams 2000). In a brilliant analysis of boom and bust in the new economy Robert Brenner points out that the period was one dominated by the availability of cheap money which corporations used, not only to over invest in capital and equipment, but also to buy back stock in their own corporations thus further separating the share prices from corporate profitability. This was a period of 'irrational exuberance', captured in the work of Yale economic professor Robert Schiller (2000), in which the ratio of capitalization to earnings reached astronomic proportions. It was an exuberance that lacked accountability. Indeed the large firms of accountants, such as Arthur Andersen, auditors of Enron, were implicated in the process as they in turn developed large investment consultancy wings which preached the Wall Street message. In the frenzy of speculation that characterized the new economy boom, the leaders of the large corporations gained enormous personal wealth. Brenner reports that between 1995 and 1999, the value of stock options granted to US executives increased from $26.5 billion to $110 billion, representing one fifth of non-financial corporate profits, net of interest. In 1992 he points out that CEOs held 2% of the equity of US corporations, today they own 12%, which is 'One of the most spectacular acts of appropriation in the history of capitalism' (Brenner 2003).

Horizontal and Vertical Transmission of the New Capitalist Narratives

The growth of management literature in the 20th century also evolves in terms of its message and its readership. The literature from the

1930s specifically addressed the management cadre of large corporations, whereas in the third spirit of capitalism management authors have a much broader audience in mind, which testifies to its ideological significance.

> As the dominant ideology the spirit of capitalism has the ability to permeate the whole set of mental representations specific to a given era, infiltrating political and trades union discourse, and furnishing legitimate representations and conceptual schemas to journalists, and researchers, to the point where it is simultaneously diffuse and general. (Boltanski and Chiapello 2006)

The narrativity of concepts thus depends on their take up, relevance and appeal to a broad constituency. These are ideas that can be deployed in a variety of settings and provide reference points and meanings for different agencies and audiences. The narratives of new capitalism transcend audiences and have a transferability across different media format. There are two dimensions to this narrativity which can be seen as *horizontal*, a set of idea articulated across different milieux and as *vertical*, stretching from the board room to a mass audience. Vivien Schmidt similarly distinguishes between a 'coordinative discourse', between policy actors and a 'communicative discourse', between political actors and the public (Schmidt 2006). An appreciation of both dimensions reveals the ideational strength of the new capitalist narratives.

The importance of the vertical or communicative dissemination of new managerial ideas helps explain their power and appeal. When Tom Peters co-wrote *The Pursuit of Excellence* the book sold 5 million copies and the author purchased a 1,300 acre farm in Vermont on the proceeds. Francis Wheen makes the point well when he looked at this curious phenomenon of business writing for the mass market.

> After that [Peters' success] the deluge: *The Seven Habits of the Highly Effective People*, by Stephen R. Covey, *The Fifth Discipline* by Peter Senge, *The One Minute Manager* by Kenneth Blanchard and Spencer Johnson, *Awaken the Giant Within* by Anthony Robbins . . . *The New York Times* list of non-fiction bestsellers soon became so clogged with inspirational tracts that the paper established a separate category for 'Advice, How-to and Miscellaneous'. Even men who had already made fortunes hastened to cash in: the Chrysler Boss, Lee Iacocca, the gloriously vulgar property developer Donald Trump and the rebarbative media mogul Al Neurath all dashed off inspirational, ghost written blockbusters that sold by the ton. (Wheen 2004, p. 42)

Nigel Thrift also describes 'a cultural circuit of capital' as a discursive apparatus that connects business schools, management consultants, management gurus, and the media.

> the cultural circuit represents . . . the dissemination of what had hitherto been high flying management theories on a mass scale in the guise of all manner of small-scale 'how to' practices through a new conglomeration of social networks, in a mass sharing of management expertise. (Thrift 2005, p. 6)

While Landay describes an integration of agencies involved in promoting the corporate visions of societal transformation this can refer to different forms of linkage across sectors connecting government think tanks, broadcast media, management consultancies, fund mangers, business schools and other academic experts. Print journalists echo the messages put out by television broadcasters and vice versa. Self-styled 'management gurus' become media friendly commentators on matters of technological change, economic trends or government policy. Other kinds of experts are also pressed into service in the contemporary representation of social transformation. Educationalists, psychologists, sociologists and economists, whether they are based in a university or in the head offices of financial institutions, lend credibility to the prevailing accounts of economic transformation. Overall there is an increasing sense that the boundaries between milieux, whether academic, corporate, government, think tank or the various mass media are being undermined.

The transferability of these concepts across different sectors and milieux adds to their pervasiveness and their legitimacy. If the same story is told by journalists, academics and management consultants its acceptance is greatly enhanced. The narrative format that can transcend media will prioritize particular rhetorical styles. This narrativity is expressed in the use of stylized facts, sound bites, attention grabbing headlines, memorable story lines, the stress on novelty and newsworthiness and anecdotal evidence that captures changes in life style, and generational shifts in attitudes. Large concepts are expressed in small settings. The impact of global processes are emphasized in their ability to penetrate the minutiae of daily experiences influencing what we eat, read, wear or watch. The growing significance of the narratives of new capitalism has been sustained by shifts within social science, most obvious in the rise of postmodernism, which have licensed a lay understanding of contemporary social transformation and privileged ahistorical perspectives of social change. As Mike Savage (2000) points out, commentators such as Beck and Giddens do not seek empirical support for their position, but seek to convince rhetorically by setting themselves up as more plausible and 'common sense' than other discredited accounts.

This transmission of ideas across different sectors has been particularly noticeable in the United States. Stories of labour market change have been headlined in the news media and then reproduced by other types of narrators. *The Downsizing of America, The Outsourcing of America* and the *The Temping of America* are particularly powerful stories that have shaped public discussion of employment change in the United States. The case of temporary employment in America is especially illustrative of this narrativity. 'The Temping of America' first emerged as a six page article in *Time* in March 1993 and was echoed less than a year later by Fortune's cover story on 'The Contingency Workforce'. Both features reported that Manpower Inc., the temporary employment agency, was the largest employer in the United States, with 600,000 on its payroll (two key ingredients – the headline and the key fact are the wheels on which this story runs). None other than Tom Peters also wrote in the *Chicago Times* at this time, 'It is spooky to realize, as *Time* reports, that Manpower is now America's largest employer.' The story's recycling continued year upon year and almost a decade later Will Hutton trotted out the Manpower 'fact' to his British readers (Hutton 2002). Hutton is former editor of the Observer, the chief executive of the Work Foundation, and has academic appointments in the Universities of Manchester, Bristol and Oxford, and so he powerfully exemplifies this articulation of ideas across different milieux. Another new economy story of life in today's America is told and retold by journalists, management gurus, and academics as this single fact speaks volumes of job instability in this fast changing world we live in. Later discussion in Chapter 6 demonstrates that the story is bogus, but for the present it is worth noting the discursive devices that travel across milieux and enhance a particular form of representation that is peculiarly unaccountable and, while it does not sustain any empirical generalization, it enjoys a rhetorical credibility.

This chapter has emphasized the development of a specific mode of representation central to those accounts of societal transformation, based on new forms of engagement between employers and workers. This is to be understood, not as some spontaneous shift in public sensibilities that gives rise to a new spirit of capitalism, but as a confluence of narratives that emerges with the rise of neoliberalism.

Neoliberalism serves to externalize social transformation and to confine policy response to market compliance. Chapters 3 and 4 will explore the principal determinants of societal transformation and examine the role of technological change and globalization in generating new relations of employment.

2

Technological Change: Autonomization and Dematerialization

The previous chapter advanced the concept of the narratives of new capitalism as a mode of representation of the forces, mechanisms and outcomes of societal transformation. The importance of the ideological platform of new capitalism was highlighted in the rise of neoliberal managerial discourse and the transmission of these ideas across different milieux. This chapter progresses the discussion by considering the substantive or thematic content of these narratives, such as weightlessness, flows, connectivity and ubiquity, and suggests that the representation of new capitalism systematically exaggerates the transformativity of the social processes under discussion. Thus the overstatement of the mobility of capital, the impact of new technology and the retreat of the state, are products of the way that change has been (mis)represented and understood. It is suggested here that the transformativity of technological change and globalization, specifically, is tied to their perception as autonomous and disembedded processes that run on their own momentum and according to their own logic. Additionally the representation of new capitalism relies on ways of conceptualizing the world that are both abstract and ethereal, particularly in relation to the 'weightlessness' of technological change and social transformation.

Towards the end of the last chapter the discussion of new capitalism mentioned that postmodernism had licensed the rhetorics of the new economy and the common sense perceptions of social change. However postmodernism has given rise to other methodological shifts within social science that have occurred over more than twenty years. The unease surrounding discussion of ideology generated by the influence of postmodernism has already been mentioned, but more importantly the desire to understand the world in its totality has also been undermined. Postmodern sensibilities are offended by totalizing epistemologies that support the grand narratives of modernity. While this animosity towards 'metanarratives' is widely acknowledged, post-modernists are in fact highly selective in their approach to metanarra-tives. As Terry Eagleton has pointed out in his insightful discussion of the 'illusions of postmodernism', a scepticism of totalities whether they be of left or right (as with Thatcher's denial of the notion of society) is spurious.

> It generally turns out to mean a suspicion of certain kinds of totality and an enthusiastic endorsement of others. Some kinds of totality – prisons, patriarchy, the body, absolutist political powers – would be acceptable topics of conversation, while others – modes of production, social for-mations, doctrinal systems – would be silently censured . . . [Moreover] grasping the shape of totality requires some tiresomely rigorous thought, which is one reason why those who don't need to do it can revel in ambiguity and indeterminacy. (Eagleton 1996, p. 12)

Thus the desire to frame a comprehensive understanding of society based on its determinants, its structures and social outcomes has waned. But following Eagleton, the abandonment of the metanarra-tive is partial and selective. It is suggested here that the discussion of the causes, processes and outcomes of social change has been modified and a narrower framework has cohered around *new meta-narratives of process*. There is much less concern with metatheoretical concepts such as the 'the capitalist system', from which the dynam-ics of capital accumulation might be derived, but it is possible to observe the construction of highly elaborate metanarratives that provide the overarching frameworks for discussion in terms of social processes. In contemporary accounts 'globalization', 'knowledge economy', 'network society', 'informationalism' and 'flows' are sig-nifiers that enjoy all the currency and status of metanarratives. Whereas discussion of 'old capitalism' might invite consideration of social classes as agencies and the distribution of income as outcomes, new capitalism is a confluence of narratives that captures and repre-sents the world in terms of abstract, self-sustaining social processes. In the absence of strategic actors such as governments, corporations or classes, social processes appear disembodied, 'all motion no matter'. Market forces appear *naturalized,* 'emptied out' of govern-ment regulation and projected as stateless realms of economic exchange. Little wonder then that this mode of representation finds such appeal in neoliberal circles. But despite all the down to earth plainspeak of new managerial discourse, what is presented is wholly abstract as a way of understanding society. If there were an equivalent shift in medical science it might lead to a 'new haematology' exclusively concerned with the flow of blood round the body, yet remaining wholly uninterested in the heart.

Autonomous Social Processes

For Manuel Castells, society is

> constructed around flows: flows of capital, flows of information, flows of technology, flows of organizational interaction, flows of images, sounds and symbols. Flows are not just one element of the social organization: they are the expression of processes dominating our economic and political life. (Castells 1996, p. 412)

In their 'definitive work' on the subject, Held, McGrew, Goldblatt and Perraton have defined globalization as

> a process or set of processes, which embodies a transformation in the spatial organization of social relations and transactions – assessed in terms of their extensity, intensity, volume, and impact – generating transcontinental or interregional flows and networks of activity interaction and the exercise of power. (Held et al. 1999, p. 16)

Grand narratives based on social processes, comprising networks, knowledge and communication flows, as opposed to systems and structures, are less deterministic but, ironically, all embracing in their reach and scope. In contrast to the materiality of structural explanation the metanarratives of process have a greater ethereality, expressed in nebulous concepts that offer immunity from empirical critique and evidentiary challenge. Commentators deploy ideas and themes that privilege descriptive content that speaks to the experience of, or shifts within, global processes, networks and flows, instead of fundamental explanations of social structure. Rather than the 'static world' of structures or the apparent stability of fixed systems, the discussion of processes is imbued with a dynamic quality, that stresses flexibility, constant adaptation, movement and flows. In the modern economies of 'signs and space', postmodern political economy is based on the ever more rapid circulation of subjects and objects (Lash and Urry 1994). It is therefore geared towards the sense of impermanence, tenuous connections and short-term engagements.

Any assessment of societal transformation couched in terms of technological, global or organizational processes in isolation, abstracted from discussions of class, corporations, governments or economic outcomes, inevitably promotes a view of the world that is hypermobile, precarious and beyond control. The autonomization of social processes, which envisages self-sustaining, self-generating natural phenomena greatly exaggerates the pace and significance of their impacts. Thus globalization, knowledge, networks and innovation are ideas that are formulated as processes, per se, with their own internal logic, momentum and outcomes. Writing about '*Autonomous Technology*', in the mid 1970s Langdon Winner noted

> The attribution of an inherent dynamism to the process of change is particularly evident in the use of 'ization' suffix words. Here, perhaps unintentionally, connotations of a self-generating, self-sustaining process frequently creep in . . . There is a tendency to speak as if industrialization, modernization and the other 'izations' are similar to such physical processes as ionization in the sense that once they are underway, they continue on their own with a kind of in-built inertia . . . In many instances historians and economists wish to maintain that the 'ization' that they are studying is a phenomenon *sui generis*, inertial and self-sustaining. (Winner 1977, p. 50)

Furthermore autonomous processes are seen to have consequences of their own. In those accounts of the 'economy of signs and space', social relations are constituted in and through flows of information and communication (Lash and Urry 1994). Globalization, as rendered by Giddens, is an autonomous process in that we are said to live in a 'runaway world' that is out of our control, moreover, in this reading of globalization the very presence of global communication flows has profound societal effects. However, the analytical significance of this emphasis on process is often concealed in a discussion that can at times appear both banal and weirdly overstated. Giddens, for instance, suggests,

> Instantaneous electronic communication isn't just a way in which information is conveyed more quickly. Its existence alters the very texture of our lives, rich and poor alike. When the face of Nelson Mandela is more familiar to us than the face of our next door neighbour then something has changed in the nature of our everyday experience . . . For globalization is not incidental to our lives today. It is a shift in our very life circumstances. It is the way we now live. (Giddens 2002, p. 11)

This is an argument that becomes stranger the more it is considered. My neighbour is not an international celebrity but, according to Giddens, this somehow makes him (or his face) less familiar to me. In which case Giddens needs to be brought back to earth. My neighbour does not have global public recognition, but I would not leave the house keys with Nelson Mandela when I go on holiday, nor would I ask Victoria Beckham to look after the kids for an hour while I go for a hospital check up. The media have been celebrity conscious since the rise of Hollywood, but it is debatable whether the celebrity of Mandela is greater than the stars of the pre-globalization era such as John Wayne or Elvis. Moreover, even if it is true that a 'celebrity culture' is more obvious in contemporary society this says little about social relations in the neighbourhood, the workplace or wider society. In Giddens' perspective life chances are less explained by access to education, the level of income and form of employment, the quality of diet, sanitation and health services, but somehow more determined by global flows of symbols, images and sounds. While it is not unreasonable to seek their impact on cultural life, in our sense of aesthetics or fashion and in shaping our leisure activities, it is a leap of imagination to see global information and communication flows reshaping social relations in any fundamental sense.

Dematerialization

The new capitalist narratives mark a break with the past in that they seek an immaterial representation of change. Periods of human history since its earliest days have been defined in relation to tool making (stone, wood or metal), or in forms of production, hunting or gathering, agriculture etc. More recent transitions from feudalism to capitalism, have been correlated with material changes in technology as with Marx's dictum that 'the handmill gives you society with the feudal lord, the steam mill; society with the industrial capitalist'. Previous phases of capitalist development have been powerfully symbolized in machines or engines that embodied the possibilities of the day. John Zysman and Abe Newman summarized the clusters of technological innovation over the past two centuries and connected machines with specific periods of development: (1) the industrial revolution and the Awkright Mill; (2) the age of steam and railways; (3) the era of steel, electricity and heavy engineering; and (4) the automobile and mass production (Zysman and Newman 2004). Thus from the industrial revolution through to the middle of the 20th century, transformation in productive capacity and in living conditions had a mechanical iconography expressed in a variety of forms such as the steam engine, the automobile, and the electric light bulb (Winner 1977).

However the new capitalist narratives describe technological possibilities by emphasizing the extent to which they have overcome material constraints. There are several strands to this representation of societal transformation that might be grouped under the heading of *dematerialization*. In relation to information and communication technologies, miniaturization and exponential increases in processing speeds and memory capacity, combine to show how modern technologies have escaped, in Gilder's words 'the tyranny of matter'. Danny Quay, a leading proponent of dematerialization, combines the rise in computing power with miniaturization to describe the weightlessness of modern economies.

> In 1949 when ENIAC – one of the world's first viable computers was turned on – the streetlights of Pittsburg would dim. By the beginning of the 1990s anyone could walk into a local supermarket and purchase a Hallmark greeting card, for two pounds sterling, that performs a reasonable rendition of Happy Birthday, and which contains more computing power than existed on all of planet Earth in the 1950s.

It is a good story of the immense growth of computing power, in new gadgets that take up a miniscule proportion of the space and energy requirements of the early computers. It is an example also used by Diana Coyle in her discussion of the weightless world. Thus the narratives stress the decreasing size of computing alongside their explosive growth in their 'power'. Lawrence Summers and Bradford DeLong's description of the new economy argues that in the 1950s there were 2,000 computers in the US, by 2002 there were three hundred million – a 4 billion-fold increase in raw automated computing power, an annual average rate of growth of 56% (quoted in Zysman and Newman (2004)). In looking at what is new about the new economy, Cohen Delong and Zysman have suggested that,

> In the 1960s Intel Corporation co-founder Gordon Moore projected that the density of transistors on a silicon chip – and thus the power of a chip – would double every eighteen months. Moore's Law, as it came to be called, has held. Today's chips have 256 times the density of those manufactured in 1987 – and 65,000 times the density of those manufactured in 1975 . . . In ten years time computers will be more than 10 million times more powerful than those of 1975 – at the same cost . . .

The past 40 years have seen a billion fold increase in the installed base
of computing power. (Cohen, DeLong and Zysman 2000)

In these narratives time, space and distance do not limit the capacities of the new information technologies. High speed, high capacity
fibre optic transmission technologies, which can download the contents of the Library of Congress in a second, also ensure that the cost
of long-distance communications has shrunk to a 128th of what they
were some 20 years previously. According to Francis Cairncross
(2002), former senior editor of the Economist, this leads to a new
phenomenon, 'the death of distance'. Additionally, such is the preju-
dice of this ethereal mindset, that many commentators seem oblivious
to the material advances in transport and communications which have
helped make the world a smaller place. Thus the expansion of freight
containerization which has greatly reduced the transportation costs of
everything from Australian wine to Chinese electrical components
features rarely in the contemporary accounts of social transformation.

To fetishize ICT processes in this way, reinforces the sense of
autonomous self-sustaining growth, and indulges all sorts of speculation as to the social outcomes of technological change. Discussions of
dematerialization operate at two levels. In the first instance it advances
the theme that products are getting much lighter or smaller and
require far less energy inputs in their production. There is a second
meaning of dematerialization that relates to the shift in the balance
between matter and information in the shift from atoms to 'bits'.
Nicholas Negroponte, Director of the Media Lab in MIT and colum-
nist for Wired, uses bits to refer to the binary digits, the zeroes and
ones of computer language, and argues that the ICT revolution is
manifest in the shift from atoms which are physical material to bits
which have no colour, size, weight and can travel at the speed of light.
In this account dematerialized knowledge embedded in digital codes
is increasingly the source of economic value in the new economy.
Technology offers us tools that can organize, store and transmit information in digital form, which can generate increased data and also
enhance their analysis, and in this way there is a self-expanding
element to the digital revolution. However, this is not just a question
of speed of transmission of large volumes of information but a fundamental shift in the relationship between information and its medium.
Since knowledge is immaterial and independent of its medium,
increasingly, Quay argues, dematerialized commodities show no
respect for space and geography . . . wealth creation and economic
activities will occur in disembodied, dematerialized processes.

Manufacture of the world's most valuable commodity is already location blind (Quay 1996).

The dematerialization of knowledge and information is premised on the conceptual separation of motion and matter. The philosophical or theoretical flaw is that the production and consumption of knowledge and information remains materialist even if its circulation is immaterial. Negroponte waxes lyrical that time is becoming meaningless, and supports his case by arguing that a five-hour piece of music can be downloaded in five seconds. This is a clear example of the fetishism of knowledge transmission, in that, even if downloaded in five seconds, it is still a five-hour piece of music that cannot be played or listened to in anything less than five hours. Where and how commodities are produced and consumed remain central to the understanding of economic activities and to regard knowledge as somehow independent of such mundane considerations is to indulge in very abstract and ultimately distorted conceptualization of societal transformation.

The idea that production or consumption can be simply derived from changes in information and communication is a common but a fairly crude expression of technological determinism. It is true that new technologies have had particular impact on specific sectors such as the print industry. Images of giant printing presses have been replaced by desktop publishing, and the arrival of word processing inspired visions of office automation which would give rise to the 'paperless office'. The editorial of Administrative Management in 1970 suggested that, by the end of the 1970s we should have climbed out of 'the Gutenberg rut'. The 'Office of the Future' was first discussed by Business Week in 1975 and highlighted office automation and the paperless office (Haigh 2006). Yet the further development of ICT has prompted an exponential growth in the consumption of paper. Annual world consumption of paper has increased from 131 million metric tons in 1975 to 352 million metric tons in 2005. The United States, presumably the most obvious beneficiary of any trends towards paperless environments, has seen annual paper consumption rise from 48 million metric tons to 89 million in the same period (World Resources Institute 2007). Electronics did not become a substitute for paper as many predicted, it has greatly increased its usage. In other words dematerialization cannot be derived from the storage and transmission of information, no matter how impressive the speed of download and memory capacities of today's computers. To focus on the transmission of information, and the chimera of weightlessness it conveys, to the neglect of the production and consumption of knowledge, can only serve to distort analysis of the transformativity of technological change. For this reason alone social and economic outcomes are especially difficult to derive purely from changes in technology.

Castells' Network Society

The implications of this methodological shift, which sees the reification of social process, are highlighted in Castells' account of the Network Society (Castells 1996). In this work the author studies the emergence of a new social structure associated with the emergence of 'a new mode of development' – 'informationalism'. The informational mode of development is based on the technology of knowledge generation, information processing, and symbolic communication. While knowledge and information are critical elements in the development of all societies throughout history, the novelty of the informational mode of development is the action of knowledge on knowledge as the main source of productivity. Castells posits a new 'technological paradigm' based on information technology. It has five characteristics:

(1) That technologies act on information in a self-sustaining process in which knowledge acts on knowledge.
(2) Because information is an integral part of all human activity the pervasive effects of new technologies characterize the new paradigm.
(3) Any system or set of relationships using the new information technologies are impelled to a networking logic.
(4) The information paradigm is based on flexibility. In a society characterized by 'constant change and organizational fluidity' the distinctive feature of the configuration of the new paradigm is its ability to reconfigure.
(5) The convergence of specific technologies into a highly integrated system. Microelectronics, telecommunications, optoelectronics and computers are now integrated information systems.

Related to the impact of knowledge acting on knowledge Castells suggests a technological convergence and growing interdependence between the biological and microelectronic revolutions, both materially and methodologically. He accurately points to the advances in genome mapping that were facilitated by the rapid improvements in computing technologies. However this serves to bolster a more contentious position that all technologies, whether they are biological or microelectronic, are generically described as informational. Arguably this can only be true at the broadest level of generalization, yet the informational paradigm is questionable on more substantive grounds.

Before examining the critiques it is worth noting that Castells' work represents a very impressive reading of a large volume of material, surveying research and reviewing literature, using insights from urban sociology, international political economy and human geography. Yet a systematic review of his work can be a deeply frustrating experience. In a very insightful evaluation of Castells, Peter Marcuse (2002) notes that Castells' style makes criticism difficult, because it is inherently contradictory. 'For any particular quote, one can generally find another, apparently contradictory elsewhere. . . . The evidence that is adduced to prove one point often contradicts a point made elsewhere' (Marcuse 2002, p. 136).

This internal inconsistency might be explained by a desire on Castells' part to make grand statements about the process of social transformation, but at the same time cover his tracks through qualification and counterclaim. Castells might be, in the words of the Irish rugby captain, 'getting his retaliation in first'. The internal consistency, however, might be better understood as part of the baggage he has carried on his political odyssey from neo-Marxism to Third Way social democracy. In Castells' work Marcuse detects a 'ghostly Marxism' in which echoes of Marxist analysis are still presented, albeit denuded of their radical political content. Thus his mode of development strongly resonates with Marx's concept of the forces of production, although the latter was firmly connected to capitalist relations of production. In Castells' case there is ambivalence and inconsistency in suggesting a social process that, not withstanding historical, cultural and institutional variation, to a considerable extent runs on its own accord.

Castells contrasts the mode of development in the informational age with the mode of development in the industrial age. 'Industrialism is oriented towards economic growth, that is towards maximizing output; informationalism is oriented towards technological development, that is towards higher levels of complexity in information processing' (p. 17). On this reading technological innovation has gained its own internal logic and momentum, significantly different from earlier developments in industrial society which were motivated by economic imperatives. The emergence of a ' new technological system in the 1970s must be traced to the autonomous dynamics of techno-logical discovery and diffusion, including the synergistic effects between various key technologies' (Castells 1996, p. 51).

Thus the informational paradigm is the master concept through which the new social structure is analysed. Theoretically all other processes and systems are derived from, or at least are profoundly influenced by it. At times the relationships between the mode of devel-opment and broader political or institutional changes are presented in an offhand manner. Thus Castells discusses the 'informational/global economy' which seems a casual coupling of concepts at best. At other times, and not withstanding his desire to present a new social struc-ture, he talks about 'informational capitalism'. The greater inconsis-tencies are however revealed in his treatment of the dynamics of the technological paradigm, rooted in the largely autonomous processes of scientific discovery and its relationship with political and institu-tional change. If previous modes of industrial development were eco-nomically motivated, then informationalism is oriented towards the accumulation of knowledge and towards higher levels of complexity in information processing. Knowledge accumulation for the sake of knowledge might seem a noble idea, but is increasingly difficult to rec-oncile with the growth of knowledge-based companies. In this schema scientists and innovators appear as computer geeks with all the earthly impulses of Tibetan monks, yet it is difficult to square with the work-ings of knowledge-based industries and companies like Microsoft. Was the XBOX developed to satiate the thirst for complexity as knowledge acted on knowledge, or did Microsoft have an eye on the huge profits in the games market that were enjoyed by SONY and NINTENDO?

The autonomy of technological development might be seen as a dubious theoretical construct, emerging out of his need to establish a new social structure driven by impulses and dynamics distinct from the industrial mode of development. Castells, however, also recog-nizes historical, institutional cultural diversity that presents the actuality of developments and raises fundamental difficulties for his theorizing of informationalism. Thus while Castells says that infor-mation technology in the 1970s was technologically induced rather than socially determined he then goes on to say that 'Profitability and competitiveness are the actual determinants of technological innova-tion and productivity' (Castells 1996, p. 81). The distinction between theoretical exposition and analytical determinants, which are rooted in historical and institutional contexts, runs throughout his work. In the abstract the informational mode of development is characterized by the autonomous accumulation of knowledge. In actuality, in terms of agency 'the state, not the innovative entrepreneur in his garage, both in America and throughout the world, was the initiator of the Information Technology Revolution' (Castells 1996, p. 60).

Given that Castells suggests that the new mode of development gives rise to a 'new social structure' his treatment of organizational or institutional change is of critical importance. In this regard theory and analysis are even more incongruous. At a theoretical level, network society 'is the convergence and interaction between a new technological paradigm and a new networking logic that constitutes the historical foundation of the informational economy' (p. 152). Yet on the following page he notes the organizational changes within the economy 'by and large were independent, and in general terms, preceded the diffusion of the information technologies in business firms' (p. 153). If institutional change has a prior, independent existence then corporate restructuring had its own rationale and procedures before the diffusion of information and communication technology. While the *pace* of corporate restructuring may have been increased to a limited extent by new information technologies, its logic and pattern would not have been decisively affected by it. Accordingly the explanatory significance of technological developments in determining some new social structure must be significantly, if not fatally, undermined.

However in the broader connection between theory and empirical evidence of the transformation of work Castells is much less circumspect. Large scale statistical evidence of employment changes are presented, not only to bolster his technological paradigm, but to offer an even more radical vision of the new social structure in which the fundamental transformation gives rise to the individualization of work and the fragmentation of societies. Yet his use of statistics is open to analytical challenge on fairly basic grounds. At an early stage his survey of labour market change confronts an interesting conundrum in that employment expansion in information processing has seen a fairly modest expansion across the advanced economies. This is a difficulty which is only circumvented by drawing the distinction between information employment, per se, and the epochal development of an information society as a whole. Informational technology is most productive, Castells argues, when it is embedded in material production or in goods handling rather than as a stand-alone activity. Therefore the ability to pin down the informational elements in production or services through direct statistical measurement is severely limited. It can only be inferred.

Given the weight of a theory that postulates a new social structure, informationalism is seen in every aspect of industrial, occupational and compositional change in the labour market. Just as Castells conflates most, if not all technological process and applications as having the similar or convergent informational characteristics, institutional restructuring is increasingly defined as informational, regardless of the technological input into the reorganization process. Organizational changes, such as outsourcing, quality control and team working are embraced as the new business practices of informational companies. While it is true that new systems of stock inventory are used in 'lean production' and testify to the importance of data gathering and throughput monitoring, to reduce lean production to an informational process is to neglect the reorganization of workplace practices through changes in management and union relations, working conditions and remuneration, and employee representation and bargaining. When a hospital outsources its catering services or a local authority contracts out its refuse collection it is a leap of faith to imagine that they are informational employers. Yet in Castells' schema, new information technologies have become the critical ingredient of the labour process, because it determines innovation capability and provides the infrastructure for flexibility and adaptability throughout the management of the production process.

The 'Productivity Paradox'

For all the 'buzz' about the knowledge economy it is surprisingly difficult to find any clear systematic connections between the meta-themes of technological change and the transformation of work. Moreover to consider 'the role of new technology' tacitly assumes that all technologies have similar form, shelf life and rates of dissemination, generalized application and comparable outcomes. Yet the impact of advances in bio-technology, electrical engineering and information technology cannot be compared easily. Their specific and/or combined impacts require further refinement in terms of product development or process development. Evidence of direct changes in labour process and employment can be detected at the level of the firm or perhaps the sector, but the ability to make any broader generalization is limited. Consequently researchers who wish to conduct macroeconomic research into the relationship between new technology and growth, productivity, and employment change are often forced to use proxy indicators which are of questionable value in supporting broader generalization. Such proxies include the percentage of research and development expenditures as a proportion of gross national expenditures, the value of e-commerce sales, and some have used patent data as a way of establishing rates of techno-logical change. Research and development embraces very different aspects of the invention, application and dissemination of technolo-gies. As seen in Bell's discussion of the knowledge economy, research and defence expenditures are embedded to significant extent in military defence spending which can seriously inflate R&D estimates. Moreover technological innovation does not guarantee the ability to develop and exploit the benefits of such advances, and there is a crit-ical distinction between industries that produce new technologies and those that use new technologies.

Information and communications technologies (ICT) have the most widespread dissemination in the economy and application in terms of labour process, but the extent to which ICT allows any macroeconomic generalization is also questionable. Despite the huge increase of ICT investment the impact on productivity growth is highly contested. The 'productivity paradox' first enshrined in Robert Solow's famous quip, 'you can see the computer age everywhere but in the statistics', has aligned sceptics and supporters since that time. Robert Brenner makes the point well.

> The capital stock of computers and peripheral equipment increased at the phenomenal average annual rate of 30% between 1975 and 1985, and near 20% between 1985 and 1993. The fact remains that even by 1993, the share of computers and peripheral equipment in net capital stock was just 2%. This was more than triple its level in 1975, but even granting huge productive powers to computers, clearly too small to make much of a dent in aggregate private business productivity. (Brenner 1998, p. 248)

The debate about the significance of ICT to productivity growth intensified during the boom of the mid to late 1990s and since that time. Federal Reserve economists Oliner and Sichel (2000) have led these discussions and concluded that 0.6 percentage points of US growth in the period 1996–9 were attributable to computing hardware and that some 0.5% points were attributed to software and commu-nications technology. Even on this generous estimate less than a quarter of the growth rates in the new economy boom were explained by the economic impact of ICT in the economy. Jack Tripplet of the National Bureau of Economic Research pointed out that in some of the industries with the most extensive use of ICT such as finance, wholesale trade, business services and communication, productivity was either very slow or declining (Tripplet 1999). Robert Gordon of Northwestern University, however, was the most significant sceptic about the ICT role in explaining the new economy boom. Gordon stresses the difference between computer production and computer use, suggesting that productivity gains in the production of computers did not spread to the rest of durable goods manufacturing. Significantly, productivity in industries such as finance, insurance and real estate that were big users of computers lagged behind national growth trends.

> There is no sign of a fundamental transformation of the US economy. There has been no acceleration of Multi Factor Productivity growth outside of computer production and the rest of durable manufacturing. Responding to the accelerated rate of price decline of computers that occurred between 1995 and 1998 business firms throughout the economy boosted purchases of computers, creating an investment boom and 'capital deepening' in the form of faster capital growth relative to labour. But computer capital did not have any kind of magical or extra-ordinary effect – it earned the same rate of return as any other type of capital. (Gordon 2002)

International research comparing the productivity and employment effects of the knowledge economy in the European Union and the United States has distinguished between ICT-producing industries, ICT-using industries and non-ICT industries (van Ark, Inklaar, McGukin and Timmer 2003). Looking at the 2000 evidence it notes that productivity growth was greatest in ICT-producing industries, namely computers and semiconductors, but that this sector does not have a large impact on the total economy due to the small weight of this sector, with a GDP share of 5.9% in the EU and 7.3% in the US. In the year 2000, ICT-using industries accounted for 27% of GDP in the EU and 30.6% of GDP in the United States. Contrary to the views of Castells, the non-ICT industries accounted for 67% of GDP in the EU and 62% of GDP in the US for the same year (van Ark, Inklaar, McGukin and Timmer 2003).

From New Economy to Telecoms Crash

The irrational exuberance of the 1990s stock market boom in the United States was fuelled by the deregulation of the finance and telecoms sectors. Clinton's Telecommunications Act of 1996 allowed for the arrival of new entrants into the market and set in motion a frenzy of mergers and acquisitions in the telecoms sectors. According to Brenner (2003), in the five years after 1995 some 1670 mergers and acquisitions occurred in the communications industry valued at $1.3 trillion. Fuelled by an almost limitless supply of finance from Wall Street and the promise of fantastic opportunities arising from the rise of the internet, expansion in telecoms companies meant that by 2000, market capitalization had reached $2.7 trillion, representing 15% of the total for all non-financial corporations. Despite the decline in profitability in the telecommunication sector since 1997, the rise in the share price led to huge investment and employment gains, with 331,000 new jobs in the sector. However, like the coyote in the Road Runner cartoons, eventually the sector could only run for a limited period without the profits to fuel further expansion. Brenner points out:

> In 2000 no fewer than six US companies were building new mutually competitive nationwide fibre optic networks. Hundreds more were laying down local lines and several were also competing on sub oceanic links. All told 39 million miles of fibre optic line now criss-cross the US, enough to circle the globe, 1566 times. The unavoidable by-product has been a mountainous glut: the utilisation rate of telecom networks hovers today at a disastrously low 2.5/3%, that of undersea cable at just 13%. (Brenner 2003)

Corporate bankruptcies in the telecoms sector ensued after investment collapsed in 2000, the value of shares plummeted by 95% and within two years more than half a million workers in the industry were laid off. Moreover the collateral damage in those sectors of manufacturing linked with telecommunications, such as semi-conductor and electronic equipment, contributed greatly to the three million jobs loss for manufacturing after 2001. Brenner's account of the new economy miracle and the subsequent bursting of the bubble reveals the unfolding of a classical business cycle of expansion and overproduction, albeit one intensified by market deregulation and rampant speculation and concentrated in a narrow time frame. It was then followed by a series of bankruptcies and scandals in which CEOs of companies like Enron and World Com tried to hide the extent of their losses. Behind all the talk of epochal change and new informational modes of development, and an economy driven by a new impetus to innovate, lies a legion of fund managers, consultants, brokers, bankers and business leaders whose self-interest seduced a broader public into believing in the new technological dawn.

The Employment Effects of Technological Change

Ever since the term 'knowledge industries' was coined by Fritz Machlup, the statistical evidence of rising informational employment has been thin on the ground. Even using Machlup's methodology, the expansion of information-related employment seems to have slowed down after 1970. In 1980 another study, using the same methodology, showed that informational labour accounted for only one third of all jobs in the United States (May 2002). In the year 2000 the international research carried out by van Ark and colleagues, mentioned previously, considered the employment effects of ICT-producing, ICT-using and non-ICT sectors in the US and the EU. In terms of total employment levels ICT-producing industries accounted for 3.9% of employment in the EU and 4.9% in the US. ICT-using industries accounted for 27.3% of employment in the EU and 28.7% in the US, while non-ICT industries accounted for 68.6% of employment in the EU and 66.4% in the US. In terms of employment growth the rate of expansion in the latter half of the 1990s was greatest in ICT-producing industries (2.8% in the EU and 4.9% in the US) but the small size of this sector means that the contribution of the sector to employment growth overall was very modest – one fifth of the non-ICT sectors. Interestingly, during the so-called new economy boom the research shows that annual employment growth rates in the US in non-ICT sectors were greater than ICT-using sectors, at 2.0% compared to 1.6%, while comparable figures for the EU were 1.3% and 1.1% (van Ark, Inklaar, McGukin and Timmer 2003).

If the link between labour productivity and new technology is tenuous, the relationship between new technology and employment and working arrangements is even more difficult to pin down. The record of futurologists who predict social and employment consequences is less than impressive, indeed there have been some spectacular misjudgements about the employment implications of technological change. Thus in the early 1970s the US telecom giant AT&T predicted that by the 1990s the majority of the labour force would be working at home. The relocation of work from the office and factory to the home is a trend that has been hugely overstated in the last 20 years. Whilst it is true that the falling costs of word processors and home based internet and email provision has allowed more work to be done at home, the extent to which this can effectively replace face to face contact in the workplace is highly debatable. Alan Felstead and colleagues have suggested that the option to work at home is another perk for those who occupy a privileged position in the labour force (Felstead et al. 2002). Moreover there is an important distinction between working from and at home, as well as distinctions between telework and homework, which have been the subject of heated debate (Sullivan 2002). More recent debates around the work-life balance (Warhurst et al. 2008) have explored the nature of the boundary between home and work and whether it is flexible or permeable (de Majn de Bruijn and Groeneveld 2008), but overall little evidence has been presented to suggest a fundamental shift in the nature of employment relations.

The case for the transformative potential of ICT rests to some extent on the growth of computing power available either as desktop or laptop. Consumers have become aware of the adjustment in units used to classify computing capacity as we ascend the Kilo-Mega-Giga-Terra-(Peca?) range of byts. However, a larger question is posed as to the practical significance of the increase in computing power. The PC on the desk might be replaced every three years and the processor speeds ratcheted up each time, but what impact does this have on the labour process? Only a very small proportion of the workforce, it appears, exploits the full potential of enhanced computing capacity. Freeman (2002) points out that the widespread use of computers at work is concentrated among white collar workers, particularly managers and professionals, who use their computer for email over the internet, word-processing, spread sheet and data base analysis and for calendar scheduling, which suggest a very basic use of the technologies. Relatedly, a larger question is raised as to whether improvements in computing technology are driven by the requirements of production or leisure and consumption. At home the increased broadband width and processor speeds are used to good effect in downloading MP3 titles and movies, yet during the day these machines resemble Rolls Royces that are used to do the work of electric milk floats. While it is certainly true that the contents of the Library of Congress can be downloaded in seconds, for most jobs this is not relevant.

The employment effects of new technologies are operationalized differently at the level of the firm and industry. In retailing, new technologies have prompted rationalization of the industry and also the concentration and centralization of corporate structure, particularly in the US and the UK. Thus employment for the sector as a whole can decrease due to rationalization but expand rapidly at the level of the company. Electronic point of sale technologies, including bar coding and scanning, have introduced huge efficiencies in stock control, delivery of supplies and the monitoring of customer through-put, sales and labour performance. This has afforded extraordinary exploitation of economies of scale in retailing and the concentration of ownership and centralization of organization within the sector. Names like Wal-Mart and Tesco are among the largest private sector employers in Europe and North America. There are over one million 'associates' of Wal-Mart worldwide, while Tesco employs a quarter of a million people in Britain alone. Such technologies facilitate greater monitoring and surveillance of work and the capacity to schedule staff to meet fluctuations in customer demand (Lichtenstein 2006). This in turn drives 24-hour shopping, which creates demand for labour to work at different times and in different shift patterns. New technology is therefore associated with changes in the form and composition of employment, but it must be stressed that changes in sales technology would not have changed retailing on their own. Organizational changes in retailing, particularly in the food sector, also relied on changes in transportation, distribution and supply systems. Moreover, the extent of international variation in part-time working and women's participation in the labour market also suggests that technological impacts are not largely determinant of labour market outcomes in these sectors.

Overall the employment effects of new technology appear to be significantly overstated. There certainly appears to be a gap between the claims for the transformative capacity of technological innovation and its material presence in the economy. The rising speed and power of computer processing, together with the fall in cost of their manufacture and the expanding width of broadband, have created a climate in which the public are receptive to ideas of pervasive societal change, but the extent to which this has left its occupational imprint is confined to small sectors of the workforce. It is interesting to note that the Charles Handy of the 1990s who spoke of a period of 'discontinuous change' arising out of technological innovation and corporate restructuring, in 2001, at the age of 68, in more reflective mood suggested that 'new technology reinforces what already happens. It does not replace it. Most of the occupations that we are familiar with today will still exist in twenty years' time' (Handy 2001).

Technological change plays a part in the reorganization of labour processes alongside other changes in work practices. Improvements in transport, information and communication technologies will feed into any corporate relocation strategies, if companies are minded to set up in other countries, but to imagine that ICT is driving some capital flight and shaping some new international division of labour is to overstate the case. Where many commentators see social relations constituted in information and communication flows, in relation to the workplace the opposite is true. In the workplace, technological change is, to a large extent, circumscribed by the pre-existing institutional structures and forms of work organization. The rise of 'immaterial labour' appears greatly overstated and consequently there is very limited evidence to show that technology is creating the conditions for the new employment relations that are the focus of this inquiry.

Overall, this chapter has argued that the autonomization and dematerialization of new technology constitute a wholly abstract way of representing economic development which gives a greatly exaggerated and unbalanced assessment of the transformativity of technological change. This abstraction fits well with those neoliberal perspectives that seek to naturalize the working of market forces and inculcate the sense of exogenous change in society. It therefore has to be seen in its ideological context, connecting technological change with neoliberal managerial discourse and expressing a set of ideas about changes in society which are articulated across different milieux. Dematerialization can be conceived at different levels and in different arena as a form of institutional filtering in which the instrumental role of governments, classes and corporations fades into the background while societal transformation is expressed in disembodied social processes. If technology is seen in isolation from changes in work organization, market conditions and production processes, it is given an independent explanatory role that it is unable to sustain. It therefore follows that critical analysis must rematerialize the discussion of societal transformation, reinstate the role of strategic actors, and subject the claims to societal transformation to empirical critique.

3

Globalization: Mobility, Transnationality and Employment

In progressing this materialist critique of new capitalism, this chapter moves on to discuss globalization. Globalization is a multidimensional concept but the principal approach adopted here relates to its perceived role in promoting relational change within capitalism. In Bauman's *Liquid Modernity* globalization creates new forms of engagement between capital and labour based on tenuous connections between firms and workers and a much greater sense of individualization, whereas for Giddens globalization gives rise to a 'post-traditional society'. Traditional roles within the family and the community are undermined by a greater awareness of, and engagement with, modern life styles, non-traditional work outside the home and new expressions of sexuality and intimacy. In his view the transformation of work is emphasized in the decline of traditional industries, traditional skills and crafts and the spread of non-traditional 'a-typical' forms of employment which give rise to new social relations in the home, at work and wider society.

Parallels between narratives of globalization and the network society are evident in that both accounts, to varying degrees, stress the autonomy of social process. Moreover, just as Castells is keen to abstract informationalism from industrialism, Giddens similarly stresses that new dynamics express modern forms of globalization.

The first phase of globalization was plainly governed by the expansion of the West, and institutions which originated in the West. No other civilization made anything like so pervasive an impact on the world, or shaped it so much in its own image. Yet, unlike other forms of cultural or military conquest, *disembedding via abstract systems is intrinsically decentred, since it cuts through the organic connection with place upon which tradition depended* (emphasis added). Although still dominated by

Western power, globalization today can no longer be spoken of as a matter of one-way imperialism. Action at a distance was always a two way process; now increasingly there is no obvious direction to global-ization at all as its ramifications are more or less ever present. The current phase of globalization should not be confused with its preced-ing one, whose structures it acts increasingly to subvert. (Giddens 1994, p. 96)

Giddens implies that the globalization of 'late modernity' is distinct from the cultural practices and military structures of imperialism, which raises some interesting questions about the wars in Iraq and Afghanistan. But for present purposes in this 'runaway world', as Giddens puts it, there is no obvious direction to globalization, strongly suggesting an autonomous social process that erodes the social structures of earlier phases of development. Finally there is no conceptual horizon beyond the contemporary landscape of globaliza-tion. Post-traditional society is no longer 'out there' acting on 'others'. It is truly ubiquitous and inclusive – 'the first truly global society'.

The globalization debates have been mapped out in Colin Hay and David Marsh's survey of the literature (Hay and Marsh 2000). They argue that the globalization debate has evolved through two waves and their own contribution prefigures a third wave of discussion. The first wave was characterized by overblown generalizations about the inex-orable and immutable globalization of capital, culture and communi-cations. This sets in train the decline of the nation state, the welfare state and distinct civil societies, all of which adds up to a shift of epochal proportions. This is a 'business globalization' literature that employs a casual empiricism characterized by the selective and unscrupulous use of evidence. It is endlessly trotted out in business, political and media circles and in certain academic domains. Hay and Marsh cite Ohmae (1990), Levitt (1983), Reich (1992) and Sachs and Warner (1995) as high profile contributors to this first wave of debate. A second wave of debate emerged in the mid 1990s in which the con-tributors were profoundly sceptical of neoliberal triumphalism and the 'globaloney' of the informational revolution. Detailed empirical studies questioned the hypermobility of capital, reinstated the salience of the domestic economy, the continuing presence of the state and the lack of convergence in international macroeconomic indicators. Chief among the sceptics mentioned are Bairoch (1996), Evans (1997), Hirst and Thompson (1996), Rodrik (1996) and Weiss (1998).

In its first and second wave the Hay and Marsh survey is also not wholly different from Held, McGrew and Perraton who distinguish between hyperglobalist, sceptics and transformationalists. However the usefulness of the Hay and Marsh contribution is the speculation about future prospects for a third wave of debates. While clearly in the sceptical camp they suggest that discussion will become increasingly complex and focused on global processes per se. In considering 'the global ideology of globalization' they seek to observe the impact of perceived effects as well as actual outcomes. Thus, regardless of the actual propensity of capital to relocate to other parts of the world, perceptions of capital flight have an impact on politics, policy and industrial relations in specific national settings. The ideas about globalization have a material effect 'in shaping the social, political and economic contexts in which we live'. If the contribution of Hay and Marsh is placed alongside the emphasis on the ideological changes in the new spirit of capitalism described by Boltanski and Chiapello, as well as Thrift's discussion of the cultural circuit of capitalism, then it is clear the debates about 'the new economy', 'globalization' and 'new capitalism' have increasingly recognized the space between rhetoric and empirical reality, and have addressed the impact of ideology and ideational factors in explaining this gap. Further advances in these debates suggest that scepticism is an insufficient response to the hype and hot air surrounding globaloney or the new economy. There are powerful ideological forces at work which remain unnoticed and go unchecked if intellectual disdain is the dominant response to such representations of societal transformation.

As with the discussion of technological change, the critique of globalization presented here will examine the accounts of autonomous processes which express exogenous change. Disembeddedness, which assumes the separation of activities from their local contexts, is central to the transformation of work which portends the rise of new capitalism. Thus since the industrial revolution, companies and workforces were said to express a co-dependency, but globalization has now loosened the connections between workers and employers. Firms are no longer bound to localities or communities and can decamp with the flexibility of a travelling circus, giving rise to a new form of capital that is 'spatially indifferent'. The global economy is seen to be *extranational* along two dimensions that might be thought of as horizontal and vertical. Horizontal, in that market forces have transcended national boundaries and are now positioned beyond the territorial limits of government control, and vertical, as a global process operating on a higher plane of activity. The United Nations Conference on Trade and Development (UNCTAD) describes 'the universe of TNCs' made up of 77,000 parent companies with over 770,000 foreign affiliates. In 2005 these foreign affiliates generated an estimated $4.5 trillion in value added, employed some 62 million workers and exported goods and services valued at more than \$4 trillion (UNCTAD 2006). In this vein, global processes operating on a higher spatial plane are contrasted with the pre-globalized capitalism of closed economies, territorially bounded firms and state controlled societies.

Capital Mobility and Transnationality

The analysis of globalization is beset with a number of challenges and it is necessary to get a balanced assessment of the scale of the activities observed and have a sense of the absolute and relative dimensions of economic trends whether considering trade, investment flows or employment. Take trade statistics as an example, America is the largest exporter in the world economy in absolute terms, but in relative terms the picture is very different. Thus according to government figures, US exports at the end of the Second World War accounted for 5% of GDP, but in the first decade of the 21st century have only increased to some 11% of GDP. Relative to the rest of the economy this is small and much smaller still when compared to other countries where exports and imports can account for three quarters of GDP. Furthermore, in the case of US trade, import penetration is highly uneven and is heavily concentrated in specific consumer goods. As Misha Petrovic and Gary Hamilton show, import penetration is extensive in shoes, luggage, toys and low-end consumer electronics (Petrovic and Hamilton 2006). It is possible that import penetration in a small number of sectors with high public visibility might also help to overstate its significance for the home market, and so for a variety of reasons a balanced assessment of trade in a large, relatively self-sufficient economy such as the US, must consider both relative and absolute dimensions and also its sectoral distribution.

The growth of transnational corporations in recent decades also tests the analysis of global economic integration. On one indicator a third of the world's output 'comes under the common governance' of 77,000 TNCs and 770,000 affiliates whose internal transfers account for a half of world trade (UNCTAD 2007). This provides a strong case for those exponents of global integration, and yet the transnationality of TNCs is much smaller than is initially apparent. *Because a corporation owns affiliates in other countries it does not imply that all, or even a majority of its operations can be considered transnational.* Thirdly corporate globalization connotes the linkage between third world producers and first world consumers and a rebalancing of activities between the developed and less developed economies. The dramatic growth of the Chinese and Indian economies featured in many accounts prefigures the shifting of the centre of gravity from the west to the east. Again, while acknowledging the significance of strong economic growth in China and India, in the greater scheme of things it is necessary to balance particular and general trends and assess overall changes in the regional share of overseas investment.

The critique of globalization presented here focuses on three issues. In the first instance it considers the mobility of capital, since disembeddedness is offered as the primary factor in generating new relations of employment. Secondly it explores the conceptual separation of national and global spheres of activity, since the global appears as a higher order extranational concept which underpins ideas of epochal change. Thirdly it challenges the idea of the ubiquity of capital flows and seeks to identify within the fog of global capital dispersal the specificity of the spatial distribution of capital investment overseas. In continuing with the attempt to rematerialize capital flows, this critique involves the analysis of the regional and sectoral distribution of foreign direct investment (FDI), the role of transnational corporations (TNCs) and the transnationality of capital, and, finally, the employment implications of free trade.

Domestic and Overseas Investment Patterns

A reasonable starting point for the discussion of globalized capitalism is a baseline appreciation of the relative weights of national and international investment patterns. During the period 1990 to 2003, according to Investment UNCTAD's world investment report in 2004, world Foreign Direct (FDI) flows accounted for a mere 8% of world domestic investment (gross fixed capital formation). In this 'era of corporate globalization' a very basic premise pertains that investment in the domestic economy dwarfs any overseas investment. The UNCTAD report shows that the proportion of FDI flows to domestic capital investment was high in some of the smaller developing countries, as in Singapore where FDI is 36% of gross fixed capital formation, but for the large economies it was much smaller, with FDI in the US representing 7% of domestic capital formation, with Germany 4% and Japan 3%. The movement of capital overseas in the form of FDI reveals much about the distribution of mobile investment in the world, but this must be recognized as playing a secondary role compared to domestic capital formation.

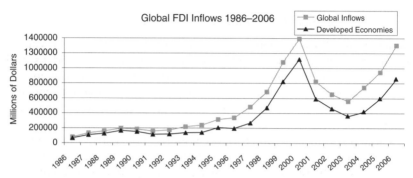

Figure 3.1   Global FDI Inflows and Developed Economies Share
Source: UNCTAD World Investment Report 2007 and preceding years.

Moreover, inward and outward FDI movements appear very sensitive to changes in the domestic business cycle. The FDI recession of the early 1990s was tied to economic downturn, particularly in Japan (UNCTAD 1994), but as Figure 3.1 clearly shows, FDI flows greatly increased with the new economy boom of the 1990s and fell precipitously with the telecoms crash at the turn of the century. FDI inflows grew at an average annual rate of 39.7% between 1996 and 2000, with FDI outflow growth of 35.1% for the same period. In 2001 FDI inflow declined by 41.1% and outflow 39.2%, in 2002 FDI inflow declined by 17.0% and outflow 17.3%, and in 2003 FDI inflow declined by 17.6% with outflow a very modest growth of 2.6%. The decline of cross border mergers and acquisitions (M&A) was even more dramatic in the same period with 48.1% in 2001, 37.7% in 2002 and -19.7% in 2003. This is also part of a longer global M&A trend which ebbs and flows with the domestic economy (Evenett 2003, UNCTAD 2007).

The global economy is represented and perceived as 'extranational' or 'supranational' acting above and beyond the national economy and outside the regulative capacity of the nation state, but for the large advanced economies this is a false dichotomy. The pattern of domestic and overseas investment reveals that the global economy is not some separate sphere of market forces with its own cycles and business imperatives, but one that echoes the rhythms of the large advanced economies. *The coincidence of international capital movement with domestic booms and slump, not only serve to emphasize the synergies between the domestic and global economy, it also challenges those who explain domestic job losses as part of a jobs migration propelled by the exodus of capital overseas.*

The Spatial Distribution of Foreign Direct Investment

Whereas the flows of communication and flows of financial capital invoke the ubiquity of global processes imagined by Giddens and others, an examination of the spatial distribution of overseas investment reveals a highly uneven spread of mobile capital and its concentration, not only in the Triad (the core regions of the world economy made up of the EU, Japan and the US), but also in a small number of developed countries within the core regions. The distribution and dispersal of overseas investment within the world economy is central to the claims of the transformationalists. An authoritative study of globalization by Held, McGrew, Goldblatt and Perraton, whilst acknowledging the concentration of FDI inflows in the OECD countries, suggested that their global share of FDI inflows had declined steadily since 1989 and that overseas investment patterns were becoming less concentrated in the OECD and more diffused, the analytical significance of which should not be understated. 'These are important developments which distinguish the contemporary era from earlier historical phases of cross border activity' (Held et al. 1999, p. 248).

If the deconcentration and dispersal of FDI flows are used to support the claims for epochal transformation, it must be pointed out that the pattern of FDI flows since the early 1990s moves in the opposite direction. The surge in FDI associated with the new economy boom of the 1990s was overwhelmingly directed towards the developed economies. At its peak in 2000 when FDI inflows reached almost $1.4 trillion, some 80% of FDI flowed into or between the advanced economies. This is the stark opposite of the global dispersal of investment flows predicted earlier by Held and colleagues, and has culminated in a growing concentration of FDI inward stock in the developed economies. Figure 3.2 describes the distribution of overseas inward investment stock between 1980 and 2006 and reveals that the developed economies share of global FDI inward stock has grown from 56% to 70%, consolidating their position as the prime target for overseas investment.

Furthermore to consider the core region as a category also understates the concentration of cross border investment *within* the advanced economies. For instance, in 2005 the United Kingdom was the largest recipient of inward investment, when it was the beneficiary of $165 billion, which accounted for 18% of global inflows of investment. This represented five and half times the total inward investment received by Africa in that year. The United States received the second largest intake of FDI at $99 billion,

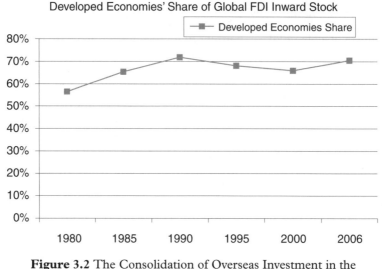

Figure 3.2 The Consolidation of Overseas Investment in the
Developed Economies

Source: UNCTAD World Investment Report 2007 and preceding years.

representing 11% of global inflows of FDI. Thus between them, the
US and the UK accounted for almost 30% of global inflows of FDI.
If the inner circle of large FDI recipients is widened just slightly the
2005 figures reveal that the UK, US, France, The Netherlands and
Canada received three quarters of all inward FDI flows to the developed economies. At the other end of the global spectrum, far from
the ubiquity of global capital flows, cross border investment is vir-
tually absent in the poorest areas with just 0.8% of FDI stock
located in 50 countries ranked as 'least developed' in the world
(Keochlin 2006).

The Sector Share of FDI

In terms of the industries targeted by foreign direct investment there
is a similar concentration of activities. Since the late 1980s it is noticeable that the stock of FDI investment into manufacturing has declined
relatively with more investment moving into services. Between 1990
and 2004 the stock of inward FDI in manufacturing fell from 42% to
32% while FDI Inward Stock for services grew from 49% to 63%.
UNCTAD'S world investment report in 2006 noted the downward
trends in FDI in manufacturing but noted a more recent sectoral concentration of investment patterns.

FDI in mining (including oil and other mining), which accounts for the bulk of the primary sector, has been largely responsible for the recent growth of global FDI . . . Current FDI growth seems to be led primarily by a few specific industries, rather than being broad based sectorally. Specifically in 2005 oil and gas, utilities (e.g. telecommunications, energies), banking and real estate were the leading industries in terms of inward FDI. (UNCTAD 2006, p. 7)

From all these data there is a very limited sense in which mobile investment patterns can substantiate the idea of the ubiquity of capital flows, spatially indifferent and disembedded. Indeed to describe the recent surge in investment in oil and mining and telecommunications as in someway 'disembedded' is more than a little ironic with companies drilling or mining miles below ground or, as mentioned above, laying millions of miles of cable on the sea bed. More generally a materialist account of investment flows challenges the general dispersal and deconcentration of capital and reveals the specificity and unevenness of capital flows that is expressed both geographically and sectorally.

Transnational Corporations

The role of transnational corporations (TNCs) reveals much about the nature of economic globalization in contemporary society but, as will be seen, it also exposes the limits of capital's transnationality. Transnational companies are often invoked as signifiers of globalization and Brands names such as 'McDonalds', 'Nike' and 'Coca Cola' have iconic status in many accounts of cultural change in contemporary society, but the role of TNCs has a surprisingly low profile in many reflections on the nature of contemporary capitalism. TNCs are central to Leslie Sklair's analysis of globalization as the 'most powerful globalizing institutions in the world today and by virtue of this fact make the capitalist global system the dominant global system' (Sklair 2002, p. 7). He cites Dunning's research which showed in the mid 1970s that 8 TNCs held 30% of the global oil market, 7 TNCs controlled 25% of the global copper market, 6 TNCs controlled 58% of the bauxite market, and 7 TNCs controlled 50% of the iron ore market. Sklair suggests that TNCs represent, not only the emergence of a transnational capitalist class but also *the separation* of TNCs from national economies. The large number of TNCs and their affiliates supports those hyper-global perceptions suggesting the decline of the national economies, but a closer investigation of TNC activity further questions the demise of nationally embedded capital.

The World Investment Reports published by UNCTAD examine the top 100 non-financial TNCs ranked by foreign asset ownership. While the world's largest 100 TNCs represented 0.2% of all TNCs they accounted for 11% of assets, 16% of sales and 12% of employment of all TNCs operating in the world. The concentration of economic power in the hand of mega-sized multinational corporations reflects the accumulation and centralization of asset ownership on a grand scale. The concentration of foreign assets, sales and employment in the hands of the largest TNCs also reveals that the distribution of international investment is highly uneven rather than dispersed throughout the globe.

A regular feature of UNCTAD's study of TNCs is the calculation of a transnationality index for each company based on the average of three ratios; foreign assets to total assets, foreign sales to total sales, and foreign employment to total employment. Oil companies like BP and Shell have high transnationality indices of 81% and 62% respectively, suggesting their foreign operations are much larger than domestic activities, while the transnationality index for General Motors is 34%, which indicates that two thirds of its assets, sales and workforce are based in the United States. TNCs headquartered in countries with small domestic markets, such as Nestlé in Switzerland, will have higher transnationality indicators but, conversely, TNCs headquartered in countries with large domestic economies will have less incentive to migrate and have a lower transnationality index as a consequence.

Overall, the transnational indicators of the top 100 TNCs are surprisingly low. These companies constitute the big overseas players of the corporate world, but their transnationality index since the beginning of the 1990s has ranged between 47 and 55%, with an average transnationality index for the top 100 TNCs of approximately 50%. This suggests that the domestic operations of TNCs on average are as important as their combined international activities. Thus of the 14.85 million people employed by the top 100 TNCs in the world some 7.37 million were based in the home country, giving a transnationality index of 50%. Together these indicators strongly suggest that even amongst many of the largest globally networked companies in the world the domestic economy provides the key market and base of operations (UNCTAD 2001, 2004 and 2006).

The Mobility of American Capital

One of the great contrasts between Europe and the United States lies in the prominence given to the issue of capital mobility and the associated 'jobs migration'. Perhaps because deindustrialization has been a more protracted process in the US, which has become entangled with issues of free trade, or perhaps out of a stronger culture of economic nationalism in the US, it appears that jobs are not just lost in the United States, they are often seen to have gone overseas. Politically the issue has a much higher profile compared with Europe. Free trade has been connected to the loss of American jobs in the presidential campaigns of a number of candidates, from Ross Perot, who in the 1992 election famously referred to 'the giant sucking sound' of jobs heading to Mexico with the implementation of NAFTA, through to Obama and Clinton sixteen years later, who both vied for popular support by professing opposition to free trade agreements that lead to American job losses. In recent years *The New York Times*, *The Washington Post*, and Forbes have published well cited articles on white collar work becoming 'a boom export'. Louis Dobb the prominent CNN broadcaster has written a book on 'Exporting America: Why Corporate Greed is Shipping Jobs Overseas', as have Ron and Anil Hira with a book on 'Outsourcing America'. As will be discussed below, the AFL-CIO's campaign against 'Exporting America' has also entered the fray determined to counter 'the corporate myths about outsourcing'.

This is a topic that is passionately debated across the political spectrum. Writing about the *Global Class War*, Jeff Faux, founder of the Economic Policy Institute, places capital mobility at the heart of his analysis of the deterioration of the American economy and the conditions of American labour.

> As the rest of the world recovered from World War II, America's unusual commercial advantages faded. In the late 1960s jobs in the apparel and shoe industries began to move out of the country as producers found cheaper labour overseas. The assembly of television parts and consumer electronics followed, and in the mid 1970s the US trade balance turned into a chronic deficit. Soon heavy industries like steel followed and autos were losing jobs to overseas competition. (Faux 2006, p. 18)

In Faux's view there is a long-term deindustrialization in the United States, tied to the export of capital to cheap labour countries which is evidenced in America's trade deficit. Accordingly the ills of the economy and the weakening of labour's position hinges on the migration of jobs and capital to cheap labour countries. Faux's position can be usefully contrasted with Tim Koechlin, writing in the Review of Radical Political Economy, who considers US non-financial capital to be extraordinarily immobile.

These data tell a remarkable and remarkably consistent story. The extent of the globalization process – by several measures – appears to be shockingly limited and the globalization of investment appears to be growing very slowly over time. (Keochlin, p. 377)

Naturally both accounts cannot be correct and it would appear that statistical evidence reveals American capital with a relatively low propensity to move. Research into US multinational corporations over the period 1977–2006 compares the distribution of activities between the domestic and the global economy by comparing the presence and the role of the US parent companies within the worldwide activities of American multinationals. The research based on the annual survey of US direct investment abroad conducted by the Bureau of Economic Analysis, shows a very stable pattern over three decades in which the ratio of domestic to global activities has hardly changed (Mataloni (2005), Mataloni and Yorgason (2006)).

Domestic and Overseas Operations of US MNCs 1977–2005

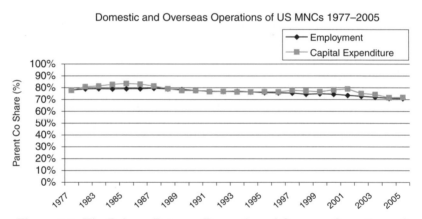

Figure 3.3. The Balance Between Domestic and Overseas Operations of US MNCs 1977 -2005

Source: Bureau of Economic Analysis.

Figure 3.3 shows the pattern of capital expenditures and employment for the domestic and overseas operations of US MNCs. It is striking that investment and employment in the domestic economy have kept apace with expansion overseas and shows that three decades of corporate globalization has left little impression on the balance between the domestic and foreign activities of US multinational corporations. *This also means that many of the mechanisms and processes of globalization have a strong national dimension and to conceive of globalization as a process of denationalization is difficult to sustain.*

There are several different motivations for corporate expansions overseas. It is not difficult to imagine that prominent among left wing or trades union perspectives would be the view that companies venture abroad in pursuit of cheap labour. However, given the direction of FDI flows already discussed, their increasing concentration in the developed economies, and the declining share of manufacturing in total FDI flows, such perceptions need to be reappraised. In relation to the inward or outward movement of investment in US manufacturing overseas, Kim Moody makes the important point that the US has been the recipient rather than the donor, with more capital coming in than going out since the early 1980s (Moody 2007). During this time some four million manufacturing jobs were shed, so it is difficult to explain job losses in relation to capital flight.

Moreover, the evidence of international capital movement, in line with the UNCTAD evidence of foreign direct investment, shows that when US capital moves abroad it invests in rich rather than poor countries. Foreign affiliates of US multinational corporations hosted by rich countries accounted for 81% of the value added by all affiliates. In relation to manufacturing, 80% of overseas affiliates production is in high wage countries where investment in stimulated by non-wage factors such as market access, transports costs, tax incentives, local support activities (Landfield and Kozlow 2006).

There are two characteristic forms of transnational organization, in which firms are either integrated vertically or horizontally. Typically vertical integration is based on a 'top down' control system that links different stages of the production process across different countries, while horizontal integration reproduces identical processes in different countries. The latter is market seeking and is most commonly associated with FDI targeted at the developed economies, while vertical integration is more cost sensitive and aimed at the developing economies. While some overseas investment occurs in vertical production networks which are labour cost sensitive (Hanson et al. 2005), overall the evidence strongly suggests that foreign investment is driven by foreign market access rather than the opportunities of exploiting cheap labour resources.

If there is a gap between public perception of jobs migrating to cheap labour countries and the statistical realities of market-seeking investment in high wage developed economies, it is clear that such views have been inculcated by employers' organizations seeking to create a favourable environment for workforce bargaining. Kate Bronfenbrenner from Cornell University points to the propaganda value of exaggerating the fear of job losses, outsourcing and corporate

relocation overseas. Bronfenbrenner's work is part of a long programme of research into employer responses to union organizing
drives in the US. She has focused on election campaigns to win union
bargaining rights under the National Labor Relations Board (NLRB)
certification process. The more recent research, which was commissioned by the Trade Deficit Review Commission, took a random
sample of more than 400 NLRB election campaigns and concluded
that capital mobility and the perceived threat to capital mobility had
a profound impact on the rights of American workers to exercise
their right to freedom of association and collective bargaining
(Bronfenbrenner 2000). Thus the spectre of capital mobility and the
economic insecurity it engenders has served to constrain wages and
union activity in a period of tight labour markets.

She demonstrated that the threat of plant closure was unrelated to
the financial health of the individual company with the closure threatened in the financially precarious companies as well as those enjoying
buoyant market position. Threats were largely associated with 'anti-
union animus' rather than genuine concern about market uncertainty.
Perhaps not too surprising is her finding that

> Despite the high percentage of plant closing threats during organizing
> campaigns, after the election, employers followed through on the threat
> to shut down all or part of the facility in fewer than three per cent of the
> campaigns in our sample where threats were made. (Bronfenbrenner
> 2000, p. vii)

Networked Production

The line of argument developed here is primarily concerned to counter
those accounts of 'turbo capitalism' (Luttwak 1999), which portray an
international economic order that emerged with the demise of national
economies and the systems of government regulation that circumscribed them. This is not to adopt a fully sceptical position which, in
some cases, has suggested that the openness of advanced economies
had actually declined over the 20th century. Hirst and Thompson in
particular have pointed to the decline of exports as a proportion of total
production from the beginning to the end of the century. Whilst this is
factually true it neglects the significance of what Bressand and
Nickolaides (1990) have called 'networked production'. While trade in
raw materials and finished products from coal to cotton comprised the
bulk of international trade in the early part of the century, networked

production, made up of intermediate goods and services, that links inter- and intra-firm production across several countries, accounts for much cross border trade in the late twentieth century. Networked production underpins trends towards regionalization in the world economy, particularly in the European Union. It encourages the formation of regulatory regimes that allow intra regional trade and some degree of policy convergence between member states, but to suggest that networked production presages the deterritorialization of economic activity and the decoupling of national institutional frameworks from global enterprise is to take the argument a step too far.

Gary Gereffi and colleagues have made the major contribution to the study of networked production in his work on 'global commodity chains'. Gereffi distinguishes between producer driven and buyer driven commodity chains. Producer driven chains typify integrated production systems in such industries as automobiles, semi-conductors, electronic equipment, while buyer driven chains characterize the supplier networks that provide for the large retailers and brand name merchandizers, such as those discussed by Naomi Klein's bestseller 'No Logo'. There are variations of the global commodity chains perspective in an alternative formulation of Global Production Networks (Henderson, Dicken, Hess and Coe 2002), which seeks to provide a less linear set of inter and intra firm linkages, a network model framework that can apply across industries, whilst recognizing new governance structures.

Discussion of network production, particularly that offered by Gereffi, has made an important contribution to the study of transnational linkages and the cross border activities of firms. However it remains important to separate internationally networked production from disembedded or footloose forms of capital. Gereffi's global commodity chains are situationally specific, socially constructed and locally integrated, underscoring the social embeddedness of economic organization. For Henderson et al. global production networks have a 'territorial embeddedness', in that 'GPNs do not merely locate in particular places. They become embedded there in the sense that they absorb, and in some cases become constrained by the economic activities and social dynamics that already exist in those places' (Henderson et al. 2002). The second important feature of networked production is that while it assists discussion about the *form* of economic integration it nonetheless does not reveal the *degree* of transnationality. The existence of global production networks does not mean that all, or even that the majority of a firm's operations within a chain or network can be described as 'cross border activities' – the chain may link transnationally but the operations of the individual firms within it remain domestic. The existence of transnational networks of territorially embedded firms informs discussion of the integration of capital, but it must be stressed that it says little about its propensity of firms to move which lies at the heart of the perceived changes in employment relations. Goods and services can flow through supply chains or networks, but this does not mean that firms do the same. Just as electricity flows through networks the transmission system is static. A dematerialized understanding of flows and networks is completely one sided in its abstraction, only able to imagine current and movement and oblivious to circuits, grids or infrastructure.

Offshoring and Outsourcing

In considering the externalization of production or services the concept of 'tradability' is important. The globalization of manufacturing rests on the degree to which it is possible to separate in space and time the production of goods from their consumption. The tradability of services has until now been limited because they need to be consumed where and when they are produced. The extent to which technological and institutional changes have overcome the tradability constraints of the service industries will have a bearing on the offshoring and outsourcing of employment. It will also inform discussion of consequent changes in the domestic labour market. If the tradability of services has been greatly enhanced then employment prospects in the home country are ominous. On the other hand if the relocation of services is constrained by propinquity to consumer markets, high level of interactivity with customers, synergies with other corporate functions such as research and development, the availability of skills, and infrastructure, then anxieties of job losses should be assuaged.

In looking at the jobs migration that has captured many recent headlines it is worth examining offshoring and overseas outsourcing. Offshoring is the overseas relocation of activities where it is carried out by a foreign affiliate; examples include the establishment of BT Call Centres in Bangalore and Hyderabad in India. Overseas outsourcing occurs when activities are externalized and then provided by a third party. Examples of overseas outsourcing to local companies include the Bank of America buying software development from Infosys in India, but services can also be externalized to foreign affiliates of other TNCs. Offshoring and overseas outsourcing create media interest and focus much public concern and anxiety and so it is necessary to assess how widespread is the phenomenon and what are the consequences of offshoring and outsourcing for employment in the home economies. The World Investment Report is again helpful in these matters.

Offshoring has a long way to go before it matures and settles down in pattern and location. A World Bank assessment of the mid 1990s concerning the number of jobs for which long-distance provision is technically feasible and for which cost savings of 30–40% would be plausible suggested that some 1–5% of total employment in the G7 countries could be affected. More recent estimates by business research groups of the likely impact concluded that some 3.4 million service jobs may shift from the United States to low-income countries by 2015; another concluded that 2 million offshore jobs could be created in the financial service industries alone, and that the total number for all industries could be 4 million. However, this should be compared with turnover of 7–8 million jobs every quarter in the United States. (UNCTAD World Investment Report 2004 Overview, p. 29)

Finally it is worth stressing that offshoring and overseas outsourcing is a small-scale activity. Despite the headlines of jobs migration most outsourcing occurs in the home country while only 1–2% of all business outsourcing is done internationally. There is some international movement of call centre employment, but this grows alongside call centre employment was the home economy. In the UK the growth of call centre employment was predicted to rise to 650,000, in the US it was expected to grow from 3% of the workforce in 2001 to 5% in 2010 (UNCTAD 2004). Where it occurs internationally the image of third world call centres in Bangalore or Ghana also suggests that the lion's share of business outsourcing is to the third world but, according to the World Investment Report, it is interesting to note that overseas business outsourcing is concentrated in developed countries with Canada and Ireland featuring as amongst the most attractive of locations. In all, some four countries (Ireland, India, Canada and Israel) accounted for over 70% of the market for offshore services.

A report on offshoring produced by the National Academy of Public Administration for the US Congress and the Bureau of Economic Analysis looked at offshoring and outsourcing for four industry groups, pharmaceutical and medicine manufacturing, architectural engineering and related services, computer systems design and related services and business support services industries (National Academy of Public Administration 2006). The research examined industry and firm level data, the former between 1998 and

2004, the latter between 1999 and 2003. It examined services out-sourcing and outsourcing to domestic firms. It concluded that the extent of services offshoring is not as extensive as popular perceptions concerned would suggest and, if it occurred, it was not related to busi-ness restructuring. 'One reason is that fewer than 20% of all MNC parents imported services.' It also reported that there was little con-sistent growth in services and interestingly showed that in business services, information and data processing, broadcasting and telecom-munication, offshoring had declined between 1998 and 2004.

Left Wing Harmonies in the Neoliberal Chorus?

One of the more controversial aspects of the case presented here is that the strength of the neoliberal perspective is abetted, almost per-versely, by left wing commentators and trades union representatives who offer their own curiously sympathetic, but ultimately self-defeating approach to labour market restructuring. Many of the authors already cited, from Hardt and Negri, to Hutton and Sennett, would identify themselves as critical or of left wing sympathies, yet their assessment of impact of institutional change is both pessimistic and self-limiting. The approach of the AFL-CIO to outsourcing in its campaign against outsourcing, must represent one of the more extreme examples of those who support the cause of labour yet are wedded to a perspective that can do little other than undermine its capacity to defend itself. The AFL-CIO has entered the debate on the 'Exporting of America' appearing determined to 'counter the corpo-rate myths about outsourcing'. As part of this campaign the AFL-CIO seems eager to present the American workforce in the most precari-ous of circumstances. Thus the union website on Exporting America finds it helpful to recycle the direst of predictions of the employment consequences of outsourcing. Thus,

> Since 2000, corporations have shipped more than 525,000 white collar overseas (sic), according to the AFL-CIO's department of professional employees. Some estimates say up to 14 million middle class jobs could be exported out of America in the next ten years. (AFL-CIO 2007)

The AFL-CIO campaign warns that 'some estimates say 14 million white collar jobs are at risk from outsourcing'. Not only is the argu-ment weak in the extreme, there is no conceivable benefit in exagger-ating the possibilities of offshoring. The projection offered is based on a research report for the Fisher Center for Real Estate and Urban Economics at the University of California, Berkeley, by Ashok Deo Bardhan and Cynthia Kroll. Their method was to estimate potential job losses by identifying the 'outsourceability attributes' of occupations. They suggested six attributes including those with a high wage differential with similar occupation in the destination country, those jobs with high information content, no face to face customer requirements, low set up costs etc. These attributes were then associated with jobs which are thus deemed to be at risk from outsourcing. The potential job loss due to outsourcing was then calculated on the number of such jobs in the US labour force that were seen to have these attributes. Having run the figures, the authors concluded that 'the *outer limits* of potential direct job loss in these occupations, without taking into account many of the dynamic adjustments that may take place . . .' was precisely 14,063,130 or 11% of the US workforce.

The merits of the analysis are highly debatable and their conclusions are exceptionally pessimistic, but it must be acknowledged that the authors are suggesting that this is the 'outer limits' of potential job losses and offer some caution in adopting these figures. The AFL-CIO however seems extraordinarily eager to recycle this doomsday scenario without any hesitation or qualification. Thus a perverse logic prevails when trades unions recognize that employers use the threat of capital relocation as a bargaining tool but seem to prepare the ground for them in stressing the vulnerability of the American workforce to cheap foreign labour.

Major American job losses occurred in the first quarter of this decade, due to overproduction in key sectors such as telecommunications that in turn deeply affected employment in manufacturing, which fell by some 3 million jobs in the first five years of the new millennium. This telecom-led crash was born out of the surge of speculative investment fuelled by Wall Street financiers. Corporate greed and market irrationality, leading to the enormous waste of resources and the resultant job losses, could have been the target for a union campaign, but instead the unions appear to accept that outsourcing is the scourge of American labour. The threat is effectively posed by foreign labour, who can take American jobs at a fraction of the wages paid at home. In addition to the underlying xenophobia such a response is quite irrational as the recession in American manufacturing, occurred during a precipitous decline in overseas investment. As Kim Moody points out, trends in relocation in American manufacturing indicate a shift to southern states where wage levels and trades union organization are very low. 'Union leaders throughout this period (since 1980), with few exceptions, talked themselves into the idea that these jobs were going overseas when, in fact, at least half of them just moved down the Interstate' (Moody 2007 p. 45). This suggests that the difficulties for American labour are at home and not abroad.

The Employment Implications of Free Trade

The economic analysis of the impact of the North American Free Trade Agreement (NAFTA) has covered a broad spectrum, which portrays minimal influence on the one hand, to 'sea change' on the other. The United States Congressional Budget Office, for instance, conducted a study of the effects of NAFTA on US–Mexican Trade and GDP. The results of their investigation are surprising since they impute to NAFTA a near negligible impact on trade and GDP. It concluded that US trade with Mexico was growing for many years and would have further expanded regardless of NAFTA. That growth, the report claimed, 'dwarfs the effects of NAFTA', a conclusion which it claims is consistent with other papers and studies in the literature (Congressional Budget Office 2003).

Under the auspices of the American Trade Deficit Commission the prominent labour economist David Blanchflower has produced an analysis of the impact of international trade on the US labour market (Blanchflower 2000). His intention is to produce an empirically based analysis of the labour market consequences of trade, as opposed to theoretical constructions of trade advantages and disadvantages. He makes one very important observation, but his treatment of it is less than adequate. Blanchflower points out that, contrary to most public perceptions, the United States is '*a fairly closed economy*', not because of barriers to entry, which he suggests are low, but the degree of openness is small because the size of the economy offers a degree of self-sufficiency that smaller countries cannot entertain. He follows Krugman and Irwin in suggesting that only since the 1970s has the flow of trade achieved the levels pertaining at the end of the nineteenth century. He then constructs a 'degree of openness indicator' based on an average of import and exports as a proportion of total GDP, and concludes that the level of American trade is 'very low by international standards'. America and Japan are among the least open economies, while the Netherlands, Belgium and Norway are the most open, with the UK, Germany, France and Canada mid range. In these circumstances where trade levels are relatively low, the labour market significance of trade is deemed to be negligible.

Two pieces of research, published by the International Labour Organization (ILO) in Geneva and the Employment Policy Institute (EPI) in Washington, on the labour market impacts of NAFTA, are necessary in order to complete the range of labour market impact assessments of liberalization and free trade. Key contributors include Bruce Campbell of the Canadian Centre for Policy Alternatives in Ottawa, and Robert Scott of the EPI. Theirs is a comprehensive analytical framework which sees the free trade agreements as the cornerstones of the development of neoliberal policy in North America over a twenty year period. Campbell notes that it was Reagan who, in his presidential campaign, first floated the idea of a 'common market' stretching from 'the Yukon to the Yucatan'. Mexico's structural reforms began in 1983 following the 1982 financial crisis, which prompted a rescue package developed and delivered by the US and IMF. The common repertoire of neoliberal policies were embedded in the rescue package, including investment and trade liberalization, domestic deregulation, privatization and public sector cutbacks, and culminated in GATT membership in 1986. Thus in furtherance of this programme the Salinas government entered into NAFTA negotiations in 1990.

The predecessor to NAFTA was the free trade agreement covering the United States and Canada (CUFTA), which came into effect in 1989. It emerged out of the cumulative changes in government policy that emanated from the arrival of the Mulroney government in 1984, which brought in the deregulation of energy, financial transportation and foreign investment sectors and the privatization of airline, oil, aircraft and telecommunications industries. Thus CUFTA/NAFTA agreements are seen as the centre pieces in the longer programme of deregulation and privatization spanning two decades. Campbell adopts Grinspun and Kreklewitch's concept of free trade as the 'external conditioning framework' which limits the range of policy options and enables the implementation of unpopular political measures. Cuts in Canadian social programmes were legitimized as part of 'the war on the deficit', since there is 'no alternative in this era of free trade and globalization'. Such a position is bolstered by the views of Donald Johnston former Liberal Government minister and head of the OECD, who suggested that 'free trade agreements are designed to force adjustments on our societies. Countries, he said, should push the pace of adjustment . . . by reducing social benefits that encourage the unemployed to turn down low paying jobs' (Campbell 1999). Therefore, while it is important to recognize that the relative size of the trade flows are diminutive it seems extraordinarily blinkered to imagine that the export and import sectors are hermetically sealed free trade zones of activity dissociated from the domestic economy. Competitive pressures are not simply confined to the export industries, since profitability in the domestic economy is as important as in the export industries. Moreover, government policies developed to make the economy as a whole more competitive transcend distinction between home and overseas markets. Public expenditure and fiscal policy adjustments in terms of social services, education or health are justified by the need to be more adaptable, innovative, flexible, efficient and dynamic than the competition. Whether that competition is local, regional or global is often not clearly articulated and is implied with a vagueness and uncertainty that seems to add to its threat.

Any kind of 'NAFTA on NAFTA off' evaluation, which seeks before and after differences in jobs gained or lost is, therefore, ill-founded, and it behoves analysis to cast a broader assessment of the impact of a range of neoliberal policy changes. However Campbell and Scott get drawn into the numbers game. From a Canadian perspective Campbell argues that economic growth in the 1990s was worse 'than any other decade of the last century except the 1930s'. Average per capita income fell steadily in the first seven years of the 1990s and only regained 1989 levels in 1999. The level of unemployment was similarly higher than any other decade since the 1930s and averaged 9.6%. The difficulty of job counting in this way is that if any improvement occurs in national economy, as has happened subsequently, then such ground for opposing free trade agreements are undermined.

Scott in particular is keen to engage in job counting. The United States experience of NAFTA, according to Scott, has been one of job loss, growing inequality and wage suppression. He argues that since NAFTA was signed in 1993 the rise in the trade deficit with Canada and Mexico has resulted in the displacement of some 879,280 US jobs. This extraordinarily precise figure is based on the not unreasonable premise that any calculation of the employment effects of free trade should take both exports and imports into the equation. However, the net effects in Scott's analysis are calculated on the idea that exports create jobs and imports destroy jobs, and so job losses must accrue when the balance of trade favours imports. Moreover, the argument further suggests that the jobs lost are from higher quality positions in manufacturing and their losses help to drive wages still lower as workers take up positions in lower paid service employment. While many will find Scott's intentions laudable there are some methodological and political questions associated with his stance. Any advocacy of protectionism must address the crude economic calculus of alternative scenarios. Would life be so much better in the absence of trade? How many domestic jobs are gained by importing cheaper components and how many jobs would be lost by obliging companies to use more expensive domestic supplies by restricting competition? A final comment on the Scott-Campbell positions relates to their view of employment change. Scott acknowledges that NAFTA's impact has been obscured because of the surge in the domestic economy in the latter half of the 1990s, which reduced unemployment levels to record low levels. He suggests that while the US economy created 20.7 million jobs the growth in the trade deficit eliminated 3.2 million jobs, which resulted in industrial and compositional change shifting workers out of good jobs in manufacturing to low quality and low paid work in the service industries.

Campbell's argument in particular may have been more helpful if he maintained his concern with the broader implication of neoliberal policy rather than entering into the job counting debates. It is also noticeable that estimates of job losses or gains in relation to exports and imports seem oblivious to the much larger story of NAFTA and labour migration. One of the major differences between regional integration in Europe and North America was freedom of movement for people in the Single European Market whereas free trade in North America was confined to business freedoms. If migration was discussed in the early 1990s it was hoped that the anticipated job gains in Mexico would reduce the incentives to migrate (Hufbauer and Schott 2005). However regional economic integration has been associated with large increases in the migration of Mexicans to the United States. As J. K. Galbraith has suggested – 'The goods headed south and labour headed north.'

In looking at foreign born workers in the US economy studies have shown that nearly half the net increase in the US workforce between 1996 and 2000 was generated by immigrants, of which half were Mexican (Mosisa 2002). Estimates for the number of illegal immigrants suggest that two thirds of the Mexican born US workers are unauthorized (Hufbauer and Schott 2005). Whereas previous migrants were largely employed in agriculture in California and Texas, today's migrants are much more dispersed throughout the US and employed outside the primary sectors. They account for a quarter of workers in the meat and poultry industry, 27% of the construction workforce, while female Mexican immigrants accounted for 20% of retailing employment (Akers 2005, Hufbauer and Schott 2005).

Foreign born men earn 70% of the income compared to native born men while foreign born women earned 82%, as much as native born women. Yet another feature of the 'new economy' boom of the late 1990s appears in a different light, shorn of its glitzy high tech image. Approximately a quarter of the increase in the labour force in the United States during the new economy boom was provided by undocumented Mexican workers. Far from the image of 'the borderless world', a different, yet altogether more familiar globalization script reflects the plight of illegal migrants from central and western Mexico, propelled by the Peso Crisis of 1995 and the privatization of 'ejido' lands, who escape to work unofficially in the low wage sectors in the US for a fraction of the wages obtained by native born workers. This seems to represent a far more significant drama than the United States jobs losses that are alleged to be directly related to exports and imports.

Any labour market assessment of NAFTA should acknowledge that precise evaluation of cause and effects tied to exports and imports is unattainable. It is important to recognize that trade levels are relatively low and their impact will be masked by broader shifts in the macroeconomy. In passing, this also means that the significance of large trade deficits are accordingly diminished. However, despite the fact that trade flows may be small, free trade agreements are the centre-pieces in a wider neoliberal policy framework, which do have broader consequences. *Free trade policies can lead to denationalization but most significantly in the form of privatization and liberalization, i.e. the declining role for nation state involvement in economic and social policy.* Therefore the discussion returns once again to the question of ideology and politics. To oppose free trade because it exposes the domestic workforce to competition from cheap labour economies, which increases the risks of a jobs exodus, is to adopt an introverted, nationalistic mindset that detracts from the broader neoliberal offensive on earnings, jobs and social protection.

There are three elements to the critique presented so far. The ideology underpinning new capitalism was discussed in relation to the emergence of a managerial discourse that came into prominence with the growth of neoliberalism. These ideas have emphasized technological change and globalization as key forces for societal transformation, which compel labour market adjustment, giving rise to new relations between employers and workers. Thus far the critique of technological change and globalization has focused on their representation as disembedded autonomous forces which express exogenous change in society. This dematerialized representation of change systematically exaggerates the significance of technological developments and greatly overstates the mobility of capital.

The discussion now moves to consider the labour market and suggests that it acts both as conductor and insulator in relation to institutional change, expressing shifts in employment patterns, but also articulates different dynamics which inhibit labour market adjustment.

4

Theorizing the Labour Market

This section looks at the mechanism or the medium through which new capitalism is said to emerge. Rather than seeking to generalize from iconic technologies or models of advanced labour processes the present account looks at employment relations in the wider context of the capitalist labour market. This approach presents a different strategy to that which sees external economic or technological factors compelling institutional adaptation and corporate restructuring, which then finds passive reflection in labour market adjustment. In the present discussion the labour market is brought centre stage and theorized 'in its own right'. This requires a much broader assessment of the nature of the capitalist labour market and the factors that both drive and constrain labour market adjustment. The materialist approach displayed in the discussion of informationalism and globalization will be pursued here in seeking to reveal the institutional frameworks that govern the operation of markets in general and the labour market in particular. There are two purposes to this theorizing: first, to situate the labour market within contemporary accounts of societal transformation; second, to examine the commodification of labour power from which the principal determinants of labour market adjustment can be established.

Although changes in the nature of work are said to lie at the heart of societal transformation it is remarkable that there is no theory of the labour market as such. In fact it is extraordinary that the market as a concept has been little theorized within social science. The economic historian Douglas North (1977) wrote that 'It is a peculiar fact that the literature on economics . . . contains so little discussion of the central institution that underlies neoclassical economics – the market'. In the same year the sociologist Bernard Barber (1977) noted 'a surprisingly small amount of attention (is) given to the idea of the market (in economics literature)'. Robert Coase the Nobel Prize winning economist argued that contemporary economists are interested only in 'the determination of market prices' which has led to the situation in which 'discussion of the market place itself has entirely disappeared' (Coase 1988). Apparently the market is posited as an article of faith rather than a focus of intellectual inquiry. Within this broader context in which the market possesses the chameleon's ability to avoid theoretical attention it is not surprising that the labour market per se is not theorized in its own right, but appears as a prop in the wider edifice of social theory.

Another perspective on the nature of markets has been outlined by Fred Block in his critique of economic discourse, which has particular relevance to the study of the market for labour (Block 1990). He considers the idealized market of economic theory with multiple sellers and buyers, in which transactions occur on a one time basis. He suggests that the best example of this idealized market is a 'spot market' of the type commonly found in stock or commodity exchanges. Most transactions, however, do not conform to this model as consumer purchases are generally made in retail outlets where single sellers use fixed prices on goods and services. Moreover, when a service is to be provided over a period of time the buyer and the seller must agree on factors additional to price and enter into a contractual relationship, which is some remove from the market of economic theory. Block suggests that there is a continuum of the 'marketness' of economic transactions with spot markets at the top of the scale and transactions or exchange organized through hierarchies at the lower end of the scale. 'High marketness' means that transactions are purely dominated by price while, at low marketness, price is one of many factors affecting the exchange. In general Block suggests that the longer the level of the contractual relationship the lower the degree of marketness. With the recruitment and retention of labour there is a low level of marketness, and within the hierarchies which characterize large employers there is a further distinction between the external and the internal labour market. The former is more often used for recruiting to new positions and especially entry level posts. The latter is a system for remunerating and retaining staff, by developing workforce skills and training, inculcating corporate culture and company loyalty and by maintaining the professional status of key groups of the labour force. If the labour market were to act like a spot market it would force workers into occupations that were not commensurate with their training and experience leading to a reduced supply of skilled labour. If memory recalls the situation in Russia after the collapse of the Soviet Union, in which highly trained scientists were compelled into working in the tourist industry, then institutional inertia might be seen more as long-term virtue than short-term vice. Therefore the labour market is unusual in that there is a very limited sense of buying and selling as a form of transaction between individuals and with this low level of marketness it is a rather imperfect medium through which technological and institutional change might generate new capitalist employment relations.

As a mechanism for transmitting change in society the labour market is limited, but in addition, a broader transformation of work cannot be simply 'read off' from changes in production as often occurs in contemporary debates. In these discussions employment change is inserted, often randomly, into broader theoretical construction in a manner which suggests the labour market is the repository of socio-economic and technological developments. Like fortune tellers studying tea leaves in a cup, commentators embrace labour market changes as 'signifiers' of institutional restructuring. Just as Toffler saw rentalism as symbolic of post-industrial society, contemporary accounts mobilize specific employment patterns as proof of wider societal development. In this way, for instance, the rise in part-time employment in the 1980s is offered as confirmation of some post-Fordist regime of accumulation, but the statistically more significant increase in part-time employment in the 1950s and 1960s recedes from view. In this theory driven climate, models of the labour market restructuring are advanced and sustained on meagre empirical foundations. Atkinson's (1986) core and periphery model of the labour force was based on a relatively small number of 'flexible firms', but it has been widely received and sustained on account of its 'heuristic productivity' (Hirst and Zeitlin 1991). Hakim's (1990) large scale survey of flexible labour practices demonstrated very limited evidence of employers using flexible labour strategies yet the absence of supporting data has done little to dent the popularity of the model. It is hardly surprising in these circumstances that Bradbury et al. (2000) have inveighed against the 'myths at work' in contemporary social science.

Transformation Theory

One of the more controversial aspects of the argument advanced here is that the narratives of new capitalism, or elements of them, are expressed across a wide spectrum of political views and analytical perspectives. Indeed it is possible that the case for societal transformation draws its strength from an implicit acceptance of the common ground that technological innovation and/or globalization stimulates institutional changes which have had far reaching consequences for the world of work. More specifically it is not unreasonable to note the overlap of concerns between post-industrialism and post-Fordism. While the former emphasized change in industrial structure, the latter is preoccupied by change in the systems of mass production, both of which are associated with the decline of the traditional labour market. As suggested in Chapter 1, the shift from post-industrial perspectives to new capitalist employment relations owes a significant debt to those left wing commentators whose sympathies with the casualties of industrial restructuring, and perhaps whose nostalgia for better days, may have strengthened the view that work conditions and employment relations in the flexible labour markets of new service industries are qualitatively different from that experienced by the preceding generation. More specifically while discussion of post-industrial society resisted broader sociological conclusions, accounts of post-Fordism directly tied institutional changes to transitions between periods or phases of development within capitalism (Albritton et al. 2001). Arguably the shift from structural to relational change or from social to societal development has been encouraged by the contribution of transformation theories associated with post-Fordism or flexible specialization.

It is therefore necessary to turn attention to transformation theory which provides the academic backcloth against which much of the accompanying research has been conducted. Ash Amin (1994) has provided probably the best summary of the lines of analysis arising from the regulation approach, the flexible specialization approach and the neo-Schumpterian approach, and comment here is confined to certain features of the debates that pertain to the determinants and outcomes of labour market adjustment. In the first instance it is significant that transformation theory has had a greater resonance in Europe than in America. This is not to say that there is no American input to the debate over post-Fordism or flexible specialization (e.g. Harvey, Sabel and Storper) but the major contributions are largely European (e.g. Jessop, Aglietta, Lipietz, Boyer, Lash and Urry, Hirst and Zeitlin). This may be due to the fact that restructuring in US manufacturing during the 1980s was not as severe as in Europe, but it is also possible that debates in America were more influenced by economic sociology. As a consequence the emphasis is laid on fundamental restructuring within accumulation and labour processes as opposed to institutional economics which highlight 'embeddedness' in the structures of capital and the labour market.

Transformation theories differ in emphasis, whether they are retrospective in identifying *transition from* Fordist systems of mass production, or prospective in considering *transition to* systems of flexible accumulation. Acknowledging the potential offence to the differing schools of regulation theory, for present purposes it is sufficient to include, under one heading, a broad school of transformation theory which sees a movement from the rigid systems of mass production, with mass markets for standard products, and a transition towards niche markets with an emphasis on much greater flexibility in labour processes. Such theories rose to prominence in the wake of the economic recession of 1973 and the prolonged period of industrial restructuring in the advanced economies that sought to address the crisis of profitability within the system. Having experienced the long boom of the post-war period, characterized by sustained growth and low levels of inflation and unemployment, the contrasting conditions of the last quarter of the 20th century could not have been starker. In the depth of the recession news broadcasts announced redundancies almost every other day, as the map of company closures came to resemble grim weather forecasts of unrelieved depression. The spectre of mass unemployment, not seen since the 1930s, dominated the economic landscape in the early 1980s and claimed disproportionate casualties among manufacturing and the heavy industries of steel, coal, shipbuilding and mining. Such a context gave the transformation theorists an audience for their institutionalist account of capitalist crisis.

The explicit connection between the formation of a 'new regime of accumulation' and the flexibilization of labour markets is a strong theme within transformation theory. Alain Lipietz, one of the leading lights in regulation theory, draws attention to the crisis of Fordism which was expressed in changes in the wage relation. 'The Fordist wage relation was characterized most of all by the combination of Taylorist principles of labour organization and rigid forms of wage contractualization', such that the flexibilization of the wage relation that attended post-Fordism involved 'a notable shift away from rigid ties to the firm and the progressive reduction in the range of guarantees of unemployment insurance. Accordingly workers become not only poor but also precarious' (Lipietz 2001). David Harvey, in a similar vein, suggests that the shift from Fordism to flexible accumulation was significantly based on new forms of 'numerical flexibility' on the recruitment of part-timers, fixed term contract staff, casuals and temporaries. Labour market flexibility will be covered in Chapter 6 in detail, suffice it to say at this point, that institutional restructuring was presented by transformation theory as leading to an increase in non-standard forms of employment with a more tenuous connection to the firm. Thus they have helped to lay the ground for those who claim that new employment relations characterize contemporary societal transformation.

Rather than considering the whole cycle of the circulation of value, including production, distribution, exchange and consumption, the post-Fordists are preoccupied with formally defined manufacturing industry. There are several implications of the focus on institutional changes in the production industries: (1) the overstatement of the trend towards capital deconcentration; (2) the extrapolation of the process of corporate restructuring from production to services; (3) the identification of labour market change as primarily emanating from production; and (4) the conceptualization of the external world of the firm in terms of partnerships, networks and alliances rather than a restructuring framework that transcends sector boundaries. The implication for the discussion of work is that transformation theory overstates the fragmentation of labour markets and the end of mass employment. It is disinclined to explain labour market adjustment that is unrelated to changes in production, such as the rise of part-time employment and it is not attuned to new forms of restructuring that transcend production, finance and consumption.

As a consequence of the narrow perspective on manufacturing a central tenet of Marxist theory of capital accumulation in the tendency towards centralization and concentration is effectively removed from discussion. This is significant since one of the features of capitalist restructuring in the last two decades is a pattern of reorganization that transcends sectoral, spatial and statutory boundaries. The waves of mergers and acquisitions witnessed in the 1990s, and notably in the utilities, telecommunications and financial services as part of a process of 'consolidation', seriously challenge any trend towards the deconcentration and decentralization of capital suggested by transformation theory. In telecommunications, in particular, the drive towards concentration and centralization has involved a small number of giant international companies formed through spectacular mergers and takeovers. The Silicon Valley imagery of small high tech companies as the engine of research and development and innovation has been convincingly challenged by Benedict Harrison's account of the continued dominance of large firms across industrial sectors. In exploring the myths surrounding small firm dynamics Harrison showed that while 85% of all the individual enterprises in the computer industry employed fewer than 100 employees, and that only 5% of firms employed more than 500 workers, these large firms accounted for 91% of employment in the industry (Harrison 1994).

Additionally, when the field of investigation is widened beyond sector boundaries and examined across spatial scales a different perspective on restructuring emerges. If the 'concatenation' of capital accumulation is taken into account, as Aglietta (1980) initially suggested, then the processes of concentration and centralization reappear at different points in the cycle of production, distribution and consumption. In this cycle, end-point concentration of capital ownership, most notable in, but not confined to retailing, has produced employers of larger size than has ever arisen in the manufacturing sector. The second dimension of a new 'transcendent restructuring' within contemporary capitalism, which expresses a reconfiguration of corporate activities that cut across sectoral boundaries, also greatly modifies the claims of transformation theory. Commercial capital diversifies across the boundaries of sectors, as Fine and Leopold (1993) have pointed out, into activities such as transport, distribution, production and also financial services. These are the days in which a British record company becomes one of the largest players in the British railway industry, in which shopping centres spring up inside hospitals, in which food retailers, that generate 8% of sales on petrol, challenge the high street suppliers of white goods. When very large firms are able to dominate end point of contact with the public there are strong pressures to diversify product and service range. Moreover, their economies of scale, eschewed by many post-Fordists, afford them a buying power with suppliers that gives them enormous competitive advantage and which in turn drives specialization and concentration in the supply industries.

In the public sector the restructuring of the utilities, following privatization, has fuelled the 'globalization of public services' (Dunleavy 1994). Very large multinational firms come to dominate water supply and energy industries which were previously organized on regional and sector lines. If the relocation of work did not immediately put out activities into large multinational companies, the subcontracting of services leads to downstream reorganization of utilities and service provision in large organizations. Ironically, when subcontracting is associated with the fragmentation of large bureaucracies and the externalization of work into small companies, in reality work is often transferred to larger organizations (Doogan 1997). Thus while transformation theory, with its preoccupation with manufacturing industry, suggests the decline of mass production and the rise of small and medium size enterprises, the tendencies towards centralization and concentration are revealed on a broader canvas that transcends spatial scale and sector boundaries.

Given its preoccupation with manufacturing, the extent to which transformation theory can address the world outside of production is debatable. While it is not wholly unreasonable, for theoretical purposes, to consider Fordism as synonymous with mass production, to present corporate restructuring in manufacturing as the template for wider institutional change across all sectors is far less plausible. Some have attempted to extend the model into services with the emergence of a 'post-Fordist welfare state' (Burrows and Loader 1994) or a 'post-Fordist local government' (Stoker 1989). This is questionable on two important counts. In the first instance, the extent to which all sectors conform to some manufacturing model is highly doubtful. There are whole swathes of the service sector, and welfare services in particular, that are funded out of the public purse and are mass employers of the Fordist stereotype. More importantly for present purposes, there are different forms of labour market flexibility in the public sector that do not apply in production industries. For instance, there is a much greater incidence of part-time employment in welfare services, particularly in health and education, than in manufacturing. Therefore the translation of the post-Fordist model from the production industries to services is quite inappropriate. If anything welfare state restructuring creates very large employers, based on the massification of service delivery and intensification of labour process, and sustains traditional employment relations which maintain high levels of trades union membership.

Institutional Economics, Embeddedness and Deep Structure

Many, if not most, economists would adhere to the view that markets are inherently self-regulating mechanisms that allow the most efficient allocation of resources and factors of production. If markets fail to conform to this ideal the fault is laid at the door of institutional rigidities and imperfections which provide external interference in the workings of price signals. This idea of external interference and exogenous shocks is highly instructive, implying as it does, ceteris paribus, some natural order of monetary exchange and interaction in which demand and supply are eventually balanced. There are occasional references to internal constraints or endogenous malfunction, relating to imperfect knowledge on the part of buyers and sellers, but the over-whelming source of market failure is externally derived. These external sources of 'imperfection' in the market are often taken to mean government intervention, the monopsony powers of trades unions and the monopoly powers of dominant firms. If rational and knowledgeable individuals express their utility preferences, as neoclassical theory implies, then supply and demand, mediated through monetary exchange and price setting, find their equilibrium at optimum positions.

Sociologists, however, have long argued against such models of human behaviour and motivation, and have countered with concepts of social structures that shape the opportunities available to individuals and groups within the labour market. Sociologists and, to some extent, psychologists have introduced an alternative and more complex set of explanations for motivations and behaviour in the labour market, which relate to social norms, values and orientations of groups and individuals. If one branch of social science is concerned with wage levels and supply and demand, the other appears concerned with individuals and groups, as bearers of social norms and cultural practices, who operate within 'structures of opportunity', their choices constrained and their options conditioned by a variety of social factors. To this extent there is some overlap between the two disciplines in that, for some, personal choices and utility maximization imply a focus on individual behaviour.

The 1980s witnessed a further development in the sociology of the labour market with a return to the Polanyian concept of 'embeddedness', which situated the economy or the market within a larger social structure. Granovetter introduced the idea that the economy is embedded in social networks that make up the social structure. Later DiMaggio (1990) argued that economic action is also culturally embedded. In the same year the concept of embeddedness was further extended with Zukin and DiMaggio's exploration of the social organization of the economy. In this work four forms of embeddedness are offered: the cognitive; the cultural; the structural and the political. This was suggested in an attempt to integrate political economy and social-organizational themes in economic sociology (Zukin and DiMaggio 1990; Tilly and Tilly 1994; and Smelser and Sweberg 1994). Therefore in many contributions within geography and sociology, labour markets are now seen as embedded within (local) culture and history and situated in space and time (Harvey 1996).

However, there is a sense in which labour markets are enmeshed in *external* networks and milieux of various kinds, but there is also an *internal* dimension to embeddedness which is peculiar to the labour market. To capture this internal and external dimension of embeddedness it may be possible to adapt Chomsky's notion of 'deep structure' and 'surface structure' to understand the establishment and development of the labour market. Surface structures express the international variation in institutional arrangements governing the interactions between employers and workers. Deep structure directly represents the foundational character of relations between capital, labour and the state, that constitute the commodification of labour power. Coming from the 'varieties of capitalism' approach, Kathleen Thelen has examined institutional formation in the labour markets of 'coordinated market economies' such as Germany and Japan, and 'liberal market economies' such as the United States and the United Kingdom. She asks why different countries pursue different trajectories in workplace training and skills formation and she concludes:

> Contemporary differences in skill formation go back to important differences in the character of the settlement between employers in skill based industries, artisans and early trades unions. I show how the development of skill formation in the early industrial period interacted with the development of collective bargaining institutions and nascent labor unions and employers organizations in ways that set countries on different national trajectories. (Thelen 2004, p. 5)

Thelen thus seeks to explain both international variation and to suggest what is common to all economies based on waged labour. Comparative industrial relations literature also stresses that labour market agencies and bargaining systems have enduring historical and cultural roots. It is clear that in many countries the main characteristics of national industrial relations are established at an early stage in a country's industrial development (Bean 1994), and that according to a study of 27 countries, the form of industrial relations reflects the national culture concerned (Blum 1981). In developing countries national liberation struggles have also had an important bearing on subsequent relations (Poole 1986). Labour market systems are often forged in the heat of social conflict and upheaval, such as the German Works Council in 1918, or periods characterized by upsurges in industrial action such as those witnessed in Western Europe in the late 1960s. Comparative historical-institutional analysis, therefore, goes further than many sociological accounts of embeddedness, which often appear more contextual than structural, and thus reveals the labour market as a deep structure. This deep structure expresses the foundational or essential character of the relations between capital, labour and the state. It derives from the commodification of labour power and 'locks in' employers and workers representatives to modes of bargaining for wages, to regimes for welfare provision, whether state funded or occupational insurance or employer benefits, and to systems for skill development and retention.

The concept of embeddedness is a welcome counterbalance to the transformation perspectives that stress deconcentration, decentralization and the fragmentation of labour market structures, but in the way it is widely understood today, it does not go far enough. Embeddedness regains the sense of tradition, history, and continuity while others stress the fleeting, transient nature of social and economic engagement, but its 'rediscovery' often fails to embrace fully Polanyi's idea of the market as an 'instituted process'. To establish the idea of deep structure, we need to turn to Marx and Polanyi to explore the commodification of labour power by considering the establishment and maintenance of the labour market.

Moving the Labour Market to the Centre Stage

The strategy proposed here takes the labour market as the focus or object of theorizing rather than treating it as some derivative category. This strategy also recognizes that labour power is itself a commodity whose value relates to the social investment in its development and maintenance. Since the immediate requirements of production, per se, only affect a minority of the workforce, a comprehensive conceptual framework of the labour market will need to include the full range of sectors. While one set of labour market pressures is generated by the immediate requirements of production, when considering employment as a whole, there is another set of reproductive imperatives that impact on the labour market. In short, a large part of the workforce is engaged with the maintenance of the physical and social infrastructure necessary to support the further development of capital accumulation and to guarantee the next generation of labour. *Labour market theory therefore requires two points of reference based in the spheres of production and reproduction.* This is a very simple strategy, since it plainly looks at all the range of factors determining the market for labour, but the implications are deceptively consequential.

The term 'service industries' is not particularly helpful, embracing, under one umbrella category, a range of activities so diverse as to encompass residential care provision for the elderly, merchant banking and electricity generation. The vagueness of the term, however, should not detract from the theoretical significance of the range of reproductive activities and services that are distinct from production industries, from education, health, social services, public administration, to financial services, distribution, transport and utilities. Within the service industries it might be helpful to distinguish between the repair and renewal of the physical and technical infrastructure, financial institutions and welfare services. In relation to welfare services it is also possible to draw distinctions between the reproduction of the next generation of labour, which provides a growing focus for state intervention, and care and services for those already retired from the workforce who are increasingly dependent on forms of user provision. In essence a large part of the labour force is engaged in 'its own' maintenance and reproduction. Thus from the perspective of employment, the requirements of reproduction are as important to the structuration of the labour market as the immediate needs of productive industry, if not more so. Accordingly the implications for labour market theorizing are highly significant.

The market for labour, therefore, is not simply, or even largely, derived from the immediate requirements of production, but is determined significantly by the reproductive requirements of the system as a whole. Changes in employment patterns, whether they are compositional, occupational or temporal will be driven by the requirements of welfare specifically and reproduction in general. While labour market flexibility is tied to the idea of 'the flexible firm', numerical flexibility is often a function of the new patterns of recruitment in public services, particularly with women working part-time. As will be argued later the expansion of the part-time labour force in recent years also relates to the availability of student labour which is a function of the expansion of mass higher education. Therefore it is argued here that labour market theorizing must fully acknowledge reproductive determinants, broaden its institutional dynamics to take on board public and private agencies and, in particular, to consider the changing roles of the state in 'instituting the market for labour'. This requires an understanding of the commodification of labour power, exemplified here in a case study of British labour market history, which reveals the productive and reproductive imperatives that structure labour market development.

The Commodification of Labour Power

In order to theorize the capitalist labour market it is necessary to have a basic grasp of the commodification of labour power, which provides the framework within which labour markets have developed. The commodification of labour power reveals the institution of the labour market by the state, and obliges the consideration of welfare and reproductive activities, which is essential to capture the range of determinants that structure the contemporary labour market. This will be attempted here by drawing on both Karl Marx and Karl Polanyi who provide the insights into the nature of the labour power as a commodity and the establishment of the market for its purchase and sale. These authors are not often brought together for these purposes. Polanyi was a life-long socialist, but he was not a Marxist (Pearson 1977). Moreover he considered labour power to be a 'fictitious commodity', believing that, since man was not born and produced for sale, he could not be classified a true commodity. Nevertheless, he argued, 'the commodity fiction, supplies a vital organizing principle in regard to the whole of society affecting almost all its institutions' (Polanyi 1957, p. 73). Thus despite their differences, there are potentially important connections between Marx and Polanyi which allow the crucial link between the realm of capital accumulation, which is Marx's domain, to the realm of the market, which is Polanyian territory.

At first sight, however, Marx does not seem a particularly useful starting point for the development of a theory of the labour market. The volumes of Capital are concerned with production rather than markets. Labour, or labour power, is a largely undifferentiated concept, measured quantitatively in terms of the time required for its reproduction and in the labour time of surplus value production. In Marx's economic writings there is little concern with complex or skilled labour. Furthermore, wages are largely determined by the level of unemployment and business cycle. Thus;

> Taking them as a whole, the general movements of wages are exclusively regulated by the expansion and contraction of the industrial reserve army, and these again correspond to the periodic changes of the industrial cycle. (Capital, vol. 1, p. 596)

Obviously these propositions are inadequate for the development of labour market theory. Yet it is Marx's desire to understand and reveal capitalism as a profoundly social process that expresses the forces and relations of production and reproduction which underpins the explanatory power of Marxism and sustains its contemporary relevance to social theory. If the correct procedures are used it will be possible to extrapolate from production of capital and reproduction of labour power to the labour market itself.

In relation to a theory of the labour market there are two dimensions to the commodification of labour power that arise from the relations of production and reproduction. One aspect relates to the difference between surplus value and exchange value of labour, the exploitation of labour, while the other relates to the value of the labour power commodity itself. Although the more Marxian versions of regulation theory have concerned themselves with surplus value extraction, there has been little attention paid to the value of the labour power commodity and the 'socially necessary labour time' needed for its reproduction. It is suggested here that a theory of the labour market must articulate both productive and reproductive imperatives in assessing the determinants and outcomes of labour market change.

The commodification of labour power, as revealed by Marx, penetrates the surface appearance of monetary transaction in the market place. Thus, under the guise of market exchange between formally free and independent individuals, the appropriation of surplus labour takes place. One of the oldest mottoes of the labour market is 'a fair day's work for a fair day's pay'. This exchange of wages and labour is rendered as a trade in equivalence and, in this way, the allocation of social labour and the distribution of resources are achieved through the 'economic' mechanism of commodity exchange. This is not a transparent process. There are profoundly political and ideological forces implicated in the commodification of labour power that serve to neutralize and obscure the social relations embedded in the market exchange of commodities. Markets take on a life of their own. Property 'receives its purely economic form by discarding all its former political and social embellishments and associations' (Capital, vol. 1, p. 618). Thus the establishment of the market in wage labour is one of the principal mechanisms by which economic relations are denuded of their social content. It is therefore the task of theory to get underneath the surface appearance of market exchange to reveal the social relations and institutional structures which govern such transactions.

In his discussion of the buying and selling of labour power, Marx considers two conditions which must be met before the owner of money can find labour power offered for sale as a commodity. In the first instance;

> The exchange of commodities itself implies no other relations of dependence than those which result from its own nature. On this assumption labour power can appear upon the market as a commodity, only if, and so far as, its possessor, the individual whose labour power it is, offers it

for sale, or sells it as a commodity. In order that he may be able to do this, he must have it at his disposal, must be the untrammelled owner of his capacity for labour, ie, of his person. He and the owner of money meet in the market, and deal with each other on the basis of equal rights, with this difference alone, that one is buyer, the other seller, both therefore equal in the eyes of the law. The continuance of this relationship demands that the owner of the labour power should sell it only for a definite period, for if he were to sell it rump and stump, once and for all, he would be selling himself, converting himself from a free man into a slave, from an owner of a commodity into a commodity.

(Secondly) . . . That the labourer instead of being in a position to sell commodities in which his labour is incorporated *must be obliged to offer for sale as a commodity* that very labour power, which exists only in his living self. (Capital, vol. 1, p. 165, emphasis added)

A contemporary commentator might suggest that relations of dependence other than wages can link the employer and the worker, particularly in the form of non-wage employment benefits, but in this passage Marx is comparing with pre-capitalist arrangements. A key feature of free wage labour is that the buyer of labour power is free from the burdens of maintenance associated with servile or bonded labour. The establishment of 'free labour', replacing feudal servitude and slavery, occurs through the mechanism of commodity exchange. This contractual relation involves free producers – juridically free and free from the means of production – and an appropriator who has absolute private property in the means of production (McNally 1993). However, while much energy is usefully devoted to exposing the exploitation essential to wage labour, the other element of commodification, relating to social reproduction, is obscured and often goes unappreciated.

Thus, the wages system frees the employer from reproductive responsibilities, such as education, public health and large-scale infrastructure projects, but it leaves unresolved how these functions are to be financed and delivered. At the heart of capitalism lies a dilemma as to how a system, ostensibly based on private market transactions, can pay for and deliver public goods. Are welfare and public services generally to be financed from the wages the worker receives, carried out as unpaid welfare provided within the family, or resourced out of the social surplus amassed through general taxation? How these issues are resolved, whether they are conceived as public services to be financed and/or delivered by government, welfare services financed by large scale insurance provisions, cooperative societies, or through personal savings and family provision is subject to continual adaptation.

These are questions that arose with the establishment of the wage system and remain unresolved to this day.

The new alignment of political and social forces configured by the establishment of the market economy, should not lead to the assumption that the market is some enclosed, stateless realm of self-regulation. Compared to the feudal lord, the capitalist is freed from responsibility for the maintenance, defence and reproduction of society, which passes to government, which acts in the interests of capital as a whole. In serving the interests of the whole economy the state appears 'above society', to quote Engels, standing apart from the commercial world of enterprise and struggle between contending social classes. Yet the sense of separation between government and the economy is in significant measure illusory and, in important respects, the differentiation is one which the state has created by its own actions. The differentiated and ostensibly enclosed spheres of the state and the market presuppose the successful intervention of government.

As Marx remarked in the Grundrisse:

> It must be kept in mind that the new forces of production and relations of production do not develop out of nothing, nor drop out of the sky, nor from the womb of the self positing Idea; but from within and in antithesis to the existing development of production and to the inherited, traditional relations of property. (Marx 1973, p. 278)

The supply of labour for waged work did not arrive out of the ether or as some spontaneous evolution from feudalism, but could only be guaranteed after a protracted process of government intervention, which created a dependency on wages for subsistence. This is one of the senses in which the market for labour was instituted by government both judicially and economically. If the processes of commodification are considered in terms of the institution of the market then there are two lines of discussion opened up which are, in the first instance *foundational*, and secondly *developmental* in responding to the ongoing reproductive needs of the workforce and the infrastructural requirements of the economy. This also implies that the commodification of labour in a general sense is not confined to private sector employment but transcends boundaries between production and reproduction and requires a more comprehensive framework for labour market theorizing.

In order to illuminate the foundational and developmental aspects of labour market theory a case study of the institution of the labour market in Britain is offered. Britain was the birthplace of the industrial revolution and the first country in which the wage based labour market came into prominence. There are other histories which would need to be included in a comprehensive work on the foundation of the labour market, such as the impact of the Napoleonic wars in Europe and the civil war in America, and such a study should also look at the role of convict labour and migrant labour and the availability of land. For present purposes however, the case study of the British labour market usefully illuminates the foundational and developmental aspects of the wage labour system.

Establishing the Market in Labour: The British Case

Industrial society developed within the womb of feudalism and was, to some degree, integrated with agriculture. In seventeenth-century England as many as a half of all small farmers engaged in one or more industrial employment. Probably a quarter of the farming population spent part of the working time in woollen industries. It was not just the rural poor who combined wage labour with farming, but also the relatively skilled labourers such as carpenters, masons, wheelwrights and ploughwrights. As David McNally points out, in his very useful discussion of the establishment of the labour market in England, the bulk of labourers constituted a 'sort of semi-proletariat, a group that lacked enough land to maintain self-sufficiency, but that could use its own production (either for consumption or for the market) as a substantial supplement to wages' (McNally 1993). However, it is not plausible to suggest that a complete transfer from agriculture to industry could have evolved incrementally and spontaneously. Quantitative changes ultimately involve qualitative change in social development such that state intervention was required to bring about the 'Great Transformation' to the market economy.

From the point of view of the labourer the rise of industrial society represented a complete overhaul in the form of employment and in labour process. Labour had to be disciplined into accepting a wholly unnatural change in the nature of work. The labourer had previously been accustomed to the rhythm of nature and its seasons but lacked awareness of time. Work was based on task rather than process and he or she was used to a degree of control over their leisure. The early factory masters encountered problems, not only in attracting labour, but also in inculcating the habits of punctuality, regularity and industry. The practice of 'St. Monday', taking Monday as a holiday from work was widespread (Hobsbawm 1977). As E. P. Thompson's highly engaging discussion of time and work discipline demonstrates, it was the element of control over his time and sense of independence that the new factory masters sought to eliminate (Thompson 1980). In this regard the report of The Survey of the Board of Agriculture for Somerset 1798 has been widely quoted.

> The possession of a cow or two, with a hog and a few geese, naturally exalts the peasant, in his own conception, above his brothers in the same rank of society . . . In sauntering after his cattle, he acquires a habit of indolence . . . Day labour becomes disgusting; the aversion increases by indulgence and at length the sale of a half fed calf, or hog, furnishes the means of adding intemperance to idleness. The sale of the cow frequently succeeds, and its wretched and disappointed possessor, unwilling to resume the daily and regular course of labour, from whence he drew his former subsistence . . . extracts from the poor rate the relief to which he is in no degree entitled.

Polanyi is quite accurate in stating that 'There was nothing natural about laissez-faire. Free markets could never have come into being merely by allowing things to take their course . . . laissez-faire was enforced by the state' (Polanyi 1957). Markets have existed for centuries but a market economy had never developed. From the perspective of labour, the transition to capitalism necessitated the establishment of the new forms of property rights, attacks on customary rights and entitlements, changes in the law in respect of masters and servants, new powers for the courts and changes to welfare laws. All these measures were put into place to bring about the commodification of labour power by creating a complete dependency on money wages.

The enclosure and consequent commodification of land required the establishment and guarantee of private property rights of the landowner. Not only did this allow for the concentration of landownership and the growth of large farms, it also denied whole sections of society access to land formerly held in common. Their rights to common land gave options to the labourer in seeking a livelihood. He or she could work for part of the year in a factory and at the same time maintain a small farm or keep a cow or other animals, which would provide an alternative source of income and food. Land enclosures therefore simultaneously propelled the commodification of land but also labour power. Enclosure is marked stages and appears in waves, particularly in the seventeenth century and the first half of 18th century. However, it is the great burst of parliamentary enclosures between 1760 and 1830, in which some six million acres of common land were enclosed, that effectively completed the transformation of agriculture.

There were also other customary rights enjoyed by labour in the form of perquisites which were removed in the creation of the labour market. The idea that labour should be paid solely in terms of a money wage would have been highly unusual to the experience of workers in the 18th and early 19th century (McNally 1993). There was a customary entitlement to 'thrums' for weavers (the weft ends left on the loom after the removal of the finished cloth), 'chips' for shipwrights (waste timber, ropes, sail canvas and cordage) and 'cabbage' for tailors (waste cloth). These waste products could be used by the workers or sold on the open market as a supplementary source of income. Consequently new measures were taken to police the embezzlement of stolen materials resulting in penalties increasing to three months imprisonment in 1777 (Saville 1994).

The government also passed a series of laws that attacked the rights of labour to organize collectively to improve their economic position. The Combination Acts of 1799–1800 made illegal combinations of all trades which previously only applied to specific trades such as tailors, hatters and papermakers. Further provisions to curb the right to organize were made in the Mutiny Act of 1797 and the Seditious Meetings Act of 1817 which, in tandem, provided the legal charges against the Tolpuddle labourers. Moreover, while the buyer and seller of labour power were formerly free and equal in the labour market, it did not imply that their interests were equally protected by the state. The Master and Servant Law of 1823, noted the legal historian Holdsworth, 'gave to the master remedies for the breach of contract absolutely different from those in the case of any other contract'. Saville (1994) concludes that at the heart of the Master and Servants legislation was the statutory provision that treated the employer and the worker as entirely unequal. Thus, when a master broke his contract it was a merely civil offence, but when a labourer broke or violated his or her contract, he or she could be summarily sentenced by the magistrate and imprisoned with hard labour for up to three months. The evidence suggests that some 10,000 prosecutions took place each year and it was not until the Employers and Workmen Act of 1875, that formal legal equality with employers was granted to labour.

The final element in the creation of the labour market was put in place by the government's social policy of the first half of the nineteenth century. The state created free labour but increasingly confined the expression of freedom to a choice between a freedom to starve and a freedom to work for wages. The state did not act in the manner of a slave driver forcing labour into the fields or mines, but presented the negative compulsion of withdrawing alternative sources of employment and welfare. The Speenhamland Act of 1797 and the Poor Law Act of 1834 were milestones in state social policy which finally completed the establishment of the labour market. The Speenhamland Act assumed that there was a general 'right to live' and inaugurated a system of local parish allowances as aid in wages. The scale of allowances was based on the price of bread and entitled the poor to a means of subsistence. It was, as Hobsbawm (1977) notes, 'a well meant but mistaken attempt to guarantee the labourer a minimum wage by subsidizing wage out of poor rates. Its chief effect was to encourage farmers to lower wages and to demoralise the labourers' (p. 202). With the parliamentary triumphs of the middle classes in 1832, the Speenhamland Act was replaced by the New Poor Law of 1834. This was 'a statute of quite uncommon callousness', which abolished the general category of the poor and established two categories of physically helpless paupers who were only offered poor relief within the new workhouses (where they were separated from families and received relief at less than market wages) and independent workers who earned their living by wages. As Polanyi points out,

> This created an entirely new category of the poor, the unemployed, who made their appearance on the social scene. While the pauper, for the sake of humanity should be relieved, the unemployed, for the sake of industry, should not be relieved. That the unemployed worker was innocent of his fate did not matter. The point was not whether he might or might not have found work, but that unless he was in danger of famishing with only the abhorred workhouse for an alternative, the wage system would break down, thus throwing society into misery and chaos. (Polanyi, p. 224)

Thus the first capitalist labour market was instituted as a product of several measures initiated or supported by the state. The commodification of labour presupposed: the commodification of land; the juridical guarantee of private property; changes to customary rights and entitlements of labour; the overhaul of subsistence welfare entitlements; legal constraints on the rights of labour to collective organization; and the enhancement of the coercive powers of the state. This suggests that any discussion of new capitalist employment relations, envisaging the end of the salarization of employment or the fragmentation of the contractual structures that underpin the wage system, should contemplate a confrontation with 'deep social structures' that have been established and maintained over two centuries by the strenuous efforts of governments. Any secession from the constitution of wage labour is only imaginable after the most profound upheaval in society on a scale far greater than that predicted by contemporary accounts of globalization and technological change.

The Reproduction of the Workforce, the Class Struggle and the Role of Employers

A subsequent shift in government function can be seen as a move from the foundational to the development aspects of state intervention, and a move from a proactive to reactive stance in the state's relation to the market. Having set up the framework for the labour market the state has to react to market outcomes that threaten the very survival of the economy. In particular it has to assume overall responsibility for the reproduction of the next generation of labour. In the British case, having corralled labourers into the extraordinarily harsh working conditions of the time, the very survival of the labour force was at risk. In the English cotton industries during 1834–47, the workforce was made up of one quarter adult males, over half were women and girls and the balance was boys below the age of eighteen (Hobsbawm 1977, p. 66). The rate of exploitation was such that the physical exhaustion of the workforce jeopardized the future supply of waged labour. From the early 1830s to the 1880s there developed, often in a haphazard fashion, a growing body of legislation that signalled a shift from orthodox economic liberalism towards social and national protectionism, as legislative measures were put in place to combat the worst effects of the living and working conditions in nascent industrial capitalism.

This irony is strikingly captured by Polanyi, who insisted that,

> The road to the free market was opened and kept open by an enormous increase in continuous, centrally organized and controlled interventionism . . . While the laissez-faire economy was the product of deliberate state action, subsequent restrictions on laissez faire started in a spontaneous way. *Laissez-faire was planned; planning was not.* (Polanyi 1957, emphasis added)

Perhaps because the economy was only 'discovered' when many of these institutional changes were already in place, the intrinsic role of the state has been ignored and only extrinsic features of state intervention acknowledged in neoclassical thinking. It is only the external and spontaneous aspects of government intervention that feature in the concerns of liberal orthodoxy. Polanyi cites Herbert Spencer, in his work in the mid 1880s on 'The Man versus the State', railing against liberals who had deserted their principles for the sake of restrictive legislation. In page after page Spencer listed the state measures that encroached on the rights and freedoms of industry, appointed inspectors and raised taxes and rates for health and sanitation improvements. These changes that Spencer found so abhorrent included: the extension of the Mines Act ' making it penal to employ boys under twelve not attending school and unable to read and write'; the Chimney Sweepers Act, that prevented the torture and eventual death of children set to sweep too narrow slots; the Contagious Diseases Act; Factory Inspection legislation; the extension of compulsory vaccination in Scotland and Ireland; an Act that made illegal the sinking of coal mines with a single shaft; and an Act appointing food inspectors 'for the wholesomeness or unwholesomeness of food'. Polanyi seems wholly convincing in terms of the state intervention as part of the self-protection of the society. He is also correct to draw the distinction between the constitutive and the reactive roles of the state. Because the latter can appear to individual capitalists as a set of restrictions or impositions, the external character of state intervention is reinforced. It is only within the broader conceptual context of the economy and society as a whole that they appear as essential requirements for the reproduction of capitalism.

The developmental role of government intervention increases with the expansion of capitalism. Thus in the 19th century international competition between states, expressed in terms of imperial rivalries and in technological advantage, began to articulate another set of imperatives in the reproduction to the workforce. In 1818 just 7% of children attended day school, but the impact of the industrial revolution raised the educational requirements of the workforce. In 1833 parliament approved a grant of £20,000 to improve school buildings in a small number of religious schools. During this time parliament spent more in a year on the Queen's stables than the education of the children, but the pressure for new resources built up as the demands of a modernizing industry began to take effect. By 1880, schooling was made compulsory for all five to ten year olds. In 1884 a Royal Commission on technical instruction toured Europe to report that schooling in Germany is 'overwhelmingly superior'. The commissioners were very impressed by the general intelligence and technical knowledge of the masters and managers of industrial establishments on the continent. By the 1890s from increased local level support for board schools to the issuing of government grants to the redbrick universities, the 19th century had marked a turnaround in the educational responsibilities of the state at all levels (Timmins 1996). Not only in terms of education, but also on the health front were the responsibilities of government to increase. During the war with the Boers (1899 –1902) it was discovered that almost half those volunteering to fight in South Africa were medically unfit. The First World War also exposed the same problems, even more brutally and on a larger scale, as one survey showed that one conscript in three was not fit enough to join the forces, and only a third was judged 'Grade One'. The responding change in government policy meant that by the time of the Second World War seven out of ten were put in the top grade (Timmins 1996).

Overall, and despite contemporary perspectives of the nation state as 'outmoded', the state thrives, adapts and adjusts to meet the demands of modern industry. In 1890 government spending in Britain amounted to less than 10% of GNP (almost half of which was military spending). Over the course of the following century successive governments, regardless of their political proclivities had increased the proportion of state expenditure to some 44% of GNP, some 26% of which was devoted to education and health alone (Pierson 1996).

During this last century the form of intervention has evolved to meeting changing economic and political requirements. In Britain the immediate post-war welfare needs for soldiers returning from the front included 'the building of homes fit for heroes'. The 1980s saw the rise of mass higher education, such that by the first decade of the 21st century the target was set for some 50% of secondary school leavers to progress to university or college education. Not only do policy priorities vary over time, there are also functional changes in the form of government roles and responsibilities. The changes in the ownership of public assets, the reconfiguration of the delivery and financing of services, and the development of new forms of engagement and partnerships with the private sector point to a continual evolution of state functions and responsibilities as the reproductive requirements adapt to meet the needs of modern industry. But this should not detract from the predominant experience of the last century, of an ever increasing role and changing form of state intervention in the economy which feature prominently in the key determinants of labour market change.

The thrust of this discussion should not, however, give the impression of social policy and welfare provision arising simply as a concession that has been wrung out of reluctant employers, by left-leaning governments or by militant trades unions. Some schools of thought, whether of the Marxist or particularly the 'power resources' perspectives, stress that welfare development is the outcome of distributional conflicts between unions and employers or its mediation in state intervention (Korpi and Palme 2003; Esping-Andersen 1990). Such a view would see the history of the welfare state in the United States for instance take the form of 'two big bangs', in the rising labour militancy of the 1930s which gave rise to the New Deal and the sweeping electoral success of the Democrats in the 1964 election which gave rise to Medicare for the elderly and Medicaid for the poor (Howard 2007). The welfare impact of class conflict is perhaps more evident at particular points in history when there is a more generalized pressure on the welfare state. Such a period was evident in the recent history of the European Union, when the preparations for European Monetary Union prompted widespread austerity measures which provoked generalized opposition from the trades union movement in the form of strikes and mass demonstrations which were fairly effective in resisting the rollback in welfare spending. *However in the absence of distributional conflict during prolonged periods characterized by low levels of union militancy, as recently experienced in many countries, it is also evident that welfare states do not collapse.* While it has been 'all quiet' on the industrial front recently many commentators acknowledge that the welfare state appears resilient to challenge and capable of adapting to new threats and opportunities.

There are a variety of explanations for welfare state resilience. It has been explained as a form of path dependency in which the institutional legacies of previous decisions provide major obstacles to reform measures, a school of thought opened up by Paul Pierson's 'new politics of the welfare state'. However there are more productive insights into welfare state developments provided by the 'varieties of capitalism' school of political economy which has stressed the proactive role of employers in the development of welfare state in Europe and the United States. In a very interesting discussion of the employers' involvement in social policy Isabel Mares points out that prior to the introduction of compulsory social insurance schemes many employers were involved in the voluntary provision of social insurance, particularly in France and Germany. In this account the benefits of employers' involvement in social policy outweigh the costs of their contribution because they see their role in social policy as a means of securing their investment in skills and of reducing the influence of trades unions in the administration of social insurance. Mares points out that the German Employers' Association argued for the greater involvement of employers in social insurance in order to tie the structure and generosity of insurance provision to the labour market conditions of the firm. In this light social policy is a compliment to those employment practices dedicated to the retention of labour (Mares 2001). More generally Esteves-Abe, Iverson and Soskice argue that 'social policy helps firms overcome market failures in skill formation' and therefore welfare policies appear less as the immediate outcomes of distributional conflicts between capital and labour, but as a central feature of labour control strategies designed to lower mobility, to counter staff turnover and combat skill shortages and to help firms cope with the fluctuations in the business cycle.

> Although strong unions and left governments undoubtedly affect distributive outcomes, we have argued that employment and income protection can be seen as efforts to increase workers' dependence on particular employers, as well as their exposure to labour market risk. Moreover, social protection often stems from the strength rather than the weakness of employers. (Esteves-Abe, Iverson and Soskice 2001, p. 183)

Such conclusions are important in explaining the continuing role of large firms, particularly in the United States, in offering health benefits and pension provision despite extraordinary increases in their costs, and it also reemphasizes the high priority that employers have attached to labour retention. They add to an understanding of the development of the welfare state and reveal dynamics that leave their own imprint on the labour market. In the sphere of reproduction a distinct set of determinants are evident that create new patterns of employment, generate occupational and compositional change in the labour market, especially in relation to gender, and produce 'atypical' forms of employment. Finally, in contrast to the irrationality engendered by neoliberal compliance with market forces, the reproductive requirements of capitalism confer a greater sense of rationality and order, demand long-term planning for current and future needs and act as a counterbalance to the rhetorics of powerlessness in the face of exogenous change.

Conclusion

The present inquiry focuses on the extent to which the transformation of work has evolved to the point at which new employment relations suggest qualitatively different forms of engagement between capital and labour. This chapter has attempted to explain why the labour market is not only an imperfect conduit through which new employment relations might be transmitted, it also acts as an insulator against the pressures for institutional changes imputed to technological development and capital mobility. The discussion so far has looked at the different approaches to societal transformation, including post-industrial literature, transformation theory, economic sociology and varieties of capitalism, to establish whether the changes can be viewed as structural or relational. These are questions of a societal nature and so the investigation must be broadly based, covering the range of labour market determinants, if plausible generalizations are to be offered. In this regard both post-industrial literature and transformation theory have attempted to draw conclusions from changes in production specifically, and then to extrapolate to the wider world of work. This approach is challenged in the above discussion on several grounds, but specifically because it overstates the extent and impact of institutional and technological change in manufacturing, and because its conceptualization of the labour market is essentially derivative.

The strategy adopted here is to make the capitalist labour market the object of theoretical inquiry. Once this is accepted it becomes clear that the requirements of production and reproduction, broadly defined, determine labour market adjustment. In order to theorize the labour market 'in its own right' it is necessary to have a basic understanding of the commodification of labour power and examine how the market for labour was 'instituted'. Marxism reveals the social relations that are obscured by monetary exchange in market transactions, while Polanyi shows that the labour market is a uniquely powerful exemplar of an instituted process – a deep structure established and maintained by the strenuous efforts of governments over more than two centuries. Its embeddedness is both external in relation to networks and agencies, but it is also internal in relation to the systems that govern recruitment, remuneration and retention, and structural in relation to the functions of the state. Finally, the discussion of the commodification of labour power must extend beyond production because the establishment of the labour market created a set of tensions in the allocation of responsibilities for the finance and delivery of welfare services. These tensions are amplified with the increasing skill requirement of modern industries, and the growing costs of health and social care. Having adopted this framework, Chapter 5 will consider the causes and consequence of welfare restructuring.

5

Globalization, Demographic Change and Social Welfare

In many accounts the transformation of work emanates from the realm of production, and is driven by technological change and corporate restructuring, both nationally and internationally. The thesis presented here suggests that the requirements of production and reproduction together determine employment and labour market change as a whole. Developments within the sphere of reproduction have their own dynamic and logic with specific employment impacts that must be factored into the analysis of new capitalism. In this approach welfare state restructuring is not simply an outcome of externally driven adjustments, fiscal or economic crises or demographic change, nor is the welfare state some residual category that lives off the resources of productive economy, expressing some public altruism that defends weaker sections of the community. In considering production and reproduction in this way a broader framework can conceptualize the interaction and integration of productive and welfare functions, acknowledge a constantly evolving division of roles and responsibilities between public and private agencies, and identify an interdependence between the welfare state and the market. While it is important to capture both production and reproduction to understand capitalism, new or old, as a whole, it is also necessary to identify the specific impacts of reproduction in terms of labour market activity, employment adjustment and institutional restructuring. Furthermore, if new capitalist relations of employment express a much higher degree of insecurity, it is also important to assess the effects of welfare restructuring and the weakening of social protection systems.

This attempt to theorize the labour market in its own right might offend the analytical machismo of those who think that the real business of change takes place in factories and in adjustments in labour process and not, for instance, in care homes or hospitals, to which an obvious reply is that the development of care homes and social services free up people and, of course women in particular, to work in factories and offices. Thus the expansion of health, education and care services have a specific contribution to employment but also a broader impact on the labour market as a whole, which is often sidelined by those perspectives which are preoccupied by the imperatives of production. However the approach adopted here might also grate with many contributors to the debates on welfare restructuring. For some time the preoccupations of social policy debate have revolved around welfare services and user benefits, the defence of the welfare state from neoliberal retrenchment as well as citizenship rights and social exclusion and poverty. The desire to dissociate welfare entitlement from the economic necessity is politically justifiable, but in analytical terms such a user-led perspective shows little concern with the producers of welfare services, and excepting debates around workfare and active labour market policy (Peck 2001 and ILO 2003), the wider labour market impact of welfare restructuring is conspicuously absent.

Preceding chapters have stressed the systematic overstatement of technological change and global movements of capital in a world view premised upon autonomous and disembedded social processes. This can only occur in a world that air brushes the role of government in market economies. Thus while corporations are said to become disembedded the changing relationship between the state and the economy is often perceived as a 'decoupling'. In this view economic forces are decoupled from the nation state as corporations offshore, their operations beyond territorial control. In this metaphorical decoupling, the nation state is cast in the role of jilted lover left standing on the pier tearfully watching the ship set sail on the high seas of the global market. Nigel Harris (2003 and 2004) would have us believe that the forces of global economic integration have developed to the point that the market has 'escaped' the state. A decoupling metaphor that has capital as the battered wife leaving the abusive husband. Yet, as a corollary to the corporate escape and abandonment scenarios, there are restructuring perspectives that point in the opposite direction. In this version the state appears as victim of global processes with their functions increasingly taken over by private sector agencies. Using case studies of health, transport, retailing and higher education, George Monbiot (2000) has written engagingly about 'the captive state', the product of the 'corporate takeover of Britain'. The image conjured here is of the siege at Helms Deep with the private sector represented by the Orcs of Mordor. Yet, as far as the OECD countries are concerned, this passive state is difficult to find in reality.

The account offered here suggests that the welfare state is allied to the purposes of capital accumulation and the reproduction of labour power, an approach the varieties of the capitalism school have considered as 'welfare production regimes' (Esteves-Abe, Iversen and Soskice 2001). Consequently there is a dynamic within the realm of reproduction that relates to the requirements of and for labour, which concerns the availability of workers and the quality of their skills. Thus the needs of production and reproduction combine to raise the social and technical competence of the workforce and, in different ways, the expansion of education, health services and social care. Kathleen Thelen, for instance, suggests that increased global pressures on firms, who compete on the base of quality and reliability, drive firms and governments to develop policies to stabilize the supply of skilled labour (Thelen 2001). Global competition, for instance, does not undermine but supports the expansion of university provision as the availability of suitably trained graduates emerges as a measure of the competitiveness of national economies.

However, the enhanced demand for welfare services does not determine the form in which it is delivered or financed, particularly in a period in which the sense of distinction and the boundary lines between public and private systems are blurring in many areas. It is suggested in this chapter that any welfare retrenchment should be considered alongside other pressures for welfare expansion. Consequently retrenchment should not be seen as a simple process of state or even corporate withdrawal from public services but of a *recommodification of welfare systems* (Bonoli, George and Taylor-Gooby 2000). To flesh out this perspective the subsequent discussion will consider globalization and welfare restructuring in Europe and North America, the labour market implications of welfare state restructuring and finally, the demographic time bomb and the pensions crisis.

Globalization and the Welfare State

In considering the social implications of globalization it is necessary to identify the political and economic forces that have prompted institutional adaptation amongst welfare systems. George and Wilding (2002) have, not unreasonably, characterized an influential view of globalization and welfare policy adjustment by identifying four key factors that are said to prompt welfare retrenchment.

Globalization gives finance capital and capital investors increased mobility, which reduces the bargaining power of governments, which are then forced to adopt business friendly policies that are increasingly resistant to welfare spending.

Globalization makes capital international rather than national in its orientation and as a consequence closed economies are opened up to global forces. This represents a break with the past as redistributive social policies were associated with state regulated closed economies.

Ideologically the rise of neoliberalism is fuelled by and sustains a view of globalization which is hostile to public expenditure and state welfare.

Globalization has led to the creation of a competition state whose primary concern is international competitiveness rather than social welfare and social justice.

Capital's propensity to move is central to the retrenchment position and deserves particular scrutiny. For many the increased mobility of capital means that governments' fiscal policies are subject to global competition as tax regimes compete to secure foreign direct investment, which subsequently results in a lowering of social standards and the dismantling of the welfare state (Shin 2000). The 'exit' threat of mobile asset holders has gained over the 'voice' welfare providers and recipients (see Garrett 1998), while others, moreover, suggest that globalization allows a certain amount of welfare 'regime shopping' (Crouch 1998). In these circumstances governments have been forced to abandon pro-welfare policies because of the threat of an exodus of capital. The case of the French Socialist government, which came to office in 1981 on a pledge of Keynesian expansionary policies and then performed a dramatic u-turn by introducing austerity measures in the following summer, is often cited alongside the flight of capital from Sweden in the late 1980s, as an example of governments bowing down to the will of mobile capital (Yeates 2001). Scharpf is another who suggests that market correcting policies depend on the state control of the economy, which was lost after the globalization of finance and the transnational integration of markets (Scharpf 1998). Thus if capital is mobile, governments are unable to control interest rates and taxation policy. In these circumstances welfare states cannot rely on tax revenues from capital and public spending has to be trimmed as a consequence. Accordingly, if capital is not able to take its share of the welfare burden then the redistributive possibilities of government policy are greatly limited. In such circumstances redistribution does not rebalance wealth between capital and labour but redistributes wealth between immobile factors, meaning high income labour and low income labour, a policy Scharpf tellingly described as 'socialism in one class'.

The response to these arguments seems to mirror the Woody Allen joke at the beginning of the opening chapter, in that both the level of capital mobility seems greatly overstated and secondly such cross border flows of capital as there are have the opposite effects to those stated above. Not only is the mobility propensity of capital much lower than the globalizers suggest, Dani Rodrik has also shown that any opening up of economies occurs in tandem with *increased government spending* (Rodrik 1996). Colin Hay points out that welfare spending enhances national competitiveness and that the educational attainment and skill level of the workforce is the most critical factor in determining the attractiveness of labour market regime, to mobile capital (Hay 2001 and 2005). Even though Duane Swank's account suggests high levels of capital mobility, he argues that the liberalization of capital controls and borrowing on international markets are positively associated with total welfare spending (Swank 2002).

In a very useful survey of the debates over the globalization–welfare nexus Philipp Genschel (2004) has examined the experience of the French socialist government. Recalling Oatley's exploration of capital mobility constraints he suggests that national monetary policy works through exchange rates rather than interest rates. Accordingly Genschel argues that the Mitterand government's about-turn was a conscious policy choice in which the political motivation to remain in the European Monetary system, with its fixed exchange rates, outweighed the benefits of domestic demand management. This had little to do with globalization. Moreover, Genschel points out that trade liberalization, capital deregulation and monetary integration are macroeconomic policy tools in their own right. What can appear at first as a loss of national autonomy, as Noteramus (1993) points out, might in itself be a conscious choice of government. Thus in reinstating domestic policy sovereignty Hemerijck (2002) describes 'the self-transformation of the European Social Models'. Bowles and Wagman's survey of first world governments showed the multiplicity of responses to globalization and challenged some inevitable capitulation of the welfare state to global market forces (Bowles and Wagman 1997), while Hay, Watson and Wincott's study of globalization and European integration looked at nine members of the EU and found that welfare state reform was both politically constructed and contested, and suggested the persistence of European social models (Hay, Watson and Wincott 1999). Lesley Sklair has argued that 'There is nothing inevitable about the dismantling of the welfare state under pressure from capitalist globalization. If it takes place, it is the conscious decision by those who run the government and those who control the state' (Sklair 2002, p. 240). Finally Swank's authoritative study of globalization and welfare restructuring has argued convincingly that national institutions determine the policy response to political pressures associated with globalization (Swank 2002).

Globalization and welfare change are independent or contingent processes. Their linkage is more ideological than substantive, in that the abandonment of Keynesian policies is justified by governments in terms of globalization. The construction of a world 'out there' beyond government control is central to the claims of nation states who have attempted to reduce the scope for social amelioration and the lowering of public expectations of social protection. They have forsaken Keynesian policies and embraced neoliberalism using globalization as a means of abrogating certain welfare obligations. This is a period of 'state denial' in which big government absolves itself of certain welfare functions, by presenting itself as incapable of dealing with technological, demographic and global forces beyond its control. Thus the 'myth of the powerless state' (Weiss 1998) is a central feature of neoliberal policy, yet ironically the state itself appears as chief myth maker.

Welfare Retrenchment and Expansion in Europe

It might seem odd to a public that has been exposed to neoliberal policies for more than two decades that the idea of welfare retrenchment should need to be debated. For many the only questions raised concern the extent of welfare retrenchment and the form that it has assumed in different countries. Yet the discussion of welfare retrenchment seems to have gone through phases not dissimilar to the globalization debates mentioned in Chapter 3. Earlier discussions about the dismantling of the welfare state were pessimistic, later accounts argued that such views were excessively downbeat, suggesting welfare adaptation rather than dismantling, while more recent contributions emphasize the political or discursive construction of welfare retrenchment. It is possible that Paul Pierson's account of the 'new politics of welfare' radically influenced subsequent analysis of the dismantling of welfare. Pierson's study of welfare retrenchment in the US and the UK under Reagan and Thatcher surprised many as he compared welfare reforms with other policy areas, such as industrial relations, regulation, industrial policy and macroeconomic policy, and found 'that the welfare state stands out as an island of regulatory stability' (Pierson 1994). It is now more widely acknowledged that the welfare state has, or has had, a greater resilience than many initially expected. Peter Taylor-Gooby's study of welfare reform in Europe noted that, despite concerns of the 1980s and early 1990s, the European welfare state had survived many of the challenges it faced, although he was less optimistic about future prospects and suggested that the conditions for more radical reforms were beginning to emerge (Taylor-Gooby 2001).

An important, but for many a disconcerting feature of discussions in Europe is that, at aggregate level, government expenditure on welfare in Europe has *increased progressively* since the 1960s (Bonoli and Taylor-Gooby 2000). There are several dynamics which need to be identified if this is to be fully understood. Many dismissively suggest that trends in total expenditures conceal changes in the structure of welfare provision, obscure the decline of social protection it offers, and say nothing about adjustments in the form of its delivery (see Hay 2005). There is a perfectly understandable response to welfare restructuring, which sees little other than retrenchment, austerity measures, privatization and a loss of citizenship rights and entitlements. This justifiable defensiveness should not, however, deny other determinants of welfare adaptation which are positive. The requirements of capitalism to develop 'the stock of human capital' increases pressure to raise the social and technical competence of the workforce and to increase the availability of labour. There is a basic social fact in the expansion of welfare that is forgotten in the perception of the welfare state as institutionalized altruism, that welfare expands in large part because of capital's need for labour power. Expansion and retrenchment are interrelated processes and an exclusive focus on one dynamic can only lead to unbalanced discussion of the welfare system as a whole.

Moreover there are different forms of welfare restructuring and different constituencies affected as a consequence. Reform measures can affect expenditure or delivery of services, and perceptions of change will vary between service users and service providers. In fact it is difficult to distil changes in welfare regimes to one or two key features. Esping-Andersen's idea of decommodification is widely used to capture the extent to which welfare states 'weaken the cash nexus by granting entitlements independent of market participation' (Esping-Andersen 1999). While this is useful for many analytical purposes, it is better suited to assess changes from the user perspective rather than that of the provider. Another difficulty arises from the diversity of welfare regimes which complicate any generalization about trajectories in provision. Welfare systems in Europe have been grouped according to a number or characteristics including: Nordic universalistic: Anglo-Saxon liberal; corporatist continental and Mediterranean regimes (Esping-Andersen 1999). There are key differences in management and financial arrangements, particularly those financed out of social insurance, as found in corporatist continental models, and those state financed systems in the Nordic countries and in the UK, while family provision remains central to welfare systems in Mediterranean countries. Institutional diversity has survived any external pressure as there is little sense of convergence within European systems (Sykes 1998; Bonoli and Taylor-Gooby 2000). Such institutional diversity reinforces the variety of responses to fiscal pressures, ranging from changes in welfare entitlement, in citizenship rights, in benefit levels such as income replacement rates, and a greater reliance on means testing and user co-payment (Taylor-Gooby 2001). These are changes in provision and entitlement from the individual beneficiary's perspective and are difficult to capture in expenditure statistics. Nonetheless many would be surprised with the resilience of welfare regimes in Europe. Swank's survey of welfare retrenchment in social democratic, continental corporatist and liberal welfare states took a snapshot of provision changes between 1981 and 2000 and found that unemployment compensation 'had been reduced modestly in a majority of nations', 'pension benefits have been remarkably stable' despite cuts in income replacement rates in some countries such as the Netherlands, Sweden and France, while social services for older people, families with children, and the long-term unemployed have been increased in social democratic and corporatist welfare states. Decommodification, indicating benefit levels and programme quality, has on average 'modestly declined' in most European states, with some significant declines in some countries such as Sweden, the Netherlands and Ireland, but it has increased in France, Italy and, surprisingly, the United Kingdom (Swank 2005).

Paul Pierson's discussion of welfare retrenchment is particularly insightful when he insists that retrenchment is not simply the reversal of the expansion of the welfare state. *Depending on perspective, welfare expansion and retrenchment can occur simultaneously, and from certain perspectives may be seen as complementary or contradictory processes.* It is suggested here that the finance, delivery and demand for welfare services do not move in the same direction. Welfare expenditure can expand but this may be translated into greater private delivery and the increased marketization of public services. Welfare demand can increase due to population changes or rising unemployment, but this might not be matched proportionately with increased public spending. On the contrary, increased welfare demand might be financed in part by higher levels of user payment. In the case of higher education in the UK, which, in common with most other European countries, is heading towards a government target of one in two high school graduates progressing to third level education, university revenues rely increasingly on forms of user payment. Higher education has thus witnessed unprecedented expansion of provision, but on the other hand, public funding per student in mass higher education has declined to the point at which students or their families incur significant expenses in the course of completing their university programmes. Additionally, while large investments in higher education have led to significant employment growth, restructuring in the sector has also led to the intensification of academic labour (Wilmott 1995; Parker and Jary 1995). Overall there are different constituencies affected by welfare reform measures and it is possible the term retrenchment does not capture the various impacts of restructuring and gives a one-sided view of change. Welfare retrenchment implies that the sphere of welfare is shrinking when the opposite is the case. *The debates about retrenchment serve a crucial political purpose, but this should not obscure the fact that the reproductive requirements of capitalism have led to a very large increase in the public service workforce, which has impacted greatly on the labour market in both Europe and North America.*

Rescaling, Retrenchment and Cost Sharing in American Welfare Capitalism

The assumption that welfare policies in advanced economies have adjusted in compliance with some externally constructed policy agenda is especially difficult to sustain in the case of the United States. There are several dimensions to welfare reform in the United States which strongly support a 'state-centric' perspective on federal welfare reform, which invite consideration of institutional decentralization in relation to welfare delivery. Furthermore, given the employers' role in welfare provision in the United States it is essential to consider corporate retrenchment in the health and pensions arenas. Looking at the history of welfare policy in the United States over the last century there are distinct periods which can be characterized consecutively by: (i) Corporate Paternalism; (ii) The New Deal and the Federalization of Welfare; (iii) The Rise of Neoliberalism with the Reagan administration; (iv) The Defederalization of Welfare under the Clinton presidency; and (v) Corporate Retrenchment and Welfare Cost Sharing.

To outsiders and insiders the American welfare state is an enigma. Misunderstood by Americans to the extent that leading social commentators have to point out that this 'Welfare State That Nobody Knows' is, when all forms of tax subsidy are considered, broadly comparable with European welfare states (Howard 2007). To outsiders, however, the scale of involvement of American companies in the provision of welfare through employee benefits seems extraordinary. The story is often told that General Motors, for instance, spends more on the health benefits for its workforce than it does on the steel for its cars, which is quite bewildering to many Europeans. It is a story whose explanation goes back to the early decades of the last century which witnessed the rise of 'American welfare capitalism', a period of company sponsored welfare which has been richly captured by Stuart Brandes (1976). Company programmes were dedicated to three tasks, namely the elimination of labour turnover, the opposition to the trades unions and the Americanization of the immigrant workforce. The 1880s and 1890s had been a period of bitter industrial disputes in which companies fought long and hard against the spread of organized labour. The incidence of company programmes rose over the following twenty-five years. It is in this period that company housing, indeed company towns, grew, in which tenants were obliged to buy over-priced goods in company stores, and it was a period of company education and health programmes, company unions, profit share, stock ownership and pension schemes.

Industrial unrest combined with labour turnover difficulties to increase the popularity of company welfare programmes amongst employers. These issues were further highlighted during the First World War, which created the need for federal government intervention in the economy. Labour turnover was particularly difficult in light of the war effort. One of the most significant indicators of the phenomenon was found in the Ford Motor Company which, in 1913, had a workforce turnover of 370% (Brandes 1976). In 1916 the US Congress established the Council for National Defence with an Advisory Committee on Labor, whose general purpose was to increase labour supply and productivity and to reduce industrial disputes. This in turn created a Committee of Welfare Work. The War Department created the Housing Corporation in 1916, which spent $194 million housing 6,000 families. In the same year 1,000 American firms provided company housing for at least 600,000 employees and their families, which accounted for approximately 3%

of the American population at the time. This was no expression of altruism but the strategic attempt of US companies to control labour supply and to combat the trades unions. Tenants were obliged to sign leases which were effectively weapons against strikes, not only by banning union organizers, but also stipulating that employees could be expected to vacate the premises on short notice if, for any reason, the employee left the service of the company. A clause that companies used often, as with the eviction of 10,000 miners in West Virginia between 1922 and 1925.

By the mid 1920s the popularity of company programmes had peaked. Of 1,500 of the largest companies, some 80% had one form of welfare programme and half had comprehensive programmes, but American welfare capitalism did not survive the crash of 1929 and the following depression. This was the great reforming era of President Roosevelt's legislative programme, in which the New Deal laid the foundations for the American welfare state. The New Deal was transformative both in terms of welfare and industrial relations. The historian Nelson Lichtenstein points out that the experience of the depression of the 1930s coincides with a particularly intense period of industrial conflict and insists the New Deal addressed both the question of underconsumption and industrial democracy (Lichtenstein 2002). The National Labor Relations Act of 1935, commonly known as the Wagner Act, expressed some degree of government hostility to aspects of corporate welfare programmes such as company housing and company unionism and allowed for independent representation of the workforce. The Wagner Act thus established the National Labour Relations Board and, during the eight years from 1935 to 1943, trades union organization enjoyed an explosive growth, in which membership trebled.

The Federal Emergency Relief Act included a $500 million programme of grants to state and local government. For the first time public money was used to support the unemployed and their dependants. The New Deal also involved a series of federal work relief programmes, which supported 8 million households or 22% of the population. This was followed by The Social Security Act of 1935, which established a national income support system based on social security and unemployment compensation, and a joint federal-state system of means tested programmes for Aid to Dependent Children, the Blind and the Disabled, and Old Age Assistance. Total welfare expenditures rose from $208 million to $4.9 billion and greatly increased federal involvement in welfare. Between 1932 and 1939 the federal share of public aid grew from 2.1% to 62.5%. The federalization of the 1930s missed out many of the southern states which did not come into the federal fold until the 1960s as a consequence of the civil rights campaigns. Thus welfare became a nationally constituted entitlement to social security.

Jamie Peck's excellent analysis of the rise of the workfare state suggests welfare retrenchment began in the early years of the Reagan administration with the introduction of the Omnibus Budget Reconciliation Act (OBRA), designed to achieve attachment to the labour force and self-support, while reducing public assistance rolls. OBRA removed half a million families from the welfare rolls. Significantly Peck argues OBRA gave states the workfare tool kit and that extensive local policy experimentation created the possibilities of a more decentralized welfare policy (Peck 2001). Large parts of the Republican 'Contract with America' in 1995 were embedded in Clinton's Personal Responsibility and Work Opportunity Reconciliation Act of 1996 (PWORA). PWORA abolished Federal Aid to Families with Dependent Children and replaced it with Temporary Assistance for Needy Families (TANF). TANF was to be operated by states under a new block grant regime. States gained control of eligibility rules, benefit systems, administration and programme design. There was a federal spending cap on welfare and maximum time limit of five years on welfare, and recipients were required to work or do community service. The rise of workfare represented a conscious break with the New Deal, in which the removal of a national entitlement to welfare proceeds through a process of 'Defederalization'. Such welfare reform means that the 'undeserving poor', i.e. the unemployed, are tackled at state or local level, while the deserving poor such as the retired are the subject of national programmes. Moreover, defederalization is a process that is carefully controlled and sanctioned by the Federal Government in Washington. *This is not a weak state reacting to global process – it is the author of its own reform.* Peck suggests the state appears as the active agent in its own 'hollowing out'.

Corporate Retrenchment and Welfare Cost Sharing

In recent times a significant number of high profile employers have filed for bankruptcy and, as a consequence of the proceedings, have sought to terminate pension plans and health benefit coverage. The AFL-CIO has reported that some 39 steel companies have declared bankruptcy between 1997 and 2005, and that after 11 September, many airline companies similarly declared bankruptcy, seeking to withdraw from pension and health provision (Parks 2005). In October 2005 Delphi, the component supplier to General Motors, also threatened to file for bankruptcy unless workers accepted large cuts in wages and loss of benefits. Yet, as the Wharton Business School pointed out, it is not just the loss-making corporations that are threatening to withdraw from benefit provision. High profile and financially viable companies such as IBM, Verizon, Sears, Hewlett–Packard and Motorola have withdrawn from guaranteed pension plans (Knowledge Wharton 2006). A wider sense of changing corporate strategy was evident in the retail sector. This gave rise to the 'grocery wars', which culminated in a six month strike in Southern California, prompted by Wal-Mart's insistence that workers make significantly increased contributions to their cost of health insurance. Therefore, in the first decade of the 21st century there were ominous signs of companies reducing their commitments to welfare provision, but the scale and the form of withdrawal is not as apparent as the headlines would suggest.

Health and Retirement Benefits

Any discussion of health care coverage in the United States has to consider the extraordinary increases in health insurance costs over the last two decades. The sharpest single increase in insurance costs took place in 1988, when annual premiums rose by 18%. There was some indication of cost containment emerging through the early years of the 1990s, but from 1998 to 2005 annual average premium increases were 5.3%, 8.2%, 10.9%, 12.9%, 13.9%, 11.2% and 9.2% respectively, according to a survey conducted by the Kaiser Family Foundation (2005). According to the National Coalition on Health Care, total health care spending in the United States accounts for some 16% of GDP and is predicted to rise to 20% by 2015. The cost of the annual premium an insurer charges an employee for a family of four is $10,800, which exceeds the gross earnings of a full-time minimum-wage worker of $10,712. Unsurprisingly in these circumstances some 46 million Americans are uninsured (National Coalition on Health Care 2006).

There are differences of perspective on the scale and form of corporate involvement in health insurance provision, depending on the focus of research. Thus the national survey of firms carried out by the Kaiser Family Foundation indicated that, between 2000 and 2005, the percentage of all firms offering health benefits had decreased from 69% to 60%, indicating a large decline in a relatively short period. However, in a national survey of employers small firms will be numerically dominant and potentially distort any generalizations about the workforce itself. Analysis of withdrawal by firm size shows that the decline in employer coverage was largely confined to small firms of less than 50 workers. In looking at households rather than firms, a different picture emerges, as shown in the research produced by the Employee Benefit Research Institute (EBRI), which is based on the Survey of Income and Programme Participation, a nationally representative longitudinal survey, conducted by the Census Bureau. In looking at workforce coverage, eligibility and take up rates of benefit the EBRI research shows that the proportion of companies that offered a health plan to wage and salary workers aged 18–64 *increased* from 80.7% in 1997 to 81.6% in 2002, while the proportion of workers eligible for health benefits *increased* from 70.4% to 71.4%. Some 60.7% of workers were participating in their employer's schemes in 2002, little changed from 60% in 1997. It is important to remember that some 20% of employees received health benefits as a dependant, while 2.4% had individually purchased insurance and 3.5% were covered by a public programme, which left 14.1% of workers uninsured in 2002 (Fronstin 2005).

The rising costs of health benefits have fallen on employees to a significant degree. In looking at the private sector workforce between 1993 and 2003, William Wiatrowski of the Bureau of Labor Statistics has shown that the proportion of employees required to contribute towards the cost of single coverage rose from 54% in 1993 to 78% in 2003, while the per cent required to contribute to family coverage rose from 74% to 90%. For those required to contribute to the cost of medical care coverage the monthly premium rose about 75% over the ten years to 2003, significantly faster than the rate of inflation and the rise in workers earnings (Wiatrowski 2004). The research by the Kaiser Family Foundation is even more illuminating in cost sharing strategies of companies. Between 2000 and 2005 the employee contribution to annual single cover insurance premium has risen from 11% to 16%, while the employee contributions to family coverage hover between 26% and 29%.

Furthermore, in addition to rising insurance premiums, most workers have to pay when they use health services in the form of deductibles and/or copayments for hospital admissions. Finally, there is little doubt that employer based health benefits in retirement have declined. According to the Kaiser Foundation in 1988, 66% of large firms provided benefits for retirees, but by 2005 this number had fallen to 33%. The EBRI found that between 1997 and 2002 the proportion of early retirees (pre-65) with health benefits declined from 39.2% to 28.7%, while the proportion of Medicare-eligible retirees with health benefits declined from 28.1% to 25.5% during this period.

Evidence provided by the EBRI on retirement benefits covered the period 1987 to 2001 and showed the proportion of *all* workers participating in an employment based retirement plan increased from 37.6% to 43%. For full-time, full-year wage and salary workers the proportion participating in a retirement plan was little changed at 58.3% during this period, while 75% of the public sector workforce participated in retirement plans throughout this period. In relation to retirement plans the big shift in the United States was from defined benefit schemes, which were fully funded by employers, to defined contribution schemes in which employers and employees contribute. Thus in 1992, some 35% of private sector workers participated in defined contribution schemes and 32% participated in defined benefit schemes, but in 2005 the participation in defined contribution schemes increased to 42% while the defined benefit schemes in the private sector had declined to 22% (EBRI 2003).

Overall, therefore, it seems that corporate strategy in relation to health and retirement provision is to make the employees accept a greater share of risk and pay for a larger proportion of the increasing cost of benefits. Despite the pessimism associated with corporate bankruptcies, there seems little to indicate of wholesale corporate abandonment of employer subsidized health and retirement benefit provision. The research on Employers' attitudes to health benefits carried out by the EBRI and its affiliate the Consumer Health Education Council showed that most large employers were opposed to the nationalization of health insurance. Significantly their survey of employers found that the principal reason to offer health benefits related to the recruitment and retention of workers. Some 79% of employers thought that health benefits were 'extremely or very important' to staff recruitment, while 78% thought it 'extremely or very important' to workforce retention (Christensen et al. 2002). Even though the cost of health care has seen double-digit premium rises over a long period, which has forced increased contributions from employers and employees, it would appear that, in 2002 at least, 'most large employers value the benefits of coverage to their businesses and the flexibility they enjoy in programme design and maintenance'. There are signs of reduced coverage of health benefits for those who leave work before they are 65 and some decline in health coverage for retirees. It is also unclear how sustainable in the long term are continuous price increases in health care costs, but in the meantime the provision of health benefits remains central to corporate recruitment and retention strategies.

Overall, in looking at American and European experiences, the perception of welfare retrenchment, driven by globalization and resulting in a state retreat and market expansion, appears as a one dimensional reading of neoliberal policy. Rather than state withdrawal, the account presented here stresses a reconfiguring of relationships between levels of government and between the public and private agencies in terms of finance and delivery of welfare, resulting in a diminishing sense of difference on either side of the statutory boundary.

The Demographic Time Bomb and the Pensions Crisis

Anyone who inserts the words 'Demographic Time Bomb' on a search engine will witness an avalanche of references from across the globe. The time bomb theme is played out in terms of demographic imperatives or fiscal gang planks that give a contemporary urgency for remedial measures to pre-empt future disasters. Statistical projections of old age dependency are fired off from all quarters and reinforced with the undeniable conclusion that people are living longer. The proportion of people in the older age groups at one end of the spectrum is tied to the decline of birth rates at the other. 'Something' the public are told 'just has to give . . . otherwise future generations will pay for complacency'. However, a couple of reflections on the adoption of the time bomb analogy might help introduce some balance to the forecasts of impending doom. In the first instance, the bomb appears to have been ticking for a long time by now and, in the case of America for at least three decades. In William Graebner's history of retirement in the United States the author notes that in 1977 *The Washington Post* reflected on growing government concerns with the funding problems of public pension programmes when it considered 'Defusing the Public-Pension Timebomb' (Graebner 1980, p. 243). As far back as 1936 the Republican presidential nominee Alf Landon, who challenged Roosevelt, questioned the solvency of social security (Meyerson 2005). At the very least the urgency of the debate is highly dubious. Secondly, it is perhaps the ticking element of the time bomb metaphor that is particularly effective in conveying the need for change rather than the explosion when the ticking stops. The idea that there is some unalterable feature of our society embedded in the age structure of the population or in declining fertility rates, adds to the urgency and necessity of radical policy change, and has obvious appeal to governments who seek to introduce unpopular measures.

Pension reform is a central feature of welfare policy discussion in North America and the European Union but it also features prominently in South America and Central and Eastern Europe and Asia. Reform debates reveal several features of neoliberal policy development including the discursive construction of exogenous change, the role of finance capital and global financial institutions such as the World Bank, not to mention right wing think tanks such as the Cato Institute and the Heritage Foundation.

The World Economic Forum in Davos in 2005 considered the Economic Implications of Ageing and noted the remarkably recent shift in concern from 'runaway world population growth' to worries with the onset of declining population, fertility rates and demographic change. Thus between 1950 and 2000 world population growth doubled, but is predicted to expand by 50% over the next fifty years with annual population growth rates set to tumble from 2% in the 1960s to less than 0.3% by the late 2040s. Precipitous population declines are predicted in Russia where the population is set to fall from 146 million in 2000 to 101 million in 2050, Japan from 127 million to 110 million and Italy from 57 million to 41 million over the same period. As if to convey the universality of the condition the World Economic Forum suggested that the population of 43 mainly European countries will be lower in 2050 than it is today. Within a very short period the nature of the time bomb has changed from countries experiencing 'population explosions' to 'ageing nations' (World Economic Forum 2005).

The assumptions that underpin the scientific argument deserve particular scrutiny and the degree to which they support the reform agenda needs to be challenged. The statistical forecasts rely heavily on the common sense perception that people are living longer. The common sense perception is also informed by undeniable statistical evidence that the birth rate is falling in many advanced countries (if the migrant populations are excluded). These two core perspectives underpin the statistical projections of changing dependency in old age that will become increasingly unsustainable as the years roll by. With all the guile of the magician's sleight of hand many of the forecasters present changes in the ratio of the population of working age to those who have retired from the workforce. Not surprisingly, the increase in the 65 plus group projects a new bulge as the baby boomers age and the population structure becomes top heavy. From this projection the argument proceeds, in most cases, that the welfare burden of those in work will become intolerable. The preferred solution is that people have to take measures today that will allow them to make much better provisions for themselves in old age. A range of policy options are offered, from delayed retirement, to greater personal investment in the stock market to generate funds for comfortable retirement.

The reform of pensions is a policy agenda that has been pushed aggressively by the World Bank since the late 1980s. First in Latin America, followed by the transition economies of Eastern Europe, then in the 1990s in East Asia, the Bank has promoted a multipillar reform approach which has now enveloped the advanced economies of Europe and North America. The options of pension payment range between a non-funded Pay as You Go (PAYG) system based on inter-generational solidarity in which today's contributors pay for tomorrow's pensioners, and a funded programme in which today's earners save for their own retirement income. The Bank considers two reform strategies, namely 'parametric reform' or 'paradigm shift' (Holzman 2000). Changes in the parameters of PAYG schemes could include adjustments to the retirement age, accrual factors, length of assessment and indexation. The paradigm shift favoured by the Bank is a move towards funded schemes. The compromise of a multipillar reform suggested involving a mix of PAYG and funded schemes is a recognition of the difficulties in persuading governments and their citizens of the benefits of funded programmes.

It is highly significant that the Bank's case for pension reform does not rely on statistical projections of demographic change. The developing countries, which have been the focus of World Bank endeavours, at present do not experience the demographic pressures of the ageing nations in the first world. The Bank argues the case for funded pro-grammes on the basis of fiscal and economic concerns in relation to savings effects and capital market formation. If contributions to PAYG are too large, the Bank warns, the financing of publicly man-dated pension schemes can affect 'aggregate savings' and capital market development. It is interesting to note the logic in which con-tributions towards a PAYG scheme are not perceived as savings, but contributions to funded schemes are seen as increasing aggregate savings. It has to be stressed that it is the contribution to capital market development that is the principal objective of the World Bank pension reform agenda.

> Even without any effect on saving volume, comprehensive coverage with high (income) replacement rates under an unfunded scheme reduces the need for additional old age saving devices and may impede the emergence of pension funds and similar financial market institutions, retarding the development of a sophisticated financial market. There is empirical evidence that financial market and economic growth are closely related, and evidence from Chile suggests that the most positive result of the shift to funded pensions was the increase in the efficient use of existing capital. (Holzman 2000, p. 15)

There is also an additional social control aspect in the shift to funded programmes, which aims to make the public come to terms with globalization and appreciate capital's importance in the ways of the world. The class condescension is staggering and could hardly have been scripted better by the anti-globalization movement.

> Implicit in the multipillar approach is a means to mitigate the fears of globalization. Most individuals receive their income from work, focusing their interest on high wages and job security. Any negative feedback from pursuing such goals or from high taxation on capital is generally ignored. Shifting to funded pensions broadens the citizenry's perspective, encouraging them to understand the role of, and returns to capital. This is particularly critical in a world in which workers think they are experiencing the disciplines of globalization on wage levels, but may not fully appreciate the efficiency gains. (Holzman 2000, p. 23)

When considering the advanced economies it is possible to consider a spectrum of pension and retirement policy reform from France through to Germany, the United Kingdom and the United States. France is a country which has high income replacement rates on retirement provided by the state pensions and had, as recently as 1982, reduced the retirement age from 65 to 60 in response to rising unemployment. In 2003, having made pension reform and jobs a corner stone of government policy, the French Prime Minister Jean Pierre Rafarrin announced key changes to the retirement ages and planned to overhaul the country's working hours arrangements. Thus the government has passed legislation to increase working lives from 37.5 years to 40 years by 2008, to 41 years by 2012 and to 42 years by 2020. The plan does not include changes to benefit arrangements and confines reform to the length of the working life. German reform seeks to lower earnings replacement from 70% to 67% and to introduce tax incentives to encourage private pension saving. Initially tax breaks will be given on 1% of earnings for private pension saving but this will increase to 4% of earnings. The United Kingdom has seen some withdrawal of final salary schemes in the private sector, and in the public sector the government has a multi-pronged reform agenda. This involves measures to raise the retirement ages, changes to the calculations for defined benefit schemes moving from final to career average salary provisions, and adjustments to indexation. As with France and Germany these proposals are highly contentious and have drawn opposition, prompting the public sector trades unions into national strike action.

In the United States the President devoted a significant part of his post election State of the Union address in 2005 to the question of social security reform. Reform was necessary, the President argued, because the system was set for severe financial difficulties in the short to medium term. Thus it was predicted that by 2018 the government would be paying out more in social security benefits than it would receive in payroll taxes, and by 2033 the annual shortfall would be more than $300 million. In order to meet this perceived challenge the President proposed the introduction of individual private investment accounts. These investment accounts would allow workers to contribute up to 4% of their taxable earnings into an investment account. The idea being that long-term asset accumulation from these funds would help make up for any shortfall in social security programmes.

The President's proposals were highly controversial and their eventual successful passage is by no means guaranteed. The Center on Budget and Policy Priorities has suggested that the proposals allow employees to mortgage half their social security benefits, but with significant risk to future income, and would do little to answer questions raised in their development. Jason Furman from the Center has shown that the plans do nothing to address the question of the solvency of the social security budget and is a high risk strategy for potential investors. Thus at retirement, workers with private accounts will receive social security benefit cuts up to a certain rate of return, but the individual only comes out ahead if the return on his/her investment exceeds the return that Trust fund bonds receive. If the investors were to receive a 3% real rate of return their social security cut back would be equivalent to a 100% tax on retirement savings in their account (Furman 2005). The distinguished economist Paul Krugman has demonstrated that in order for the investment account to deliver on their promises over the planned 75 year period the economy would have to notch up an average annual growth rate of 6.5

to 7% for the entire period. This would involve maintaining the growth rate obtained during the irrationally exuberant dot.com boom of the mid to late 1990s for some seven and a half decades, which contrasts starkly with the actuarial prediction of annual growth of 1.9% for this period (Krugman, 2005).

The statistical evidence of the budget crises has been challenged by a number of critics. The Center for Economic Policy and Policy Research has exposed the weakness of the privatizers' case and exposed the motivations behind the conservative reform agenda. In the first instance they point out that the social security budget has huge assets ($3.7 trillion will be available in 2018 at today's prices) which, together with payroll tax revenue, means that insolvency only becomes an issue after 2042, according to social security's trustees. The Congressional Budget Office in contrast projects that all promised benefits can be maintained until 2052. Mark Weisbrot and Dean Baker, the co-directors of the Centre for Economic and Policy Research, argue that the problem is of no grave concern and the projected shortfall for the next 75 years is less than one third of the tax cuts enacted by the Bush administration. They report that all the social security experts agree that the budget is stronger than for most of its previous 70 year history (Weisbrot and Baker 2005).

In America, as elsewhere, the privatizers' demographic case is based on the idea of old-age dependency and calculations of the proportion of the working age population to the retired populations. This is the headline ratio that the funded scheme lobbyists have used for several years. It must be stressed that this ratio is not the same as the employment to retirement ratio that reduces the welfare burden as the labour market expands. The increased participation of women has to be factored into the equation as the active workforce expands across the advanced economies. The Left Business Observer suggests that over the course of the 20th century the ratio of non-worker to worker has fallen from 4:1 to 1:1 and is not projected to change much in the future. It also predicts that in 2050 there will be more people in paid employment than there were in 1950 when Mum was at home and the baby boomers were in kindergarten.

Further research by Randall Wray elaborates this line of argument, by analysing the economic and demographic assumptions behind future projections in the United States. In relation to the ratio of workers for every beneficiary Wray notes that this ratio has been falling since 1960, when it was 5.1 workers for every beneficiary, and also that the decline is predicted to slow down from 3.3 today to 1.8 in 2070. He also notes that economic and productivity growth will make a very large contribution to any gap in pension funding. After an exhaustive discussion of factors that will affect future capacity to fund social security, including changes in productivity growth labour market participation, immigration and fertility, Wray convincingly argues that projected demographic changes are surprisingly modest and can be accommodated by small policy reforms (Wray 2006).

It is perhaps worth returning to the World Bank case for the privatization of social security, which is based on its experiences with its clients in South America since the late 1980s, and consider claims firstly for efficiency and secondly fiscal stability. In efficiency terms even the International Council for Capital Formation has acknowledged that the administrative costs associated with funded programmes accounts are a significant weakness in the privatization case. If the much-vaunted success of the Chilean experience is anything to go by, the costs are enormous. According to the Left Business Observer, Chile devotes some 30% of revenues to administrative costs, which covers everything from brokers' fees to marketing expenses. The United States life insurance industries are more efficient, devoting 10% of revenue to administration, while social security's overhead is less than 1%. If Wall Street financiers were able to benefit from Chilean style administrative costs the profits from privatizing American social security would be colossal. Hardly surprising is the financial services' support for the proposals. Secondly there are also other Latin American experiences that are not worth repeating at least in relation to financial stability. Dean Baker points out that Argentina partially privatized its social security system in 1994 with the resulting loss of revenue of 0.9% of GDP equivalent to $100 billion. Seven years later Argentina went into bankruptcy and defaulted on its debt. He argues that, had the government still received social security revenue between privatization and default, the government would have been running a balanced budget in 2001 (Baker 2005).

In a special issue of the International Social Security Review entitled 'Pension Crisis – What Pension Crisis?', the editorial noted that retirement is an economic question not a demographic issue. Otherwise, the editor noted, why were retirement ages reduced when life expectancy lengthened? (Sigg 2002). In the same issue Nicholas Barr considered a series of myths at the heart of the pension debate including the myth that funding resolves adverse demographics. Central to the success of future pension arrangements, Barr suggests, is the productivity and output of the economy: demography is a lower order concern (Barr 2002). Finally Dalmer Hoskins, the Secretary General of the International Social Security Association, noted that a 1 to 2% increase in the number of employed persons would have a significant impact on long-term pension financing. (Hoskins 2002, p. 18)

Perhaps the last word on the subject should go to Pierre Concialdi of the Paris Institute for Economic and Social Research (IRES), who has examined pension reform in Europe where population ageing is said to be greatest. He has examined the relationship between demography, the move to funded pensions and the motivations that inform the reform agenda. He notes the great diversity of fertility rates and differences in dependency ratios, and finds that it should be difficult to fashion an appropriate policy to fit all situations in Europe except that there is one – that is to reduce the level of pension expenditure. The relationship between demographic pressure and pension reform he finds highly contingent. Concialdi points out the extreme case of the United Kingdom where the ageing of the population will be one of the slowest and the drop in public pensions is expected to be one of the largest in Europe. Looking more broadly at European developments he concluded

that demography is only an alibi to move to funded commercial pensions. In short, it seems that, rather than the crisis of the public pension system, the main reason for the privatisation of pensions is to be found in financial business interests. (Concialdi 2006, p. 312)

The Labour Market Implications of Welfare Change

Despite all the hype around the technological changes in production leading to a new economy, it is suggested here that changes in the sphere of reproduction are probably more significant in relation to employment and labour market change. These functions geared towards the supply and enhancement of labour power have been overlooked in debates that have been preoccupied with production industries, but have also focused on retrenchment and changes in welfare benefits from a user perspective. Despite, or perhaps even because of welfare retrenchment, public service employment has expanded significantly, with Education, Health and Social Service emerging as key drivers for job creation. Thus in the EU between 1992 and 2002, when total employment expanded by some 8.7%, employment in Education rose at double this rate at 17.7%. In the United States, when total employment grew by 15% in the period 1992 to 2002, employment in Education grew by some 58%.

However there are other welfare functions which contributed to the stock of human capital, albeit in a less obvious manner, whose employment expansion has been of even greater significance. In particular the expansion of Health and Social Services has provided a major contribution to job creation in the advanced economies. In the 1980s and early 1990s Health Services in the United States were described as 'the real jobs machine' (Hiles 1992). Of the 17.2 million jobs added to the US workforce between 1991 and 2002 Health and Social Services contributed 4.2 million, accounting for nearly one in four additional jobs. There is every reason to expect that this will continue well into the future. In the US, between 1980 and 2000, the number of physicians increased from 453,000 to 782,000, or by 73%. This large increase was both absolute and relative in that the number of physicians per 100,000 of the American population grew from 196 to 255 during this period. The National Center for Health Workforce Analysis in the US Department of Health and Human Services has examined future needs to the year 2020 and has surveyed the range of forecasts for physician shortages. Thus in 2000 there were approximately 782,000 physicians and the five forecasts of physician requirements by 2020 varied between 996,000, representing an increase of 28% to 1,090,000, representing an increase of 40% (HSRSA 2002).

Between 1980 and 2000 the number of registered nurses in the United States had grown from 1.27 million to 2.2 million, while the number of registered nurses serving 100,000 people had risen from 560 to 807. The National Centre report of 2002 points out that in 2000 there was a shortage of 111,000 registered nurses representing some 6% of the registered nurse workforce, a number that is expected to increase to 808,000 or 29% by 2020. This calculation is based on a 40% increase in demand and a 6% increase in supply. It should also be noted that the distribution of this shortage is uneven across the states with California set to experience a shortage of 120,000 registered nurses, representing 46% of its registered nursing workforce. Labour shortage has not been confined to registered nurses and there are also significant shortages predicted in licensed practical nurses (300,000 by 2020) and nurse aides and home health aides (800,000 by 2020) (HRSA 2003). The shortages were not predicted to grow evenly across both decades but to gather pace after 2012. In 2005 the headline figure reveals that 1 million additional nurses must be recruited in the United States over the next fifteen years.

While America experienced a surge in employment in Health and Social Services in the 1980s the European surge occurs later in the 1990s. The EU data available to this study only allows employment change comparison between 1992 and 2002, during which time employment in Health and Social Services increased by 6.4 million or 84% in the European Union. *In the EU case employment growth in Health and Social Services was ten times greater than the EU economy as a whole. Moreover, in the EU, while total employment increased by 12.2 million between 1992 and 2002, Health and Social Services added 6.4 million jobs, representing more than one in every two additional jobs created in the EU.*

A final element of the labour market impact of welfare restructuring is that, contrary to the models of the flexible firm driving new forms of atypical employment, it is suggested here that the growth of 'non-traditional' forms of employment and compositional change are driven by changes in these sectors. As will be shown later the expansion of higher education has given rise to the student labour market, while the rise in part-time employment of women owes much to the growth of health and education and social services. The expansion of temporary employment in many countries also relates to public sector job creation measures designed to combat unemployment rather than the rise of contingent employment assumed in many accounts of new capitalism.

New Employment Relations and the Recommodification of Welfare

The conceptual separation and distinction between state and society was one of the axiomatic assumptions of political science for much of the twentieth century. The binary opposition of market allocation and state planning could not be clearer, and represented a distinction that enjoyed consensus across the political spectrum. Public and private agencies were driven by different impulses and priorities and were instituted to serve different constituencies, with the nation, society or community on the one hand, and the customer, the employee and the employer on the other. Patrick Dunleavy and Brendan O'Leary captured the idea when they clearly stated that,

> The state is a recognizably separate institution or set of institutions, so differentiated from the rest of society as to create identifiable public and private spheres. (Dunleavy and O' Leary 1987, p. 2)

In this idealized model, public–private distinctions were the basis of *statutory boundaries*, which defined the modes of financing and delivery of goods and services, and the *allocation mechanism*, whether bureaucratic planning or market transaction. Yet events began to challenge such distinctions. Peter Fairbrother and Al Rainnie have considered the reconstitution of the relationship between state and capital, and highlighted the rise of New Public Management inspired by the OECD, which supported a shift from Keynesianism to neoliberalism (Farbrother and Rainnie 2006). In America in the early 1990s Osborne and Gaebler (1992) had described the reinvention of 'entrepreneurial government', which would compete with other agencies in the delivery of the business of government. In surveying international trends Philip Cerny has considered the rise of what he has called 'the competition state', whose role is the promotion of the national and international competitiveness of firms based in their territories. More significantly Cerny argues that the competition state becomes an agent of its own transformation from the state as civil association to enterprise association. Thus the state is drawn into promoting the marketization of its own activities and structures as well as promoting marketization more widely, both in economic terms and ideologically (Cerny 1997).

Within political science a movement has thus occurred in the shift from 'government to governance' which allows for a blurring of the boundaries between public and private agencies. A new division of responsibilities has evolved in relation to the financing and delivery of public services. The financing of goods and services is increasingly complex, involving, inter alia, subsidy from the general public purse, charges to the individual user, state subsidy in the form of tax concessions, hypothecated taxes or utility charges, and tax-relieved employment benefits. Linda Weiss insists that the transformative capacity of the state does not correlate with its 'extractive' capacity to raise taxes. Esping-Andersen also stresses that the welfare regime does not correspond to the volume of publicly funded social welfare provision. None more so than in the United States, where James K. Galbraith strongly suggests that the forms of public support for welfare activities must be viewed from the broadest perspective.

Public service provision similarly transcends statutory boundaries. Publicly funded services are often contracted out to private providers or to charitable 'non-governmental agencies'. Such is the diversity of financial or management arrangements involved that singular concepts such as privatization seem too one dimensional to capture the variety of mechanisms and processes by which the public sector is exposed to market forces. Privatization suggests, once and for all time, relocation of services from the mother ship of the public sector to the alien landscape of the private company, which may be appropriate in certain sectors such as telecommunication or utilities, but is not the dominant feature of the broader restructuring across much of the public sector.

Marketization is adopted here to capture the evolutionary sense of institutional change and the social processes involved in the increased exposure of service provision to market forces. It is suggested that marketization captures a variety of mechanisms for the introduction of market forces including privatization, deregulation and contracting out. However, marketization represents more than the unidirectional externalization of services, and includes the internalization of management practices and the inculcation of cultural change within the public sector. Not only is there in-house retention of contracted services, marketization has also instituted a whole range of new public management practices that have adopted the trappings of the private sector firm, the adoption of more commercial modes of operation and a reorientation towards the service user as customer. Marketization therefore represents both external relocation and institutional adaptation, a transcendent restructuring of the public sector that has cultural, ideological and institutional dimensions.

Harman (1991) has convincingly suggested the 'structural interdependence' of state and capital. Perhaps, however, if consideration is given to the new institutional arrangements for national and global market regulation, and also to the changes in the division of tasks in the financing and delivery of services to the public, it might be helpful to consider the *interpenetration of state and capital*. The state penetration of the market raises the significance of its role in 'instituting the market' by regulating its processes, specifying its products and services, and controlling market access and terms of trade. It also stresses the importance of government support for public and private welfare and defence systems through a range of direct and indirect subsidies. On the other hand, capital penetration of the state is suggested in the marketization of the public sector, the diminishing distinction between the management practices of public and private agencies and, as suggested below, in the 'dedifferentiation' of public and private labour markets.

From the *producer's perspective* the reform of welfare has, for the majority, been largely associated with work intensification, some diminution of employment conditions and greater job insecurity. Alongside the intensification of competition in the private sector that, rightly or wrongly, is connected to global economic forces, the marketization of the public sector emerges as a primary explanation of the international rise in job insecurity and precariousness (Doogan 2001,

2005). Into the well-ordered world of state planning and control neo-liberalism has introduced the uncertainty of the market. From the public service employee's point of view the irrationality of the market's 'invisible hand' replaces the bureaucratic rationality of state agency. The distinction between public and private labour markets begins to break down as a consequence, a process described elsewhere as 'dedifferentiation' (Doogan 1997).

Esping-Andersen's study of welfare regimes examines the interplay between public and private provision, which reveals the overall distributional structure, the relation between social rights and private contracts, and the inequalities of class, gender or status that define the welfare state regimes. A central plank of Esping-Andersen's approach to welfare is the decommodification of labour provided by the welfare state. In the capitalist labour market the wage earner is treated as a commodity, albeit an unusual commodity, as they must survive and reproduce themselves and the society they live in. Decommodification is seen as the 'degree to which individuals, or families, can uphold a socially acceptable standard of living independently of market participation' (p. 37). If commodification represents the exposure to market forces, decommodification offers a possible means of capturing the social and political implications of welfare regime change. However, Esping-Andersen's analysis of public sector employment undermines the explanatory potential of decommodification. While he acknowledges that welfare state employment is based on the labour contract, he insists 'its logic is completely different. The logic of productivity hardly obtains, wages are to a degree determined politically, jobs are typically tenured, and employees normally enjoy substantially more autonomy, freedom over how they allocate their time, do their jobs and make their work-welfare choices' (p. 160). To be fair this was written in the late 1980s and developments since that time may have compelled reconsideration of the relatively privileged position enjoyed by public service employees. From the mid 1990s to the present day the public sector has provided higher levels of industrial conflict as public sector trades unions seek to defend traditional entitlements and working conditions. Public sector workers are also represented in the ranks of the low paid, and compensation in the form of state provided public pensions is the target of an international offensive.

Welfare restructuring exposes public services to market forces in new and radical ways, but there is little sense in which this constitutes new employment relations that suggest societal transformation. The idea of recommodification of welfare is helpful in conveying the sense of the greater commercialization of the public services and of rising welfare costs borne by individuals. However, from a producer's point of view, Esping-Andersen's decommodification insists on too great a distinction between public and private labour markets, which over-state changes in employment relations that attend marketization. The use of dedifferentiation seeks to capture the importance of institutional adjustment but denies that this constitutes a paradigm shift in employment relations.

The discussion presented here has surveyed the debates around welfare restructuring in relation to globalization, demographic change and neoliberalism. It has stressed that the requirements of production and reproduction together determine employment and labour market restructuring as a whole, and any macro assessment of the transformation of work, change based solely on changes in production is oblivious to a crucial set of dynamics which will be included in the following discussion of employment stability, job insecurity and labour market flexibility. This emphasis on the central role of the welfare state in the reproduction of labour power also provides an alternative view to the perception of welfare as the collective expression of altruism, and maintains its importance to the modernization of economies. This allows a better framework for analysing welfare expansion and retrenchment and is a way to see behind the neoliberal rhetoric to the basic social fact that capital needs labour.

6
The Flexible Labour Market and the Contingent Economy

The discussion now moves on to consider the labour market outcomes that are said to express new forms of engagement between
employers and workers that are increasingly characterized by precariousness and impermanence. The labour market is the 'signifier'
par excellence of societal transformation, embodying the outcomes
of technological change, industrial and occupational restructuring,
deregulation, flexibilization and individualization. Consequently if
labour market outcomes are misconstrued it will generate widespread
public misunderstanding about social transformation. This chapter
will seek to capture the dominant perspectives of the transformation
of work, attempt to place these views in the context of industrial
restructuring in the advanced economies.

It is not unreasonable to suggest that the dominant public perception is of a labour market that has changed, and not for the better.
There is a vague impression that 'things ain't what they used to be'
and the future is uncertain. This is often expressed as a departure
from a previous era that was stable, secure and hopeful. Neumark,
Polsky and Hansen (2000) have drawn attention to a *New York Times*
article in 1996 which suggested that 'the notion of life time employment has come to seem as dated as soda jerks or tail fins'. Post-war
experience of sustained economic growth imbued social expectations
of intergenerational improvements in work prospects and living
standards, but such optimism waned in the 1970s with the return of
inflation, mass unemployment and, over the course of the following
decades, three recessions in the world economy. There is now a widespread intuition that the labour market is a buyer's market. Employers
can pick and chose who they want to hire, since the numbers seeking
work exceed available job vacancies, and they are able to drive a hard

bargain in the wages they offer and in the intensity of the effort they expect in return.

The jobs created by the new economy seem to lack the substance of the past. Before, there were 'real jobs' when people were employed to make things in engineering, steel, mining or manufacturing industries. Despite contemporary environmental or gender sensibilities, there is a comfort in the smokestack nostalgia for 'proper' jobs, where men were paid decent wages to provide for their families. The imaginary landscape of today's economy is dominated by shopping malls, young people 'waiting tables and flipping hamburgers', call centre operatives, women part-timers and redundant men, 'finished at fifty', with only the prospects of part-time work in hardware stores or casual work for neighbours and friends. The growth of McDonalds, although it has taken place over decades, has a particular symbolic value in the current rendition of the new capitalist narratives. Just as Toffler saw in the disposable pen and the disposable diaper a change in the durational mindset of superindustrial society in the 1960s, the industrial correspondent of the BBC described a world of 'fast food and throw away jobs' (Jones 1986). Lash (1994) tells of '(the) post-Fordist creation of millions of "junk jobs" . . . and . . . the creation of the massive "MacDonalds proletariat" in the services (sic)' (p. 120). 'McJobs' have come to symbolize not only temporary work in hotels, catering and restaurants, but a broader 'McDonaldization' of service sector employment (Ritzer 1993). And, finally, it almost goes without saying that trades union power, once able to protect workers and negotiate reasonable terms and conditions of employment, has declined along with those industries such as mining, steel and manufacturing in which they were strongly organized. The result is the emergence of a transformation of work characterized by insecure or precarious employment and the intensification of the labour process both in terms of day to day efforts and the projected lengthening of working lives prior to retirement.

Individualization, Fragmentation and Flexibility

In describing the new capitalist labour market it is important to realize the different dimensions of changes envisaged, both qualitative and quantitative. It is not merely a question of job gains and losses in growing or declining industries, distributional shifts in the occupational structure, or adjustments in the form of contract in relation to full-time, part-time or temporary employees. Many commentators are not simply referring to jobs, but to a much more fundamental change in 'the employment relationship'. Such new relationships are characterized by a loss of reciprocal obligations between employer and worker, resulting in much weaker bonds, reduced commitment and a loss of attachment to the labour market. Therefore, the concerns within contemporary debate range between job instability and contingent employment in the workplace to a broader sense of insecurity and precariousness in society. Zygmunt Bauman, for instance, has offered a particular take on the topic by stressing the emergence of an 'individualized society'. He has argued that the contemporary experience of uncertainty is 'strikingly novel' and is a powerfully individualizing force in present day society (Bauman 2001). Since the industrial revolution the relationship between capital and labour was characterized by mutual obligations and interdependence, but, Bauman argues, this no longer pertains in a world in which capital has cut itself loose from its dependency on labour. Capital has become extraterritorial and disembedded to an unprecedented degree and has acquired a spatial mobility sufficient to bend immobile political agencies to its will.

> The present day uncertainty is a powerful individualizing force. It divides instead of uniting, and since there is no telling who might wake up in what division, the idea of 'common interests' grows ever more nebulous and in the end incomprehensible. Fear, anxieties and grievances are made in such a way as to be suffered alone. They do not add up, do not cumulate into 'common cause', have no 'natural address'. This deprives the solidarity stand of its past status as a rational tactic and suggests a life strategy quite different from the one which led to establishment of the working-class defensive and military organizations. (Bauman 2001 p. 24)

In Bauman's mind capital is both footloose, lacking any special attachment to either state or economy. Such mobility greatly enhances its bargaining power to such an extent that collective negotiation with labour is rendered unnecessary. In such circumstances collective labour is atomized and workers are left to fend for themselves, although for the most part this is speculation on Bauman's part devoid of evidence.

However, Bauman is not alone in this line of thinking and in this mode of argument. Other high profile commentators, such as Ulrich Beck, Manuel Castells and Robert Sennett, have projected a transformation of work in recent times that has particular consequences for employment stability and job security. Beck's account of 'reflexive modernity' is derived in part on the temporal destandardization of labour based on part-time and temporary employment. His more recent work describes the political economy of insecurity, characterized as a one-sided power struggle between the territorially fixed political players (governments and trades unions) and non-territorial capital, finance and commerce. This transformation culminates in the 'Brazilianization of the West', in which paid employment represents a minority experience with the majority left to eke out a more precarious existence (Beck 2000). The personal consequences of work in the 'new capitalism' according to Sennett (1998), means that there is 'no long-term' and that institutional restructuring has 'accompanied short-term, contract and episodic labour'. For Castells (1996) the informational economy is predicated on the development of a core labour force and a 'disposable labour force that can be automated, and/or hired/fired/offshored depending upon market demand and labour costs'. In common with the disaggregation and individualization of labour described by Beck, Castells' take on individualization imputes a greater role to technological change:

> we are witnessing the end of the historical trend toward the salarization of employment and the socialization of production that was the dominant feature of the industrial era. The new social and economic organization based on information technologies aims at decentralizing management, individualizing work and customizing markets thereby segmenting work and fragmenting societies. (Castells 1996, p. 265)

Many people will be amazed by the scale of changes anticipated by such luminaries of contemporary social science. The end of salaried employment, the fragmentation of labour markets and the atomization of the experience of work represent predictions of change of an order that has not been heard of since George Gilder intimated that the development of superindustrialism in the 1960s was comparable in magnitude to the transition from primitive to civilized society.

Yet the audacity of the vision is inversely related to the evidence provided to substantiate such claims. Beck's account seeks to capture the present state of fragmented and globalized work by using new conceptual frameworks. He suggests that 'it is as problematic to infer the future from current trends and data as it is to read it from tea leaves' (Beck 2000, p. 8) and that is why he is offering an account that is 'visionary non-fiction'. He presents the 'embryonic vision of a post-work society using all imaginable and available arguments, data concepts and models'. Rather than sacrificing too many hair follicles in trying to figure out what he means, it is worth noting that Beck has

scant regard for current trends and statistical data in his future projections and offers visions rather than evidence. For a highly respected
sociologist Sennett also offers a very superficial account of the corrosion of character arising in short-term capitalism. Echoes of Toffler's
decline in 'durational expectations' are again found in his reading of
the new economy in which 'experience drifts in time, from place to
place, from job to job'. Castells, by contrast, expends significant
energy in the analysis of work and the informational divide yet, as suggested in Chapter 2, his conclusions are only tenuously connected to
the statistical evidence and the argument he advances.

However, it is also possible to suggest that the end of employment
scenarios do not fall from the sky, but as Fevre argues, are a product
of theoretical and analytical developments since the 1970s, namely
the demise of Marxism and the postmodern turn (Fevre 2007).
Fragmentation and individualization are extreme versions of labour
market change that was previously considered in terms of contingency
and flexibilization. It was Audrey Freeman (1985) in the United
States who coined the term 'contingent work' to refer specifically to
'conditional and transitory employment arrangements as initiated by
a need for labor – usually because a company has an increased
demand for a particular service or a product or technology, at a
particular place and a specific time'. Labour market flexibility in turn
emerged out of the analysis of industrial restructuring and the development of flexible production systems and the prior development of
dual labour market theory in America. Furthermore the wider significance of flexible employment has been emphasized in accounts of
labour market change that reflect global processes (Felstead and
Jewson 1999). Particularly in the European debates the rise of new
patterns of employment, indicated by the increase in part-time, temporary and casual jobs, are not merely symptomatic of compositional shifts in the labour force, but are manifestations of global
transformation (Standing 1999). In this broader context of industrial
restructuring, technological change and globalization, commentators
are impelled towards excessive generalization. Small-scale adjustments in labour markets are imbued with transformative potential
because great social forces are in motion. Beck's account of reflexive
modernity is premised upon disaggregation and the destandardization
of labour processes. Thus fragmentation and individualization are
intimately bound up with the rise of non-standard forms of employment which are symptomatic of industrial restructuring and societal
transformation. In other words a huge analytical weight rests on the
significance of 'atypical employment' and new forms of intra labour

force polarization. Methodologically, this is a departure from Daniel Bell, whose analysis of post-industrial society, despite its weaknesses, at least makes a case based on the majority of the workforce, who are employed in the service industries. Castells, Beck and Sennett, by contrast, generalize from minority experience in the workforce represented by temporary, casual and part-time employment.

Labour Market Dualism and Perverse Generalization

The plausibility of any labour market analysis is tested by the assessment of non-standard employment. Atypical work represents the departure from traditional working practices and the stable employment with which they have been associated. Flexible employment assumes centre stage in the narratives of the new economy and symbolizes a tenuous attachment to the world of work. Casualization, temporary or contingent work and part-time employment are, therefore, symptomatic of a new precariousness in society. However, it is suggested here that there is a major theoretical weakness in the construction of the non-standard workforce. To define something negatively in this way compresses a broad diversity of employment arrangements into a single category, *which is defined solely in terms of what it is not, namely the standard labour market experience.* On the one hand this risks a perverse generalization of the norm, characterized by the illogical coupling of full-time and stable employment. It is illogical because full-time employment can be both permanent and temporary. On the other hand it presents as homogenous the experience of the 'atypicals' that have been banished to the dark side of the labour market, a precarious world of risk, uncertainty and temporary work. This also represents a perverse generalization in which the small minority within the minority, the temporary worker, comes to epitomize the non-standard workforce as a whole. To see how this situation has arisen it is necessary to trace developments back to the 1970s and track the growth of dual labour market theory and its legacy in the growing importance of flexible labour markets that seemed to emerge out of the corporate restructuring in the 1980s.

Dual labour market theory has waxed and waned over the years. Economists date the existence of dual labour market theory to Harris and Todaros' (1970) research into the labour market in Africa, which they analysed in terms of a qualitative difference between rural agriculture and urban manufacturing. Peter Doeringer and Michael Piore (1971) offered the more influential analysis of the effects of poverty and discrimination in primary and secondary labour markets, which stressed the role of internal labour markets within firms. Internal labour markets, characteristic of primary labour markets, rewarded the investment in human capital and correlated length of time employed with career advancement and improvements in earnings. The idea of primary and secondary labour markets drew critics from all quarters, notably from the left in the critique offered by Blackburn and Mann (1979), but neoclassical economists were also unhappy with the idea of 'two wage levels in equilibrium', and in the mid 1970s the theory fell out of favour as it was deemed to be incompatible with neoclassical economics. For many years there was little interest in dual labour market theory but in the latter part of the mid 1980s it resurfaced in economic debates, leading some to talk of the re-emergence of dual labour market theory (Launov 2004).

In the 1980s the debates over economic restructuring provided the new context for labour market dualism, this time captured in the idea of different forms of flexible labour. Corporate restructuring represented to Piore and Sabel (1984) the emergence of 'the second industrial divide', characterized by the decline of mass production and mass consumer markets and the rise of flexible specialization. The regulation school offers a Marxist variation on this theme. Regulation theory envisaged a profound institutional restructuring in society in which the Fordist regime of accumulation, based on mass production, and a mode of regulation, consisting of mass consumption and the Keynesian welfare state, gave way to post-Fordism. This post-Fordist scheme privileges the decline of mass production and asserts the significance of flexible production systems geared towards niche markets. A model of 'the flexible firm' presented by John Atkinson captured the mood of the time well. A dual labour force was said to emerge out of the growth of 'numerical flexibility' and 'functional flexibility' which, in turn, lead to the creation of a 'core' and a 'periphery' in the labour market.

Atkinson's work vacillated at times between describing a dual labour force (Atkinson and Gregory 1986) and a three tier workforce (Atkinson 1987), with the latter distinguishing between employees and external workers such as sub-contractors and temporary agency staff. For the most part his work is remembered in terms of the core and the periphery. Peripheral workers are victims of a 'tenuous relationship between workers and employers', owing to 'their unorthodox patterns of attendance'. They are more likely to be female, part-time, often temporary with shorter job tenures and deploying job skills which are readily available in the external labour market. A later version of the core and periphery model provided by David Harvey (1989) subdivided the periphery into two groups one of which was full-time workers whose skills are readily available in the labour market, such as clerical, secretarial, routine and lesser-skilled manual work. The second group, that provides even greater numerical flexibility, included part-timers, casuals, fixed-term contract staff, temporaries, sub-contractors and public subsidy trainees, who have even less security than the first peripheral group. Harvey's refinement has two merits, in recognizing that full-time employment does not automatically confer job stability and also in recognizing gradations of stability within the periphery. However, such merits are eclipsed by his lumping together of temporary and part-time employment.

Temporary, Contingent and Casual Employment

The first chapter recalled the oft repeated 'fact' that Manpower Inc. was the largest company in the US, employing some 600,000. As Ida Walters shows temporary help firms count everyone, even those who are on their payrolls for only one day, in their yearly totals. On a typical day the number of staff on the pay roll of Manpower Inc. varies between 80,000 and 112,000 (Walters 1994). To claim a workforce of 600,000 just does not stand up to close scrutiny, but this has not stopped its endless recycling. In a similar vein, the 'facts' about temporary employment deserve critical inspection.

The OECD's *Employment Outlook* of 2004 reports a very useful study of temporary employment amongst its member countries. Several qualifications are acknowledged in conducting comparative research in this area, which is beset with definitional and measurement difficulties and where there are large differences in employment trends between countries. That being said, the OECD reported an average rate of temporary employment of some 12% in 2000, which represented a fairly modest increase from just over 10% in 1985. The uneven share of temporary employment is highly pronounced in Spain, where just under one in three jobs is temporary, whilst in the United States, the ratio is less than one in 20. Between 1985 and 2000 temporary employment had risen in France, Italy, the Netherlands, Portugal and especially Spain, and has declined in the United States, Denmark, Ireland, Greece and Luxembourg. Interestingly, in Spain temporary employment almost doubled between 1985 and 1990 from just over 15% to just under 30%. In the next five years it grew more slowly and peaked at 35% and has seen a modest decline in the following five years. The report notes that where temporary employment has expanded it has done so for a variety of reasons. Temporary employment owes its relatively large share to the role of agriculture in certain countries, such as Mexico, Turkey and Greece, while in France it has grown due to the expansion of large-scale public employment programmes. The form of temporary employment varies significantly between temporary help agency workers, fixed term contracts, on-call workers and seasonal workers. Thus, more than one third of temporary workers in the Netherlands are agency staff, compared to 2.1% in Canada. The report notes that, since 1992, the headline number of agency workers has increased rapidly, at least five fold in Denmark, Spain, Italy and Sweden, and just under four fold in Austria. Overall, however, the proportions are still very small, *with just over 1% of the workforce in the EU employed as regular agency workers.*

The OECD shows a significant wage differential between permanent and temporary workers, with the wage gap as high as 47% in Spain at one end of the spectrum and 17% in Germany. Access to fringe benefits such as holiday pay, paid sick leave, unemployment insurance, maternity leave and retirement pension also distinguish the permanent from the temporary employee. In European countries these are provided on a universal basis by legislation and in other countries such as the United States it will be provided on a voluntary basis. However, where universal benefits exist, there might be entitlement thresholds in relation to minimum periods of service, contribution periods, earnings thresholds or hours thresholds, which will affect short-term employees. Minimum wage legislation in the EU covers both temporary and permanent employees, as does equal opportunity legislation. Collective agreements on pay, where they exist, usually apply automatically for temporary workers, and some countries, such as Spain, Belgium and France, have introduced legislation explicitly requiring pay equality between temporary and permanent staff for work of equal value.

The OECD study reports surprisingly high levels of satisfaction with temporary employment in relation to pay and working conditions, but greatest dissatisfaction with the degree of job insecurity. It also shows unexpectedly high levels of job tenure among temporary workers. For the OECD as a whole, job tenures of less than one year were reported for 58% of temporary workers, compared to 13% of permanent staff, with 16.9% having ongoing job tenures of 1–2 years, 4.3% with 2–3 years, 9.9% 3–5 years and 11.6% more than five years. It would seem on the basis of the OECD study that earlier claims that standard employment relationships were unravelling are not supported by changes in temporary employment. Yet temporary, casual or contingent employment has a profile in labour market studies that seems in many countries entirely disproportionate to its place in global employment trends.

The United States provides a good terrain to explore the landscape of the contingent economy. Arne Kalleberg describes in some detail 'the explosive growth' in temporary employment in the United States and traces its history to Chicago in the late 1920s (Kalleberg 2000). Kalleberg notes that by 1956 employment in the temporary help industry amounted to some 20,000 employees. Since 1972, however, from this very small starting point, employment in the temporary help industry has expanded rapidly. Between 1972 and 1998 temporary employment grew at an annual rate of 11%, which represented an increase in its relative share of employment from 0.3% to nearly 2.5%. A different slant on this might reveal that temporary employment has only expanded by 2.2 percentage points in twenty-six years, which in the scheme of things is much less impressive. Peck and Theodore (2001) have looked at the contingent economy in Chicago and have suggested 'an explosion of the temp economy' in major metropolitan centres in the US which has been sustained and legitimized by labour market deregulation and flexibilization. 'Hence, the maturation of the temp industry holds far-reaching implications for the structure and dynamics of labor markets' (p. 492). Despite the admirable sentiments of the authors in drawing attention to hiring practices at the very bottom end of the labour market, it is necessary to curb excessive generalization lest inaccurate and unduly pessimistic conclusions are drawn.

In the first instance it must be born in mind that temporary employment in the United States accounts for a very small and, in recent years, *declining* share of employment in the workforce. The Bureau of Labor Statistics has, since the mid 1990s, produced a supplement to the Current Population Survey, which looks at Contingent and Alternative Employment Arrangements and offers three estimates of contingency. The narrowest estimate is based on wage and salary workers employed on a temporary basis and excludes the self-employed and independent contractors, while the broadest estimate includes the latter. In 1995 the lowest estimate was of 2.74 million contingent workers, which represented 2.2% of the total employed, while the largest estimate was 6.03 million, which represented 4.9%. The latest available data are contained in the 2001 supplement, which reported that the narrowest estimate had declined to 2.3 million, representing 1.7% of the workforce, while the broadest estimate had declined to 5.37 million or 4.3% of the workforce. Thus the share of contingent work was very small and shrinking during the period 1995 to 2001. It would be reasonable to assume that this trend reflects a more buoyant labour market and that the decline might well falter with the impact of recession since 2000, but the broader conclusion is that the trends and prospects for contingent employment does not suggest the unravelling of the standard form of employment.

In addition to the contingent workforce, the importance of alternative employment arrangements has to be stressed. In an excellent compilation on the subject of non-standard work in the United States, Polivka, Cohany and Hipple (2000) have very usefully defined the components of the non-standard workforce and analysed the characteristics of agency temporaries, on-call workers, contract company workers, direct hire temporary workers, independent contractors and those regularly self-employed who are not independent contractors. The largest group were the independent contractors, representing some 6.7% of the total workforce and the smallest group were temporary agency staff, representing 1% of the total employed. In income terms the hourly earnings of agency staff, on-call workers and direct hire temporaries were significantly lower than those employed on a regular basis, but within the wider grouping of alternative arrangements that covered the self-employed and independent contractors, the hourly earnings were significantly higher than the non-contingent workforce. However, in the contingent workforce per se, earnings across all occupations and all industries is lower than the non-contingent workforce, with the interesting exception of the construction industry, in which the earnings of the contingent workforce is higher than their non-contingent counterparts. The occupational profile of the contingent workforce is spread across a range of jobs, with the share of managerial and professional jobs ranging between 21% and 30% of the temporary workforce, depending on the definition of contingent worker adopted, and the share of skilled, semi-skilled and routine manual jobs ranging between 24% and 27%. The industrial profile of the temporary workforce reveals higher rates of contingency, i.e. figures above 3% were found in construction (7.2%) and services (6.2%), the latter concentrated in personal services, educational services, entertainment and recreation, and social services. Low rates of contingency were reported in manufacturing, transport utilities, wholesale and retail trades, and business services (Hipple 2001). It is also very interesting to note the trades union representation among the temporary workforce. The 1999 figures show that 16.3% of the total workforce was represented by trades unions, while 7.4% of the contingent workforce was represented by unions. Surprisingly, in the construction industry the union representation of the contingent workforce of 23.1% was higher than that of the non-contingent workforce at 19.2% (Hipple 1998).

Overall, the variety of contractual arrangements suggests that contingent employment does not constitute a uniform segment of the labour market. Rather than sustaining any model of labour market dualism it is perhaps necessary to recognize that temporary employment is itself bifurcated in terms of earnings and occupational profile. Even Peck and Theodore, who are so keen to generalize from the experience of temporary employment agencies, acknowledge the different employment conditions of the large agencies such as Manpower and Kelly in the suburbs compared to the 'hiring halls' of disadvantaged inner city areas. Despite its connotation with low status work, both high and low skill occupations are employed on a temporary basis. It is interesting to note in the professional categories an exceptionally high contingency rate amongst colleges and university teaching staff at 28.4% (Hipple 1998).This suggests that, if academics can see a lot of short-term contract workers on their own doorstep, they are perhaps given to exaggerating its wider significance.

In Canada Leah Vosko and colleagues have considered the rise of temporary employment agencies in a manner similar to Peck and Theodore, but given the greater scale of temporary employment in Canada, have a more substantial case for generalization (Vosko 2000 and Vosko, Zukewich and Cranford 2003). However, it is suggested here that similar difficulties emerge in an approach that seeks to represent broad labour market experience from a minority standpoint. Vosko takes as a starting point the normative model of the standard employment relationship (SER), which has been fundamentally weakened and, with its decline, the temporary employment relationship (TER) has gained (normative) prominence. The SER is based on the norm of full-time permanent jobs with employee benefits, the TER is based on a precarious model of employment, epitomized in the growth of the temporary employment agency. The rise of TER and the decline of the SER is associated with the increased participation of women in the labour market, and hence it is possible to talk of the 'gendered rise of a precarious employment relationship'. However, there are two basic points of contention with the arguments advanced here. In the first instance, while temporary employment in Canada is approximately 12% – which is much higher than America – it is still small. Canada is not Spain, where one in three of the workforce has temporary contracts. The temporary help industry is approximately four times larger than the US, but that means it only accounts for 4% of the workforce. While employment agencies' customers have extended across sector boundaries, offering a greater diversity of work and occupational coverage, does this allow the basis for some of the claims made? Vosko states, 'In essence, the rise of the THI (temporary help industry) and the related spread of the TER reflects profound shifts in the balance of class power' (Vosko 2000). While it is essential to consider shifts in the balance of forces in the labour market, this view seems to attach too much weight to the specific impact of employment agencies and the rise of temporary contracts. The second point of contention is Vosko's basic position that the rise of women's participation, and the forms of employment, such as part-time work, with which they are often in the labour market, is a source of job instability. The evidence later presented in the statistical analyses of long-term employment in North America and Europe challenges such a proposition.

Part-time Employment

The discussion of the 'flexiworkforce' presented here and in the following chapter takes as a starting point the crucial distinction between part-time and temporary employment. It is not that these are wholly exclusive categories, but they are often bundled together in such a manner as to make them seem almost interchangeable concepts. It is commonplace to refer to divisions in the workforce between those who are employed full-time and the rest who are 'part-time, temporary and casual employees'. In this mindset, part-time workers are largely temporary, so much so that it would be hard to shift the dominant perception that full-time work is a far more stable form of employment than part-time work. In general the overlap between temporary and part-time employment is small, with the exception of male part-time workers. In its survey of 12 European countries the OECD Employment Outlook for 2004 reported that 7% of male full-time workers were temporary and 10% of female full-time workers were temporary, while some 34% of male part-time workers were temporary and 18% of women part-time workers. Even though there is a lesser correlation between full-time and temporary working it is still the case that the degree of overlap between temporary working and part-time working is fairly small, with more than four in five women working part-time on a regular ongoing basis. In the United States, for instance, the 2001 survey of Contingent and Alternative

Employment Arrangements conducted by the Bureau of Labour Statistics reported that some 24 million people worked part-time and 21.8 million were non-contingent. Expressed differently almost 91% of the part-time workforce were employed on a regular ongoing basis.

The OECD study analysed part-time employment in its member countries and considered a variety of factors including job quality, earnings and tenure as part of its assessment of the quality of jobs and its contribution to employment growth. Unsurprisingly perhaps the study points to significant international variation in the rate of part-time employment. It is relatively low in southern European countries and high in the UK, the Netherlands and Scandinavia. It is the largest element of the non-standard workforce, in most cases by some considerable measure. Part-time employment makes a very important contribution to total employment growth, equivalent to the contribution of full-time work. International trends in hourly earnings and in benefits reveal significant differences between full-time and part-time employment. In relation to median hourly earnings, part-time workers earn between 55% (United States and Canada) and 90% (Australia and Portugal) of full-time earnings. The earnings effect is greater for men where the average median hourly earnings accounts for 71% of full-time earnings, compared with 86% of earnings for women who work full-time. The narrower differential for women is explained, both by the much larger proportion of women employed part-time, and also the relatively lower hourly earnings of female full-time workers. In comparing part-time and full-time earnings across industries the biggest differential was found in business services, with men earning less than two thirds and women a little more than three quarters of their full-time counterparts. In most countries the largest concentration of part-timers is found in the retail sector, where the impact on earnings is smallest, with part-time workers earning more than 90% of their full-time equivalents. In respect of employee benefits, the difference between full-time and part-time workers is greater than in earnings. European legislation outlaws discrimination between full-time and part-time workers in relation to pay, certain benefits, working conditions and redundancy. Collective agreements also seek to provide benefits for full-time and part-time workers on a pro-rata basis. However, there are eligibility thresholds in some instances, based on hours worked, length of service and earnings minima, which might release the employer from paying old age pensions and unemployment benefits.

The connection between part-time and flexible employment practices is not as obvious as those accounts of industrial restructuring would appear to suggest. It rose significantly in the US and the UK in the 1950s and 1960s, suggesting that the growth of part-time employment predates the wave of corporate restructuring of the 1980s and the aforesaid rise in flexible production systems. However, Chris Tilly has argued, in fairly influential research in the United States, that the nature of part-time employment has changed since the second half of the twentieth century, with a shift from voluntary to involuntary part-time work (Tilly 1996). In America, a large part of the debate has focused on the question of voluntary and involuntary take up of part-time working. It touches on questions of job quality as well as the reasons for the expansion of part-time employment, whether led by the preferences of employees or constrained by employment options. It informs broader perceptions as to whether part-time jobs are 'real jobs' or not. Tilly suggests that for many a part-time job is 'half a job'.

> The expansion in the US of the part-time labor market actually gives us a great deal of worry. Most importantly virtually all of the increase in the rate of part-time employment in the United States during the last two decades is due to the expansion of involuntary part-time employment. An involuntary part-time job *is* only half a job in the sense that it is only half the job that the employee wants. About one quarter of the part-time workforce is working part-time involuntarily – most of them are unable to find a full-time job. (Tilly 1996, p. 2–3)

Another version of the 'half a job' perspective is found in a study of global labour flexibility, by Guy Standing of the International Labour Organization. In his survey of global trends, Standing has constructed an indicator of job insecurity, based on a composite measure of unemployment and voluntary and involuntary part-time employment, which together offer an estimate of 'labour market slack' (Standing 1999). Additionally, Tilly is committed to a version of dual labour market theory and seeks to distinguish between good and bad part-time jobs. Part-time employment in the primary labour market is a mechanism for retaining staff – which he calls 'retention jobs' – in contrast to secondary part-time jobs, which are low paid, low skill, lack benefits and have high turnover. After 1970 Tilly argues that the form of part-time shifted to involuntary job growth and is associated with the rise of the secondary labor market that accompanied the shift from manufacturing to trade and services. Between 1969 and 1993, Tilly argues, of the 3.3% increase in the rate of growth in part-time employment, some 3% is accounted for by the expansion in involuntary part-time work.

However, while Tilly identifies significant social processes, his commitment to dual labour market theory perhaps provides too stark a contrast between good and bad employment prospects in different sectors and occupations. Moreover, the statistical basis for involuntary employment has been challenged. Alec Levenson's detailed discussion of trends in part-time and temporary work suggests significant misclassification of those deemed involuntary part-timers. Many involuntary part-time workers were found in low paid jobs, but had options to take low paid full-time jobs, in which case the hours of work are not an issue (Levenson 2000). Arne Kalleberg suggests that, while involuntary part-time employment expands from 1970, after 1979 part-time employment expands because of growth of industries that employ mainly part-time workers, in which case full-time workers are not being replaced by part-time workers. Bruce Fallick of the Federal Reserve Board in Washington counsels against misplaced concern, because the proportion of part-time workers in the US has not grown appreciably since 1983. He does suggest that much of the hiring of part-time staff takes place in fast-growing industries, which risks exaggerating the significance of part-time job gains. In these fast growing industries, he notes, there is no indication that workers are part-time because they could not find full-time work (Fallick 1999). Finally the Economic Policy Institute's comprehensive review of 'The State of Working America for 2002/3' analysed the non-agricultural workforce and has suggested that part-time employment declined between 1989 and 2000 from 18.1% to 16.9%, and that involuntary part-time employment has declined from 4.3% to 2.4%. This study suggested that by 2000 involuntary unemployment had declined to its pre-1973 level (Mishel, Bernstein and Boushey 2003). In which case the grounds for much of Tilly's 'half a job' perspective have been removed.

The discussion of employment change as the emergence of new modes of engagement confronts the apparently semantic question of whether labour market adjustment takes place because of the characteristics of the job and the job holder, or because of the nature of the industry in which it is located. On the one hand part-time employment is particularly represented in service industries such as retailing, education and health. On the other hand, men engage in part-time work in the early and later years of their working lives, while women, who often have domestic responsibilities, constitute the large majority of the part-time workforce. Feminist researchers have stressed the impact of the gender division of domestic labour in structuring labour market opportunities for women (O'Reilly and Fagan 1998). Yet the labour market does not passively reflect gender roles, and a wider set of factors deserve consideration, including the availability of child care, tax treatment and benefit coverage. This has to be combined with the analysis of the nature of the industry in which they are employed. Companies whose operations are sensitive to changes in customer demand will require much greater flexibility in staffing arrangements than those whose product demand is predictable and/ or constant. Thus in the distributive trades the rate of part-time employment in retail outlets is much larger than wholesale outlets.

Flexibility, Disposability and Reliable Labour Supply

It is worth reflecting on the employment trends that provide the focus of attention when considering flexible labour markets, and also what has been excluded from discussion. The most extreme form of numerical flexibility is evident in the seasonal employment of migrants in agriculture. Seasonal migrant farmworkers come from the poorest East European countries such as Bulgaria and Rumania, and are hired in the summer months in Northern European farms. A similar pattern is found in North America, where fruit growers employ labour from Haiti, Guatemala and Mexico to work in Florida, Texas or California (Food Security Learning Centre 2005). While this trend has intensified to some extent with the growth of agribusiness, and while there may be new sources of migrant labour from China, seasonal migrant farmworking cannot be said to be a new economy phenomenon. Indeed it is one form of non-standard employment that has a very low profile in the discussion of flexible labour markets. Thus the debate about flexible labour is selective in what is cited in support of the new employment relationships. Shift working is a mainstream activity in production and in certain service industries, yet, with its Fordist associations is perhaps a little old fashioned to attract much interest from labour market researchers. Flexitime working might feature in background discussions of 'family friendly policies', but has not been given much airtime in the discussion of flexible labour. Perhaps because the debates over flexible labour are so connected to flexible production systems, the discussants are oblivious to new employment practices that derive from adjustments in welfare provisions, such as child care, higher education or pension programmes. Thus, theoretical bias, intellectual faddishness and government policy priorities have conspired to elevate the significance of particular employment practices such as agency staff, while larger groups go unnoticed, under-researched and undervalued.

Rather than attributing some false homogeneity to atypical employ-ment, it is necessary to deconstruct the periphery or the secondary labour market in terms of specific employment patterns. It is essential to separate the temporary from the part-time, to analyse by industrial and occupational categories and to consider the social processes that would help explain difference in terms of age, gender, ethnicity and social class. Excessive generalization is perhaps theoretically driven, but sector or group specific studies reveal a world of work that has adapted in ways that were neither predicted nor explained. Part-time employment, for instance, is concentrated in those industries such as education, health and retailing, which lie outside the normal scope of flexible production systems. Part-time employment also resists classi-fication in terms of primary and secondary labour markets. Sector specific research and company studies reveal employment practices that not only transcend the privileged and peripheral divide, but also challenge the presumption that flexible employment arrangements reflect the disposability of labour.

The deployment of part-time staff in retailing reveals some impor-tant features of the relationship between temporal flexibility and labour turnover (Doogan 1992). The retail sector in the United Kingdom has been transformed in the last twenty years through indus-trial concentration and centralization, which have produced giant retailers with six-figure workforces, making a very large contribution towards new job creation in Britain. Such chains, originally based in food retailing, have diversified across a range of services and offer the most sophisticated examples of flexible staff scheduling. The large retailers are able to schedule staff in line with variations in customer demand, which can fluctuate on an hourly, daily, weekly and seasonal basis. Advances in electronic point of sales technology enable retailers to monitor customer throughput in real time and offer the capacity to match staff schedules in accordance with peaks and troughs in cus-tomer demand. Yet this scheduling flexibility depends on the prior guarantee of a reliable labour supply. Recruitment practices are far from casual and all workers are employed on a contract. As one manager pointed out 'even school students pushing trolleys round the car park on a Saturday afternoon are expected to sign a contract with the company'. Moreover retention incentives have been developed to reduce labour turnover. Even though the retailers do not offer top of the range wages, they do offer profit share, staff discount, and pension schemes after a period of service in the company. Competition between retailers is not solely confined to price, but also extends to the quality of customer service and is reflected in the promotion of personnel practices that seek to inculcate a strong company culture. Such personnel practices would not be possible or necessary in a high turnover industry. To that extent part-time employment has enhanced flexible staffing arrangements and helped consolidate personnel practices that prioritize employment retention to some extent.

Labouring to Learn – The Rise of the Student Labour Market

A final element in the expansion of the part-time labour force in recent years is the rise of the student labour market. What is extraordinary is that this phenomenon has been largely unnoticed or ignored by social researchers. Again this trend arises from changes in welfare regimes rather than industrial restructuring. The last two decades have witnessed large increases in the proportion of young people completing secondary education and the rise of mass higher education. It was not that long ago that the majority of pupils left secondary school at sixteen years of age, but in many countries nowadays half the graduates of secondary school progress to higher education. The expansion of mass higher education has not been completely funded by the state and increasingly relies on forms of user payments that are born by students, graduates or their parents. 'Earning and learning' is the order of the day, as students increasingly need to combine work and study to earn additional income for living expenses or to avoid sinking further into debt.

The student labour market expanded during the 1980s and 1990s such that by 1994 half of employed 18 year olds were also enrolled as students in the USA, Canada, Denmark, the Netherlands and Australia (Hoffman and Stein 2003). Employment is not confined to the summer months, but also takes place throughout the year. The number of hours that students work each week is substantial. It appears that the average working week for students is 21 hours in the United States, 16 hours in the United Kingdom, 14 hours in Canada, and 11.2 hours in the Netherlands (Presley and Clery 2001; Canny 2002, Statistics Canada; Hoffman and Steijn 2003).

The rise of the student labour market in North America has not been given the recognition that it deserves given its scale. In the United States data from the National Longitudinal Survey of Youth, which is sponsored by the Bureau of Labour Statistics, reported that in 2001 most older teenagers who worked did so throughout the year. Some 65% of students who were 17 at the start of 2001 worked as an employee at some point in the following year. For 18 year olds the figure rose to 72%, and 76% for 19 year olds. Over 90% of college students aged 19 at the start of 2001 worked at some point during the year. Depending on age, the number of weeks worked ranged between 33 weeks for 17 year olds and 36 weeks for 19 year olds. A preliminary assessment of data on American college students reported by the National Center for Educational Statistics in the United States' Department of Education, shows how the expansion of mass higher education has taken place alongside the expansion of the student labour market in the United States. *In 2003 full-time and part-time students recorded very high levels of employment. Some 70% of full-time undergraduate students were in employment, working for an average of 26 hours per week, 48% working part-time and 22.2% working full-time.* In Canada, between 1976 and 2004, the earliest and latest dates available at time of writing, the year-on-year expansion of the student labour market was the key element in the changing employment profile of the 15–24 age group. In 1976 there were some 418,000 employed students aged 15–19, and by 2004 the number of working students rose to 617,000 representing an increase of 48%. For the 20–24 age group the number of employed students increased from 160,000 to 438,000, representing an increase of 173%. During this time the proportion of working students in the wider 15–24 age group, covering students and non-students, increased from 24% to 45%.

In Europe the student labour market is particularly significant in certain countries. In Denmark it is especially important accounting for 7.5% of the total workforce and 34% of the part-time workforce, but it is also sizeable in the Netherlands, Ireland and the United Kingdom. In the UK, the 1999 Students at Work Survey conducted by the National Union of Students explored the growth and significance of earning and learning.

> In the mid 1970s less than 30% of the under 20s studied and those who combined work and study accounted for less than 5% of those under 20 active in the labour market. According to the ONS (Office of National Statistics) by 2006 70% of the under 20s will be students and 53% of under 20s in the labour force will be students. In the mid 1970s only 9% of the 20–24 age group were students and this is projected to grow to 23% by 2006. In 1979 only 1% of the 20–24 age group active in the labour market were students. The ONS projects that this will rise to 10% by 2006. (National Union of Students 1999)

This is a phenomenon that British researchers have largely overlooked until recently. For too long many appear to be locked into a mindset that saw students earning 'pocket money' for luxury items, rather than working out of economic necessity. A review of research into student employment (Hakim, 1998) concluded that financial need does *not* drive the expansion of the student workforce and that poverty and low household income is an insignificant factor in the rise of student jobs (Micklewright, Rajah and Smith 1994). Hutson and Cheung (1992) suggested that teenagers spend all their earnings on luxury items rather than necessities: fashion, clothing, music, entertainment, drinking and hobbies. Moreover it is suggested that student employment is based to a large degree on self-selection and is supply rather than demand driven (Lucas and Ralston 1997). Times have changed and more recent studies have suggested that student employment has made an important contribution to the increase in total employment gains.

There is a similar story told in the Netherlands. Meer and Wielers (2001) have pointed out that the number of jobs held by students in the Netherlands rose from 12,000 in 1981 to 164,000 in 1997. In the period 1995–9, alongside Ireland, the country witnessed very significant employment gains. The 'Dutch Miracle' saw the active labour force increase from 6.01 million to 6.81 million jobs, with unemployment falling from 533,000 to 292,000, much of which was explained in significant measure by increased labour market flexibility provided by students (Hofman and Steijn 2003). Furthermore, and in parallel with the surprisingly long tenures of temporary employees in the United States, some 48% of Dutch students have worked with the same employer for 18 months or more.

Technological change and industrial restructuring in the service sector drive changes in labour process and the introduction of new forms of employment that are accessible to working students. Student employment can no longer be regarded as casual but should be seen as structural, both in terms of supply and demand (Incomes Data Services 1999). It is driven by a specific demand for student labour arising out of personnel policy and recruitment strategies in particular service sectors. Temporary employment agencies target students for recruitment to new service industries. The kinds of jobs created in the newer sectors are particularly conducive to student employment: from telesales and marketing to retailing, hotels bars and restaurants, clerical and administration, and the form of employment in these sectors offers greater access to evening and weekend working. In the United Kingdom some well-known corporations depend heavily on student labour. In 1989 Sainsburys employed 6,000 but by 1998 the number had increased to 30,000 students, constituting one quarter of their workforce. Some 35% of the 20,000 staff at Waitrose are students, who also account for 40% of Kwik Save's 20,000 employees. Students account for 60% of the 11,000 staff at Pizza Hut while 16,000 students are employed by Tesco, representing 10% of its workforce. 14,000 students account for 21% of Safeway's 68,000 employees (Incomes Data Services 1999).

The growth of the student labour market in North America and in many northern European countries raises the bar for the analysis of non-standard employment, demanding greater specification while further discouraging excessive generalization about labour market dualism. As with temporary working there are significant distinctions within the part-time workforce, between students working and studying, on the one hand and, on the other, women working a number of hours that best suits domestic responsibilities. It is not unreasonable to assume that women with such domestic responsibilities will have different orientations and assume a longer time frame for their employment. For most students there is another set of expectations which does not envisage long-term engagement with the jobs they take up while they are studying. Commentators talk about deferred entry in the labour market that has arisen with the expansion of mass higher education, which is accurate as far as it goes, but further refinement would acknowledge an earlier period, between secondary school and post-college employment. This is characterized by dual engagement in education and employment, which confers a new transient position for young people in the labour market. Its transitory nature should not trivialize its status, but it does present difficulties for those who suggest broader polarization within the labour force.

Since large theoretical positions are based on the growth of non-standard work, particularly temporary and part-time employment, it is important to recognize the degree to which such expansion is tied up with the employment of young people in the 16–24 age group. In this age group the connection between temporary and part-time employment is greatest, but the degree of overlap sharply declines in older age groups. Temporary part-time employment is therefore based in significant measure on students who will later go on to more rewarding and stable jobs after graduating from college or university. The transitory status of student employment does not support the broader thesis of a labour market fragmentation driven by new employment relationships. The incumbents are temporary, but their temporary part-time employment helps to complete an education which will enhance their labour market standing in the long run.

The lack of attention to the student labour market is an irony worth considering. When the search for novelty has driven research programmes in social science in recent years, why is it that a genuinely novel social process, evident across the advanced industrial world, should go unnoticed (except by taxi drivers who see their weekly earnings nosedive out of term time)? The numbers involved are huge – 7.5% cent of the total workforce in Denmark, almost half of those aged 15–24 in Canada etc. The lack of concern might be explained as a form of theory blindness. Earning and learning do not fit easily into the pre-existing mindset of labour market dualism, which consigns employees in the secondary labour market to a life of low paid precarious work. Feminist researchers, who often have a sharper eye for new labour market developments and who are not bound by traditional labour market categories, might find it difficult to integrate student labour with a feminization framework that sees all part-time work as gendered. Alternatively the broader oversight might be explained by the construction of the labour market as an institution that responds primarily to changes in production and not, as in this case, to changes in welfare regimes.

Downsizing and Internal Labour Markets

Corporate restructuring and its impact on the internal labour market (ILM) is a particular feature of American debate on the transformation of work. It came into prominence in the 1990s after the mass layoffs witnessed in high profile companies, some of whom had previously enjoyed a reputation as providers of stable employment. The *New York Times* series of articles in 1996 on 'The Downsizing of America' described 'the battlefields of business' in which 'millions of casualties' were sustained, pointing in particular to 123,000 job losses in AT&T, 18,800 in Delta Airlines and 16,800 in Eastman Kodak. The latter is particularly poignant given that 'Big Yellow' managed to avoid job losses in the 1930s and had prided itself on being a high wage employer. It also symbolized a company that had been particularly affected by technological development, with the rise of digital photography, which continues to exert the downward pressure for cost reduction and job cuts, as evident in the 2004 announcement of a 21% cut in Eastman Kodak global workforce.

Given that ILMs are a defining feature of primary labour markets, as suggested by Piore and Sabel, their alleged demise would have serious implications for labour retention and job stability (Capelli 2001). ILMs are characteristic of large organizations and their key features include: restricted entry points, internal promotion, long-term commitment to staff, pay not related to individual performance or to market conditions, but progression through rigid wage structures. The company benefits of ILMs range between the retention of company specific skills and the return on the investment in human capital, the organizational integration of employees and the avoidance of employee bargaining. Signs of their demise are found, not only in large scale layoffs but also in the growth of 'market mediated' employment relations in the firm, a more individualized reward system based on merit and personal performance, and a shift from movement within the company to job movement between companies that often results in wage cuts. Public perception and media commentary would support the view that internal labour markets have declined, but fortunately for present purposes there are in the United States some serious level-headed analysts who can offer a more informed assessment of the alleged demise of internal labour markets.

Researchers look for specific evidence of the decline of ILMs in a variety of ways. Since they are said to be strongly associated with large companies, signs of the decline in tenure differentials between large and small companies would be useful indicators, and declines in the firm specific component of wages would also attest to the demise of ILMs. Philip Moss, Harold Salzman and Chris Tilly (2000) cite American research that shows that tenure differentials have not changed in the 1980s and 1990s, and that the company specific wage factors show no essential change over the previous two decades. Moreover, Moss, Salzman and Tilly go on to examine case studies based in high technology and large insurance companies which showed the restructuring of ILMs and the subsequent effects on company policies. Their results are most revealing in that the companies came under pressure to reinstitute ILM systems as they expanded to take on more complex and innovative tasks and more technical functions. Later research by the same team looked at the evolution of job structures in call centres. They concluded

> The bottom line is that businesses still find it necessary to integrate substantial proportions of their inbound call center workforce into the firm via established career ladders and to respond to worker preferences for improved job quality and skill development, and much movement in recent years has been toward integrating call center jobs into the core job structures of the firm, though often in new form. (Moss, Salzman and Tilly 2008)

Another study of large private sector firms in the United States analysed retention and downsizing in 51 companies varying in workforce size from 1,500 to in excess of 80,000 workers (Allen et al. 2000). They found that job retention rates in larger companies continues to be much longer than in the rest of the labour market. The general conclusion is that retention increases as company employment grows, but also their results show that downsizing does not affect retention of mid-career employees but does impact on job retention among junior employees and the most senior employees. A study of internal labour markets by Erica Groshen and David Levine has more substantial evidence from 228 large companies in the Mid West examining pay policy over 40 years. They examined the extent of divergence between company wages and those available in the external labour market. Their study shows the persistence of wage differentials, which suggests the long-term resilience of ILMs. The internal pay structures may be less rigid than in the 1960s and 1970s, and there may be more evidence of the use of merit or performance based remuneration, but overall the conclusions strongly suggest that ILMs have survived successive waves of corporate restructuring.

There are two conclusions arising from this discussion which will be elaborated in the chapter on job insecurity and long-term employment. Overall a survey of the international evidence suggests that the separate treatment of part-time and temporary employment is a pre-requisite of labour market theorizing. It is essential to unbundle part-time and temporary employment that have been conjoined in the construction of the non-standard workforce and the discussion of labour market flexibility. Hypothetically, if there were no temporary contracts, then part-time employment would appear to be a much more stable, mainstream form of employment. If dissociated from temporary employment, part-time working might possibly be perceived in similar fashion to flexiworking, which has little effect on job status. Alternatively, if there was no such thing as part-time working, the significance of temporary employment would be marginal at most. The insecurity of temporary employment is thus amplified by its association with a much larger group within the labour force who, as will be shown, have a much more long-term attachment to the labour market.

Secondly these forms of 'numerical flexibility' have a tenuous connection with the flexible production systems of post-Fordist theory. Where temporary employment has grown, it has a multiplicity of sources, from public sector employment programmes to seasonal employment in agriculture and agency working. Moreover, the growth of part-time employment appears, in many instances, to predate the corporate restructuring that was said to give rise to the flexible firm. Its expansion in recent years owes more to changes in welfare regimes, which created the supply of male part-time workers at both ends of the age spectrum, and altered the supply and demand for women's part-time employment in health, social services, education and retailing.

7
Long-term Employment and the New Economy

The central thrust of the present discussion is the separation of job stability, represented by the length of job tenure, from job security, which is taken to mean the general sense of confidence in employment economic circumstances. It is necessary to disentangle insecurity and instability, and even to question the assumption of any obvious relationship between security and stability. Changes in the duration of job tenure or variations in labour turnover can occur for good and bad reasons reflecting either optimism or pessimism. What might appear as job instability can express excessive job changing and 'overheating' in tight labour markets or it can signal downsizing and layoffs and redundancies. From the employees' point of view, if turnover is based on voluntary job quits it is a positive expression of labour mobility and improved employment prospects. If people are subject to enforced separation from their jobs through downsizing or outsourcing then turnover and declining job tenure signal deteriorating market conditions.

Quantitative measurements of job tenure can be accurately measured and analysed to produce findings that can plausibly indicate variations in job stability or instability. If discussants enter the realm of insecurity, however, they are confronted with the messy world of perceptions and expectations and people's assessment of possibilities, probabilities and anxieties of their consequences. These can be understood at the subjective level of the individual, as 'Homo economicus' licks a finger and tests the strength and direction of the wind, or as a broader set of public perceptions of the way of the world and the future it portends. The messiness is compounded by the fact that beliefs and attitudes are very hard to pin down and quantify, and so it is pretty difficult to generate rigorous and statistically consistent measurements of perceptions and opinions. Later discussion will focus on job insecurity, but for the present it will look at job stability and, in particular, at long-term employment. If there is any truth in the mantras that proclaim the 'end of jobs for life' and the decline of stable employment that are said to witness the advent of the new economy, it is not unreasonable to expect to find statistical evidence of systemic decline in job tenures. However, when researchers go in search of job instability it is fairly elusive. Certainly there are sectors of the economy that have declined and groups of people and communities whose lives have been blighted by layoffs and redundancies. Over the piece however, there is little support for any broad generalization of a decline in job stability that would sustain the Cassandran pronouncements about the end of salaried employment.

As several researchers in Europe have shown, the national Labour Force Surveys provide little statistical support for those who seek to offer the last rites at the terminal decline of stable employment (Auer and Cazes 2000; Auer, Cazes and Spiezia 2001; Burgess and Rees 1998; Knuth and Erlinghagen 2002). In North America the discussion of job stability amongst labour economists in the United States is very well informed and, for comparative purposes quite illuminating. The most comprehensive volume on the topic is a collection, edited by David Neumark, based on the leading analysts in the field who have reflected on changes in job stability in the US labour market in the 1980s and 1990s, and asked whether 'long-term employment was a thing of the past' (Neumark 2000). The debate is engaged with a high degree of statistical sophistication, but if the reader can get past the 'Cox proportional hazard models by gender, race and education group', the findings are most revealing. They compare data on job stability from different sources, Current Population Survey (CPS), the Panel Study of Income Dynamics (PSID), National Longitudinal Surveys (NLS) and the Survey of Income and Programme Participation (SIPP) over the 1980s and 1990s. The collection covers changes in job stability by age and gender, the impact of job losses and, given the debate about internal labour markets, they also address differences between large and small employers in relation to job tenure changes. By and large the consensus view is that job stability, contrary to media representation, has not declined. Neumark's survey of the surveys is that there may be specific questions raised by the tenure changes for males in the older age groups, and while the early 1990s may have seen some loosening of the bonds between workers and firms, this does not constitute a trend decline in long-term employment nor does it 'infer anything like the disappearance of long-term secure jobs'.

Measuring Job Stability and Long-term Employment

In labour market analysis a broad range of indicators is available to social scientists to support theses, to test hypotheses or, less ambitiously, simply to gather data that might support or challenge public perceptions of the world of work. In analysing employment stability many analysts favour the use of average or median job tenures, but in the discussion presented below the concern is with long-term employment, measured by the number of people who have been with their current employer for ten or more years. While average or median indicators enable analysis of the distribution of elapsed job tenure it is suggested here that the focus on long-term employment affords greater insights into compositional, industrial and occupational change within the workforce. It allows analysis of the long-term workforce, per se, and its relationship to adjustments in the total labour force. In most accounts the complexity of this relationship has not been fully appreciated and consequently many insights into the nature of contemporary labour market change lie unrevealed. Finally the analysis of long-term employment allows comparison between North America and Europe which is important if one seeks to capture employment change across the advanced economies, that might represent the new economy at work.

Debates amongst labour economists have posited a broad counter-cyclical relationship between employment change and job tenure. Burgess and Rees (1998) suggest that, as a general rule of thumb, the length of average job tenure will increase with the decline in the level of employment. This at first appears to be counter intuitive, but, when one considers that increased employment opportunities can feed through into the recruitment of new starters, it is not difficult to imagine that downward movements in the business cycle will have the opposite effect and raise the average length of job tenure. As a general statement, while this may be plausible, it is also noted that aggregate employment can change positively or negatively with different consequences for the level and rate of long-term employment. A further concern is the distinction between absolute and relative increases in long-term employment. If the expansion of the long-service employment cannot keep pace with the total job growth then job stability can increase in absolute terms while the long-service workforce will decrease as a proportion of the total employed. In general terms if the relative growth of the long-term workforce exceeds the expansion of the workforce as a whole it suggests a significant increase in labour retention. Total job gains can happen instantaneously due to new recruitment, but long-term employment relies on historic recruitment and labour retention over a decade or more. During the period considered below the general experience is of employment expansion, and so the fact that long-term employment has increased to the extent highlighted by the statistics suggests a very significant increase in labour market attachment.

The contours of the 'new economy' can be outlined by identifying the sectors that have expanded and contracted in recent times. In turn the profile of the 'new' workforce can be mapped out by considering occupational change and compositional adjustments, while examination of different forms of employment, particularly in part-time and full-time jobs, can also assist the analysis of labour market attachment. The following tables describe variations in long-term employment in North America and Europe. The North America data are derived from the United States and Canada, and the European data consists of labour force survey data from the twelve member states of the EU in 1992. Total and long-term employment change is considered for the US, Canada and the EU by gender. More detailed analysis of industrial, occupational and compositional change is presented for the US and the EU. By studying the intrinsic features of the long-service workforce it will be possible, for instance, to identify the sources of long-term job gains and losses. Furthermore, by examining its extrinsic characteristics in relation to the workforce as a whole, it is possible to gain insights into the differential impacts of industrial restructuring, occupational and compositional change on labour turnover and job stability. Finally, some readers may find this presentation of the statistics a little dense, but each section finishes with an overview to present the key findings of the analysis.

Table 7.1 looks at employment change and the growth of the long-term workforce in the United States, Canada and Europe. The European data are drawn from the twelve member states of the European Union in 1992, which is the earliest date from which consistent statistics are available, and the North American data are based on the job tenure supplement produced by the Bureau of Labour Statistics, and Statistics Canada, covering the years 1991 to 2002. This table shows differences in the rates of total employment growth between North America and Europe and in the expansion of the long-service workforce. In the first instance employment grew by 12.2 million jobs or by 8.7% in the EU, while in the US 17.2 million jobs represented a growth of 14.9%, and in Canada the highest growth rate of 19.9% represented the addition of 2.6 million jobs. During this period the analysis by gender reveals distinct patterns in Europe and

Table 7.1   Total and Long-term Employment Change in the United
States, Europe and Canada by gender 1991–2002

UNITED STATES

| | 1991 | | | 2002 | | | LTE | | Employment | |
	Total	LTE	RLTE	Total	LTE	RLTE	Growth 91-02		Growth 91-02	
Male	62396	19962	32.0%	70053	21838	31.2%	1876	9.4%	7657	12.3%
Female	52583	12348	23.5%	62087	15789	25.4%	3441	27.9%	9504	18.1%
Total	114979	32310	28.1%	132140	37627	28.5%	5317	16.5%	17161	14.9%

EUROPE

| | 1992 | | | 2002 | | | LTE | | Employment | |
	Total	LTE	RLTE	Total	LTE	RLTE	Growth 92-02		Growth 92-02	
Male	83624	34731	41.5%	87242	37650	43.2%	2919	8.4%	3618	4.3%
Total	56653	18046	31.9%	65243	23863	36.6%	5817	32.2%	8589	15.2%
Total	140277	52777	37.6%	152485	61513	40.3%	8736	16.6%	12207	8.7%

CANADA

| | 1991 | | | 2002 | | | LTE | | Employment | |
	Total	LTE	RLTE	Total	LTE	RLTE	Growth 91-02		Growth 91-02	
Male	7060	2418	34.2%	8262	2750	33.3%	333	13.8%	1202	17.0%
Female	5791	1330	23.0%	7150	2033	28.4%	703	52.9%	1359	23.5%
Total	12851	3747	29.2%	15412	4783	31.0%	1036	27.6%	2561	19.9%

Source: European Labour Force Survey, Bureau of Labor Statistics, and Statistics
Canada.

LTE denotes Long-term Employment, measured by those workers who were with
their current employer for ten or more years.
RLTE denotes the Rate of Long-term Employment, the proportion of the total workforce who were employed long-term.
LTE Growth 92–02 records the change in the long-term workforce between 1992 and
2002 in terms of numbers and percentages.
Employment Growth 92–02 records the change in the level of total employment
between 1992 and 2002 in terms of numbers and percentages.

North America. The expansion of the male workforce of 4.3% in
Europe was noticeably lower than male job gains in the US (12.3%)
and in Canada (17%). In all three countries the contribution of female
jobs to the total employment was significantly higher during this
period. Women's employment increased by 15.2% in the EU, by
18.1% in the US, and by almost a quarter (23.5%) in Canada.

The expansion of the long-term workforce is not revealed by a
superficial examination of job tenure patterns. The rate of long-term
employment has risen from 28.1% in the United States to 28.5%, in
Canada from 29.2% to 31.0%, and from 37.6% to 40.3% in Europe.
At first sight, the changes in the proportion of the long-service workforce do not appear too radical. However, when one considers that

long-term employment should decline during periods of employment expansion then increases in job stability bear closer inspection. The comparison between aggregate changes in the labour force as a whole and adjustment in the stock of long-term jobs reveals important shifts in the balance between recruitment and retention. Comparing adjustments in total employment with the growth of the long-term workforce reveals a significant shift towards job retention that is further highlighted by considering differences by gender.

In Europe, when the labour force grew by 8.7% the long-term workforce grew by 16.6%, in the United States when total employment grew by 14.9% the long-service workforce grew by 16.5%, and in Canada when total employment grew by 19.9% the long-service workforce grew by 27.6%. In Europe the long-term male workforce expanded by 8.4% while male job gains were 4.3%. In Canada and the United States male jobs gains of 17.0% and 12.3% were larger than the increase in the long-term male workforce of 13.8% and 9.4% respectively. However the contribution of women to the long-term workforce in all three instances is highly significant. While total job expansion for women was 15.2% in Europe the growth of the female long-term workforce was 32.2%, in the United States total job gains of 18.1% were surpassed by the growth of the female long-service workforce of 27.9% and in Canada job gains for women of 23.5%, significant as they were, paled in comparison with the growth of the female long-term workforce of 52.9%.

The trends outlined above have evolved over a longer time frame as can be demonstrated with data from North America since 1983 as shown in Table 7.2. European Union data for the twelve member states are not available since several countries were not part of the EU in the 1980s. The United States data are based on the first Job Tenure Supplement produced by the Bureau of Labor Statistics which can be compared with Canadian data for the same period. The rate of long-term employment in the United States has risen from 27.1% in 1983 to 28.5% in 2002. This occurs during a period in which total employment has expanded by almost 35 million jobs, or an increase of 35.8%. During this time the growth of the long-term workforce was proportionately greater with 11.2 million long-term jobs expanding the long-service workforce by 42.5%.

The aggregate data conceal substantial gender differences. For men in the US the rate of long-term employment has dropped from 32.6% to 31.2%. This occurs because the expansion of the male long-term workforce (23%) did not keep pace with the total expansion of male employment of 15.6 million jobs, which represented a growth of 29%

Table 7.2   Total and Long-term Employment Change in the United States and Canada by Gender 1983–2002

	1983			2002			LTE		Employment	
	Total	LTE	RLTE	Total	LTE	RLTE	Growth 83-02		Growth 83-02	
UNITED STATES										
Male	54415	17755	32.6%	70053	21838	31.2%	4083	23.0%	15638	28.7%
Female	42858	8647	20.2%	62087	15789	25.4%	7142	82.6%	19229	44.9%
Total	97273	26402	27.1%	132140	37627	28.5%	11225	42.5%	34867	35.8%
CANADA										
Male	6420.5	2034.1	31.7%	8262	2750	33.3%	716	35.2%	1842	28.7%
Female	4606.6	821.8	17.8%	7150	2033	28.4%	1211	147.4%	2543	55.2%
Total	11027.1	2855.9	25.9%	15412	4783	31.0%	1927	67.5%	4385	39.8%

Source: Bureau of Labor Statistics, and Statistics Canada.

between 1983 and 2002. For women in the US the rate of long-term employment has risen from 20.2% to 25.2%. This has occurred because total employment gains for women of 19.2 million jobs (representing an increase of 45%) between 1983 and 2002 is surpassed by the expansion of the long-service female workforce, which has increased by 83% in this period.

The Canadian data describe an increase in total and long-term employment for both males and females between 1983 and 2002. Total employment expanded by 4.4 million jobs, which represented a 40% increase in the size of the workforce, while the long service workforce grew by 1.9 million, representing a growth of 67.5%. The rate of long-term employment thus rose from 25.9% to 31% during this period. The male labour force in Canada increased by 28.7%, while the long-term workforce expanded by 35.2%. However, while the female workforce has expanded by 55.2%, the women's long-term workforce in Canada expanded by 147.4%. Thus women made up 33% of the long-service workforce in the US in 1983, but by 2002 they constituted 42%, whereas for Canada the female component of the long-term workforce grew from 29% to 42% over the same period.

Since Canada and the European Union have witnessed increases in the long-term employment of men and women and the United States has seen female long-term employment increase it is important to consider what has happened to bring about a small reduction in the relative size of the male long-service workforce in the United States. Table 7.3 shows the change in total and long-term employment for women and men in the United States between 1983 and 2002. This

Table 7.3   Total and Long-term Employment Change in the United States
by Age between 1983 and 2002

	1983			2002			LTE	Employment
	Total	LTE	RLTE	Total	LTE	RLTE	Growth 83-02	Growth 83-02
Male Tot	45578	13818	30.3%	61023	17071	28.0%	3253 23.5%	15445 34%
25-34	13709	1517	11.1%	14408	1179	8.2%	-338 -22.3%	699 5%
35-44	9715	4192	43.1%	16491	5370	32.6%	1178 28.1%	6776 70%
45-54	7156	4292	60.0%	13201	6510	49.3%	2218 51.7%	6045 84%
55-64	5062	3340	66.0%	6118	3285	53.7%	-55 -1.6%	1056 21%
65+	998	475	47.6%	1558	724	46.5%	249 52.4%	560 56%
	1983			2002			LTE	Employment
	Total	LTE	RLTE	Total	LTE	RLTE	Growth 83-02	Growth 83-02
Female Tot	39575	7651	19.3%	57401	13934	24.3%	6283 82.1%	17826 45%
25-34	11425	947	8.3%	12551	787	6.3%	-160 -16.9%	1126 10%
35-44	8371	1875	22.4%	15157	4051	26.7%	2176 116.1%	6786 81%
45-54	5836	2195	37.6%	13221	5350	40.5%	3155 143.7%	7385 127%
55-64	4159	2146	51.6%	5986	3038	50.8%	892 41.6%	1827 44%
65+	895	488	54.5%	1415	707	50.0%	219 44.9%	520 58%

Source: Bureau of Labor Statistics.

table captures the ageing of the baby boomers with employment
growth increases for the 35–44 and 45–54 age groups for both men
and women, which leaves in its wake relatively small job gains among
the 25–34 age group. For men, employment expansion among the
35–45 age group was 70% and 84% among those aged 45–54, compared with women of the same age groups, who experienced job
growth of 81% and 127% respectively. For the 55–65 age group, male
job growth has been relatively small at 21%, but for women it was
44%. *Such dramatic job growth for women, together with falling activity
rates for men, means that women's employment in the 45–54 age range has
now caught up with men, with 13,221 women employed compared to
13,201 men.*

Changes in the age profile of the workforce, due to falling activity
rates and earlier retirement from the workforce, will have a bearing on
the rate of long-term employment. In 1983 the rate of long-term
employment among the 45–54 age group was 60%, and 66% among
those aged 55–64. A relative or absolute decrease in these age groups
will impact on the male long-service workforce. For men aged 45–54
the long-term workforce expanded by 51%, but for those aged 55–64
contracted by 1.6%. For women aged 45–54 the long-term workforce
increased by 143% and in the 55–64 age group by 41.6%. There has
been no increase in the rate of short-term employment, and low

growth among the older aged male workers has slightly reduced the rate of long-service employment. Thus the small declines in the rate of long-term employment are not related to increasing job instability but to earlier retirement and falling activity rates for men. Because men are withdrawing from the workforce it does not imply that jobs they leave behind are any less stable and so the general trend towards the increased retention of male and female labour can be observed in the three case study areas.

OVERVIEW

Over both shorter and longer time frames, the growth of the long-term workforce has been significant in Europe and North America. This is all the more remarkable as it has occurred during a period of substantial employment expansion. However the analysis by gender reveals considerable increases in the long-term retention of female labour, which suggests that changes in industrial and occupational structure and in forms of employment have enhanced labour market attachment, particularly for women. The theoretical and analytical implications are highly significant challenging both public perception and widely held assumptions within social science debate.

Industrial Restructuring and Long-term Employment in the United States and Europe

As the analysis considers industrial and occupational change across North America and Europe certain difficulties are encountered in terms of the comparability of categories of data and the complexity of the statistics that they reveal. There are differences in time periods provided by the statistics, industrial and occupational classifications are similar but do not offer perfect comparisons. The latter mean that statistics for the United States and Europe do not lend themselves to presentation in a single table but require separate consideration. Finally, pressure on space means that analysis of industrial and occupational change is confined to the United States and Europe.

Industrial Restructuring in Europe

Changes in the industrial distribution of employment are captured in tables 7.4 and 7.5 in terms of growing and declining industries, which

Table 7.4 Employment Decline and Long-term Employment in the European Union (thousands)

	1992			2002			LTE Growth 92-02		Employment Growth 92-02	
	Total	LTE	RLTE	Total	LTE	RLTE				
Agriculture	8047	4426	55.0%	5881	3346	56.9%	-1080	-24.4%	-2166	-26.9%
Fishing	256	107	41.8%	201	95	47.4%	-12	-11.2%	-55	-21.6%
Mining	875	453	51.8%	490	271	55.4%	-182	-40.1%	-385	-44.0%
Utilities	1402	773	55.1%	1137	687	60.5%	-86	-11.1%	-265	-18.9%
Manufacturing	32447	12788	39.4%	427	16137	43.9%	59	0.5%	-3173	-9.8%
Distribution*	23709	7195	30.3%	525	13974	34.2%	417	5.8%	-1462	-6.2%

*Due to changes in industrial classification 1993 figures are used
Source: European Labour Force Survey.

are mapped against changes in long-term employment in each sector. Table 7.4 describes industries that have experienced employment contraction with differential consequences for long-term employment. Thus Agriculture, Fishing, Mining and Utilities have experienced employment declines and falls in the number of people employed long-term while Distribution and Manufacturing have experienced total employment decline but increases in long-term employment. In the first instance it is noted that falls in the numbers employed long-term occur in industries with very stable workforces, such that in 1992 more than half the workforce were in long-term employment in Agriculture (55.0%), Utilities (55.1%) and Mining (51.8%), with some 41.8% in Fishing employed long-term. It is also noted that this group of industries constitutes a very small proportion of the European workforce, employing 7.6% of the workforce in 1992 and 5.1% of the workforce in 2002.

Thus total employment has declined in Agriculture with the loss of nearly 2.2 million jobs, which represented more than a quarter of the agricultural workforce in the European Union in 1992. Employment in Mining has fallen by some 0.4 million jobs or 44% of the workforce in the same period, while Utilities experienced almost 0.3 million job losses which represented almost a fifth of the workforce in 1992. These industries lost a total of 1.3 million long-service jobs, with contraction greatest in Agriculture, which lost over a million long-term jobs. However, the loss of long-term jobs has been eclipsed by the declines in total employment such that the *proportion* of the shrinking workforces who were long-term employed *had actually increased*. Thus, between 1992 and 2002 the rate of long-term employment in Agriculture had increased from 55.0% to 56.9%, in Fishing from 41.8% to 47.4%, in Mining from 51.8% to 55.4% and in Utilities from 55.1% to 60.5%.

Table 7.5   Expanding Sectors and Increasing Long-term Employment in the EU 1992–2002 (thousands)

	1992			2002			LTE Growth 92-02		Employment Growth 92-02	
	Total	LTE	RLTE	Total	LTE	RLTE				
Construction	10784	3444	31.9%	12071	4147	34.4%	702	20.4%	1287	11.9%
Hotels	5109	1078	21.1%	6374	1482	23.2%	403	37.4%	1265	24.8%
Transport	8499	3911	46.0%	9349	4064	43.5%	153	3.9%	851	10.0%
Financial Intermediaries	4421	1928	43.6%	5211	2465	47.3%	537	27.8%	791	17.9%
Public Admin	10922	5286	48.4%	11741	6848	58.3%	1562	29.5%	819	7.5%
Education	8831	4038	45.7%	10396	4945	47.6%	906	22.4%	1564	17.7%
Health and Social Work	7886	2854	36.2%	14328	5735	40.0%	2882	101.0%	6442	81.7%
Other Social Services	6793	1971	29.0%	7227	2451	33.9%	480	24.4%	434	6.4%
Private Households	1311	277	21.2%	1657	426	25.7%	149	53.7%	345	26.3%
Real Estate & Business Services	6966	1715	24.6%	13951	3856	27.6%	2141	124.8%	6984	100.3%

Source: European Labour Force Survey.

This describes a process of labour hoarding alongside job shedding which is particularly noticeable in Manufacturing and Distribution. Manufacturing employment declined in the European Union such that some 3.2 million jobs were lost between 1992 and 2002, which represented a contraction of some 9.8%. In respect of the long-service workforce, by contrast, there was a very modest expansion in Manufacturing such that the numbers employed long-term rose by 59,000, which represented an increase of some 0.5% of the long-service workforce. Thus, by the end of the period, the rate of long-term employment in Manufacturing increased from 39.4% to 43.9%. In the Distribution sector, total employment fell by some 1.5 million jobs, which represented a contraction of some 6.2% of the workforce. At the same time the long-service workforce increased by 0.4 million or 5.8% such that the proportion of the workforce with their employer for ten years or more increased from 30.3% to 34.2%.

The industrial sectors that experienced employment growth alongside increases in the level and rate of long-term employment are highlighted in Table 7.5. Job gains were remarkably strong in Real Estate, Renting and Business Services, which reported 7 million additional jobs, representing a doubling of the size of the sector. Similarly in Health and Social Services 6.4 million new jobs were reported, representing employment growth of 81.7%. Less spectacular, but still significant employment growth was recorded in Education, with 1.6 million job gains (representing growth of 17.7%), in Construction 1.3 million job gains (11.9%) and in Hotels and Catering job gains of 1.3 million (representing employment growth of 24.8%). Employment growth was relatively modest in Transport, with 0.9 million additional jobs representing a 10% employment expansion, while in Public Administration the additional 0.8 million jobs represented growth of 7.5% in the sector. In 1992 the rate of long-term employment varied between 21.1% in Hotels, Catering and Restaurants at the lower end of the spectrum, to Public Administration with 48.4%. By 2002 there were increases in the rates of long-term employment in Public Administration (48.4% to 58.3%), Financial Intermediaries (43.6% to 47.3%) and Education (45.7% to 47.6%). Whereas at the other end of the scale, significant long-term employment growth from lower base rates was recorded in Other Social Services (29.0% to 33.9%), in Private Households (21.2% to 25.7%) and in Real Estate Rental and Business Services (24.6% to 27.6%).

In Real Estate, Renting and Business Services the dramatic pace of employment expansion, which doubled the size of the sector and added 7 million jobs, might have depressed the relative size of the long-term workforce. However, there were 2.1 million additional long-term jobs, which expanded the long-service workforce by 125%. The expansion of the long-service workforce has also been extraordinary in Health and Social Services, which rose by 2.9 million or by 101%. Long-term employment in Public Administration increased by 1.6 million, representing a 30% growth. The expansion of Construction was expressed in 0.7 million additional long-term jobs, which increased the long-service workforce by 20.4%. Additional long-term jobs also occurred in Education, 0.9 million (22.4%), in Financial Intermediaries, 0.5 million (27.8%) and in Hotels, Catering and Restaurants, where 0.4 million long-term job gains swelled the long-service workforce by 37.4%.

An overview of industrial restructuring and long-term employment in Europe

The statistical evidence on long-term employment challenges conventional wisdom on several counts. In the first place the evidence indicates that any decline in labour retention was confined to a few sectors, namely Agriculture, Fishing, Mining and Utilities, that constituted less than 7.6% of the workforce in 1992 and some 5% in

2002. In fact, in numerical terms, the decline in long-term employment in the EU largely emanated from Agriculture. Moreover these industries have not declined under the impact of technological developments as the insecure worker thesis suggests. The principal reason for employment decline in these industries was the changes in government policies. The privatization and deregulation of Water, Gas, Electricity and Mining industries have served to reduce total and long-term employment. Changes in EU and central government subsidies for Agriculture have accelerated the rationalization of the farming industry, with the consequent loss in long-term employment. Labour market attachment therefore declines in relatively small sectors of the economy and for very specific reasons.

More widely the evidence strongly demonstrates that the expansion of long-term employment is spread across public and private sectors, and traditional and modern industries. Long-term employment is increasing in those sectors in which total employment is both expanding and contracting. In Manufacturing there is evidence of job shedding and also labour hoarding. At this level of aggregation there is no evidence to show that the new service industries place any smaller premium on the retention of staff than the traditional industries. Long-term employment is increasing relatively and absolutely in industries that have higher rates of labour turnover such as Hotels, Restaurants and Catering and Construction. Contrary to the impressions arising from the flexibility debates it appears that employers increasingly prioritize the retention of staff. The statistical evidence strongly suggests a generic rise in the tendency to retain workers long-term, with specific exceptions in a small number of sectors whose fate has been determined by changes in EU and central government policies. If any specific sector can claim to demonstrate the arrival of the 'new economy', it is probably Real Estate, Rental and Business Services, which contains much research and development activities and computing activities. It has experienced very fast employment growth between 1992 and 2002, expanding by 100% in this period. However, the long-service workforce in this sector has grown by 125%, which is one of the clearest signs that the expanding sectors of the new economy place a strong priority on the retention of staff.

Industrial Restructuring in the United States

Table 7.6 describes those sectors in the United States that have experienced employment change and long-term job losses. Employment

Table 7.6   Employment Change and Long-term Job Loss in the United States 1991–2002 (thousands)

	1991			2002			LTE Growth 91-02		Employment Growth 91-02	
	Total	LTE	RLTE	Total	LTE	RLTE				
Auto & Repair Services	2315	331	14%	1467	304	20.7%	-27	-8.2%	-848	-36.6%
Communication	2557	1344	53%	2902	1019	35.1%	-325	-24.2%	345	13.5%
Manufacturing	19481	6922	36%	17483	6345	36.3%	-577	-8.3%	-1998	-10.3%
Mining	719	263	37%	428	146	34.1%	-117	-44.5%	-291	-40.5%

Source: Bureau of Labor Statistics.

falls in Automobile and Repair Services may have a greater statistical than substantive significance, but for the record, this sector has declined by 848,000 jobs or by 37% between 1991 and 2002, although the contraction makes little dent in the long-term workforce, with the loss of only 27,000 jobs. Consequently the relative size of the long-service workforce has increased such that the rate of long-term employment has risen from 14% to 20.7%. Analytically the implications of employment change in Manufacturing, Mining and Public Utilities are more profound. Employment in Communication and Public Utilities has expanded by 13.5% but changes in this sector have impacted on long-service jobs with the loss of established posts such that the long-term workforce has shrunk by one quarter. Thus a relatively small sector, with a stable workforce, in which 53% had been employed for ten or more years in 1991, accounted for a large proportion of long-term job loss since 1991. Similarly, in Mining, total employment declines of 40% has disproportionately affected the long-term workforce, which declined by 44.5%. Manufacturing accounted for 17.4% of the American workforce in 1992 but was to lose two million jobs by 2002, representing a 10% reduction in the workforce. The decline in long-term workforce was relatively smaller at 8.3%, such that the rate of long-service employment has been maintained at 36%

Table 7.7 looks at expanding sectors and explores the implications for long-term employment. In the first instance employment expansion has occurred across whole swathes of the US economy between 1991 and 2002, which witnessed formidable employment growth, with 19.3 million additional jobs. Leading the charge was the Business Service sector, which accounted for 3.3 additional jobs, some 17.4% of total job gains, and represented a growth of 154% in this period. This spectacular rate of recruitment should have eclipsed any increase

Table 7.7   Employment Expansion and Long-term Employment Growth in the United States 1991–2002 (thousands)

	1991			2002			LTE Growth 91-02		Employment Growth 91-02	
	Total	LTE	RLTE	Total	LTE	RLTE				
Agriculture	2715	1186	43.7%	2822	1304	46.2%	118	9.9%	107	3.9%
Business Services	2163	272	12.6%	5510	625	11.3%	353	129.8%	3347	154.7%
Construction	4573	1054	23.0%	6532	1177	18.0%	123	11.7%	1959	42.8%
Educational Services	1849	473	25.6%	3016	775	25.7%	302	63.8%	1167	63.1%
Entertainment	896	127	14.2%	1758	202	11.5%	75	59.1%	862	96.2%
Finance	6764	1541	22.8%	7632	1835	24.0%	294	19.1%	868	12.8%
Government	17860	7351	41.2%	19586	8228	42.0%	877	11.9%	1726	9.7%
Health Services	3593	574	16.0%	5850	1138	19.5%	564	98.3%	2257	62.8%
Hospitals	3486	896	25.7%	4660	1568	33.6%	672	75.0%	1174	33.7%
Other Prof Services	3833	766	20.0%	5363	1218	22.7%	452	59.0%	1530	39.9%
Personal Services	2450	342	14.0%	2775	493	17.8%	151	44.2%	325	13.3%
Retail trade	16209	2215	13.7%	16981	2648	15.6%	433	19.5%	772	4.8%
Social services	1351	186	13.8%	2548	437	17.2%	251	134.9%	1197	88.6%
Transportation	3275	981	30.0%	4336	1290	29.8%	309	31.5%	1061	32.4%
Wholesale trade	3653	856	23.4%	4243	1048	24.7%	192	22.4%	590	16.2%

Source: Bureau of Labor Statistics.

in the long-term workforce, yet this has more than doubled, from 272,000 to 625,000, an increase of 129%. Thus after such rapid expansion the rate of long-term employment has only declined from 12.6% to 11.3%. Other sectors that have seen large job gains include Health Services, with 2.3 million (62.8% growth); Construction, with two million additional jobs (42.8% growth); Government, with 1.7 million jobs (9.7% growth); Other Professional Services, with 1.5 million jobs (40% growth), with Hospitals and Social Services each contributing 1.2 million jobs (34% and 89% growth respectively).

The balance between recruitment and the long-term retention of labour is revealed in Table 7.7, which allows comparison of total employment expansion with changes in the absolute and relative size of the long-term workforce. As with the European data, job stability was high in Agriculture (43.7% employed long-term), Communication and Public Utilities, in which more than half the workforce had ten years of service, and Government, with 41.2% employed long-term. At the other end of the spectrum, in 1991 low job stability was evident in Business Services (12.6% employed long-term), the Retail Trade (13.8%), Social Services (13.8%) and in Entertainment and

Recreation Services (14.2%). Long-term employment remained static in Educational Services (26%), and Transportation (30%), declined in Business Services, Communication and Public Utilities, Construction, Entertainment and Recreation Services, although in three of these cases long-service employment growth has been significant but has failed to keep pace with the total employment gains. In the ten remaining sectors the rate of long-term employment has increased and exceeded the total employment gains. In some sectors this has taken place in the face of rapid workforce expansion. Thus in Health Services and Social Services, total employment has increased by 63% and 87%, while the long-term workforce has grown by 98% and 135% respectively. In Hospitals total employment gains of 33% were surpassed by the rise in long-term employment of 75%, Other Professional Services grew by 40% while the long-term workforce rose by 59%. In some sectors growth was relatively slow such as the Retail Trade (5%) and Government (9.7%), which allowed the long-term workforce to expand by almost 20% in both cases.

OVERVIEW

The loss of long-term jobs is a particular experience confined to a small number of sectors in North America and Europe. In Europe long-term job loss was confined to sectors representing 7% of the workforce in 1992, of which the majority were located in agriculture. The decline in long-term employment in the United States is also found in particular sectors, which represent approximately one fifth of the workforce. As with Europe, Public Utilities and Mining have experienced total and long-term employment decline. Unlike Europe, the United States has seen total and long-term employment expansion in Agriculture and the Manufacturing sector contributed to the loss of long-term jobs, even though the relative size of the long-term workforce has remained static. Long-term employment has declined relatively in some sectors because rapid recruitment has taken place due to fast growth in the sector, although in most of these sectors it has increased absolutely. In both North America and Europe the rise in the long-term workforce straddles old and new industries, public and private services and low turnover and high turnover sectors. The comparison between total and long-term employment increases in the case of the United States, which has seen rapid job gains, makes the increase in labour retention all the more significant. On this industrial analysis alone, there is little connection between the new economy and labour market detachment. On the contrary the fast growing sectors increasingly prioritize labour retention.

Table 7.8   Occupational Change and Long-term Employment in Europe
1992–2002 (thousands)

	1992			2002			LTE Growth 92-02		Employment Growth 92-02	
	Total	LTE	RLTE	Total	LTE	RLTE				
Managers	11371	5105	44.9%	12536	5934	47.3%	829	16.2%	1165	10.2%
Professionals	15724	6529	41.5%	19141	8551	44.7%	2022	31.0%	3416	21.7%
Technicians	17162	6523	38.0%	23842	10168	42.6%	3644	55.9%	6680	38.9%
Clerical workers	19113	6807	35.6%	19718	8195	41.6%	1387	20.4%	605	3.2%
Service & Sales	16384	4653	28.4%	20987	6309	30.1%	1655	35.6%	4603	28.1%
Skilled Agriculture	4836	2854	59.0%	4743	2858	60.3%	4	0.1%	-93	-1.9%
Craft	23080	8733	37.8%	22092	9133	41.3%	400	4.6%	-988	-4.3%
Machine Operators	12447	5137	41.3%	12759	5284	41.4%	147	2.9%	312	2.5%
Elementary	14314	3951	27.6%	14555	4186	28.8%	235	6.0%	240	1.7%
EU12	140277	52777	37.6%	152485	59903	39.3%	7126	13.5%	12207	8.7%

Source: European Labour Force Survey.

Long-term Employment and Occupational Change in Europe

In the eleven years covering the period from 1992 to 2002, employment growth in Europe has been accompanied by occupational change with significant implications for the long-service workforce. Table 7.8 describes the shifts in the occupational profile of the European workforce between 1992 and 2002 and shows large job gains among Technicians (6.7 million), Professionals (3.4 million) and Service and Sales (4.6 million), and job losses among manual occupations, with 1 million Craft jobs lost and 93,000 jobs lost in Skilled Agriculture. The occupational distribution of long-term employment described in Table 7.8 shows that labour retention is associated with occupations that have a higher social and technical skills content and, conversely, labour turnover is similarly higher in low skilled occupations. Thus, at one end of the spectrum, some 27.6% of the low skilled workforce in elementary occupations were employed long-term in 1992, which was significantly lower than the European average of 37.6%. At the other end of the range, the higher proportions of the workforce employed long term were found in skilled agriculture (59%) with Managers (44.9%) and Professionals (41.5%). Moreover, the strong association between skill content and long-service employment increased in the eleven years to 2002. While total employment expansion has been significant among Technicians (38.9%), Sales and

Service grades (28.1%) and Professionals (21.7%), the increase in the long-service workforce has been even more remarkable, such that the long-service employment has increased by 55.9% for Technicians, by 31% for Professionals and by 35.6% for Sales and Service. Amongst elementary occupations the expansion of the long-service workforce has been modest, with additional gains of 235,000 (6.0%). In similar manner to the case of Manufacturing it is revealing that, while total employment of craft workers has declined by 1 million or 4.3%, the long-term employment of craft workers has increased absolutely and relatively. Thus the number of long-term craft workers has increased by 400,000, representing an increase of 4.6% in the long-service work-force in skilled manual occupations.

Long-term Employment and Occupational Change in the United States

At the risk of statistically overwhelming the reader, it is necessary to analyse occupational change by gender as shown in Table 7.9. Against the trend in Canada and the European Union the US data reveal that the rise in long-term employment for men has not kept pace with employment growth and has witnessed a modest decline in the rate of long-term employment. There are two credible explanations for the changing activity rates for men, discussed earlier, and for the occupa-tional change for women. Table 7.9 describes occupational change and long-term employment for men and women. In this table it is notice-able that employment growth for men is concentrated in Managerial and Professional jobs (33.4% and 30.4% respectively), with Service and Sales (19.7% and 13.6% respectively) accounting for most of the remainder. The rate of long-term employment in Managerial and Professional groups indicates that these are the most stable of jobs in the US workforce with 39% and 36% having given ten or more years of service with the same employer, while elementary and agricultural jobs are least stable, with approximately 17% employed on a long-term basis. However, while there are increasing numbers of male managers and professionals employed long-term, long service job gains have not kept pace with overall expansion, resulting in the relative decline in long-term employment.

For women the shift in the occupational profile considerably enhances labour market attachment. Table 7.9 shows an increasing concentration of women in Managerial and Professional jobs. The number of women managers increased by 53% between 1991 and

Table 7.9   Occupational Change and Long-term Employment of Men and Women in the United States 1991–2002 (thousands)

| | MALES | | | | | | | | | |
| | 1991 | | | 2002 | | | LTE | | Employment | |
	Total	LTE	RLTE	Total	LTE	RLTE	Growth 91-02		Growth 91-02	
Agriculture	1246	210	16.9%	1263	305	24.1%	95	45%	17	1.4%
Clerical	3664	1171	32.0%	3827	1032	27.0%	-139	-12%	163	4.4%
Craft	10277	3366	32.8%	10918	3319	30.4%	-47	-1%	641	6.2%
Elementary	3391	579	17.1%	3743	614	16.4%	35	6%	352	10.4%
Machine Operators	8360	2580	30.9%	8585	2551	29.7%	-29	-1%	225	2.7%
Managerial	6637	2598	39.1%	8857	3262	36.8%	664	26%	2220	33.4%
Professional	6482	2320	35.8%	8453	2629	31.1%	309	13%	1971	30.4%
Sales	5458	1155	21.2%	6531	1384	21.2%	229	20%	1073	19.7%
Service Occupations	6082	1167	19.2%	6907	1437	20.8%	270	23%	825	13.6%
Technicians	1844	497	27.0%	1940	537	27.7%	40	8%	96	5.2%
Male Total	53441	15643	29.3%	61024	17070	28.0%	1427	9%	7583	14.2%

| | FEMALES | | | | | | | | | |
| | 1991 | | | 2002 | | | LTE | | Employment | |
	Total	LTE	RLTE	Total	LTE	RLTE	Growth 91-02		Growth 91-02	
Agriculture	213	28	13.1%	326	64	19.6%	36	128.6%	113	53.1%
Clerical	14011	3271	23.3%	13964	3523	25.2%	252	7.7%	-47	-0.3%
Craft	956	291	30.4%	1087	350	32.2%	59	20.3%	131	13.7%
Elementary	775	131	16.9%	983	159	16.2%	28	21.4%	208	26.8%
Machine Operators	3350	915	27.3%	2625	766	29.2%	-149	-16.3%	-725	-21.6%
Managerial	5519	1656	30.0%	8437	2769	32.8%	1113	67.2%	2918	52.9%
Professional	7648	2271	29.7%	11065	3272	29.6%	1001	44.1%	3417	44.7%
Sales	5959	758	12.7%	6728	903	13.4%	145	19.1%	769	12.9%
Service Occupations	8121	1287	15.8%	9868	1526	15.5%	239	18.6%	1747	21.5%
Technicians	1886	430	22.8%	2317	603	26.0%	173	40.2%	431	22.9%
Female Total	48438	11038	22.8%	57400	13935	24.3%	2897	26.2%	8962	18.5%

Source: Bureau of Labor Statistics.

2002, while the number of professionals increased by 44.7%. The rise of long-term employment in these sectors of the female workforce has been strong during this time. While total employment of women professionals increased by 3.4 million jobs (44.7%) this was matched by one million long-term jobs, which represented an expansion of the long-service employment among women professionals of 44%. The increase in women managers has been rapid, with a 53% increase over the period which was exceeded by the 67% increase in the long-term employment of women managers. Managerial and Professional jobs have the highest rates of job stability so that employment expansion in these sectors will disproportionately sustain labour market attachment for women. For comparative purposes with Europe it is helpful to group together Managerial, Professional and Technical (MPT) jobs. It is noticeable that, in 1991, 28% of men were employed in MPT and by 2002 this share had risen to 31.5%. In 1991 31% of women were employed in MPT but by 2002 the proportion had risen to 38%. It is also interesting to note in the United States data that in 2002 there were more female managers and professionals than the combined total for men, with women accounting for 49% of managerial jobs and 54% of professional jobs. This is not to suggest that women have taken over the top jobs in the American economy as the managerial and professional categories include both executives, in which men dominate and jobs in teaching and administration, in which women will be over-represented. However, the occupational shifts in favour of women's employment in the higher occupational groups has significantly enhanced the labour market attachment for women and has allowed some upward movement within occupational hierarchies. One noticeable difference between men and women is found amongst machine operators which has seen a modest (3.5%) increase for men but a sizeable loss (21.6%) of machinists jobs held by women, suggesting that the decline in the textile industry has impacted on the long-service employment of women in semi-skilled manual jobs.

OVERVIEW

Since the early 1990s employment growth in the United States and Europe has been concentrated in Managerial, Profession and Technical jobs and to a lesser extent in Service and Sales. These are categories that include the elite jobs at the top of the occupational hierarchy, including company executives, lawyers and judges but also technicians, administrative staff, teachers and sales managers. Their expansion is evidence of the increasing importance of social and personal skills and technical competence, and that occupational shifts towards a more sophisticated knowledgeable workforce are associated with increasing labour market attachment and job stability. The business textbooks would suggest that new service industry jobs are inherently unstable, yet the statistical evidence points fairly clearly in the opposite direction.

Part-time Employment and the Long-term Workforce in Europe and the United States

Precariousness and contingency in labour markets has been strongly associated with the rise of what some call non-standard or 'atypical' employment. The normative assumptions underlying the use of this term are barely concealed, i.e. that mainstream employment is rooted in the male full-time labour force. A second feature of discussions of atypical employment is also significant for present purposes. The term suffers from the generalization that is a feature of many contemporary models of the labour market, which lump together disparate labour market groups into some core or periphery, or primary or secondary labour market. Thus casual, temporary, self and part-time employment can be included under one category and located in some marginal position within the labour force. This is particularly unhelpful when considering the position of part-time employment and labour market attachment.

Table 7.10 considers long-term employment change in relation to the full-time and part-time jobs held by men and women in the United States and Europe. *A major difference between America and Europe is that total employment growth is generated largely by full-time jobs in the United States and by part-time jobs in the European Union.* In the US the number of full-time male jobs increased by 6 million, representing an increase of 12.3%, while 6 million female full-time jobs represented an increase of 16.5%. In Europe full-time male jobs increased by 1.6 million, which represented a modest 2% increase in male full-timers, whereas an additional 3 million female full-time jobs increased the female full-time workforce by 7.6%. Part-time job gains in the EU were substantial between 1991 and 2002. The female part-time workforce grew by 5.5 million jobs, representing an increase of 34% and the male part-time workforce grew by 2 million jobs, representing an increase of 54.8%. In the United States the male part-time workforce grew by 1.5 million jobs, or by 28.6%, while the female part-time workforce grew by 2.8 million, which represented an increase of 23.7%. Male part-time employment increased at both ends of the age spectrum reflecting the growth of the student labour market and the reduced working hours of men in the older age groups over 55 and over 65.

Since the growth of atypical employment is associated with labour market disaffiliation and the loss of stability in employment, the relationship between full-time, part-time and long-term employment is of critical importance. In Europe part-time jobs are more stable than

Table 7.10   Part-time, Full-time and Long-term Employment in the US and the EU by Gender 1992–2002 (thousands)

UNITED STATES

Female	1991 Total	LTE	RLTE	2002 Total	LTE	RLTE	LTE Growth 92-02		Employment Growth 91-02	
	Total	LTE	RLTE	Total	LTE	RLTE	Growth 92-02		Growth 91-02	
Female	Total	LTE	RLTE	Total	LTE	RLTE	Growth 92-02		Growth 91-02	
Full-time	36501	9467	25.9%	42530	11674	27.4%	2207	23.3%	6029	16.5%
Part-time	11935	1572	13.2%	14768	2235	15.1%	663	42.2%	2833	23.7%
US Total	48436	11039	22.8%	57298	13909	24.3%	2870	26.0%	8862	18.3%

Male	1991 Total	LTE	RLTE	2002 Total	LTE	RLTE	LTE Growth 92-02		Employment Growth 91-02	
Male	Total	LTE	RLTE	Total	LTE	RLTE	Growth 92-02		Growth 91-02	
Full-time	48184	15265	31.7%	54100	16358	30.2%	1093	7.2%	5916	12.3%
Part-time	5258	379	7.2%	6762	671	9.9%	292	77.0%	1504	28.6%
US Total	53442	15644	29.3%	60862	17029	28.0%	1385	8.9%	7420	13.9%

EUROPE

Female	1992 Total	LTE	RLTE	2002 Total	LTE	RLTE	LTE Growth 92-02		Employment Growth 92-02	
Female	Total	LTE	RLTE	Total	LTE	RLTE	Growth 92-02		Growth 92-02	
Full-time	40190	13563	33.7%	43236	16921	39.1%	3358	24.8%	3046	7.6%
Part-time	16464	4483	27.2%	22007	6943	31.5%	2460	54.9%	5543	33.7%
EU12	56653	18046	31.9%	65243	23863	36.6%	5817	32.2%	8589	15.2%

Male	1992 Total	LTE	RLTE	2002 Total	LTE	RLTE	LTE Growth 92-02		Employment Growth 92-02	
Male	Total	LTE	RLTE	Total	LTE	RLTE	Growth 92-02		Growth 92-02	
Full-time	79960	34003	42.5%	81568	36392	44.6%	2389	7.0%	1609	2.0%
Part-time	3664	728	19.9%	5674	1257	22.2%	529	72.7%	2010	54.8%
EU12	83624	34731	41.5%	87242	37650	43.2%	2919	8.4%	3618	4.3

Source: European Labour Force Survey and Bureau of Labor Statistics.

their US counterparts. The rate of long-term employment in Europe in 1992 for male full-timers was 42.5% and 19.9% for male part-timers. For European women 33.7% of full-timers had long-term jobs compared with 27.2% of part-timers holding a long-term job. In the US 31.7% of male full-time workers had stable jobs in 1991 whereas 72% of male part workers had long-term jobs. In the US 25.9% of women full-timers held a job long-term in 1991 and 72% of female part-timers were employed long-term. The rate of long-term employment for European women part-timers rose from 27.2% to 31.5%. Expressed differently the total female part-time workforce in the EU grew by some 33.7%, while the long-term part-time workforce expanded by 54.9%.

OVERVIEW

Since the early 1990s job growth in the United States has been driven by full-time employment, while in the European Union total employment expansion is largely underpinned by part-time jobs. In the US part-time employment has increased for women and has enhanced long-term employment but from a low base rate. The European experience provides much firmer evidence that the expansion of part-time employment increases job stability particularly for women. Since part-time employment is the dominant form of atypical employment it is possible to conclude, particularly on the basis of the European evidence, that new forms of employment that offer alternatives to the traditional working week can enhance rather than undermine labour market attachment.

Precarious Employment and Increasing Job Stability

The broad public perception of the end of jobs for life and the decline of stable employment is extraordinary when set against the rise in long-term employment. The evidence from North America and Europe strongly suggests that Employers are increasingly prioritizing the retention of labour but they appear to retain labour that is not convinced of long-term commitment from the employer. This situation is quite paradoxical and so it is necessary to have some sort of explanation of how the two trends are possible. There are specific reasons that relate to the form of industrial and occupational change which are offered below and there are broader ideological explanations, which are pursued in the next chapter and the conclusion.

(1) The impact of the recession of 1989–91 had a particular impact on service industries and non-manual employees, which exposed new groups to the threat of job loss. Corporate restructuring together with fiscal pressures on public service jobs combined to rationalize employment and expose white collar workers who previously held expectations of job stability. Moreover the rise of mergers and acquisitions in the 1990s created an atmosphere of corporate upheaval. In the UK, for instance, the waves of mergers and acquisitions, buy-outs and sell-offs pursued relentlessly in the cause of consolidation and rationalization have generated widespread concern over corporate restructuring. Some 29% of private sector firms covered by

the Workplace Industrial Relations Survey (Millward et al. 2000) had changed hands between 1990 and 1998, almost half of which were takeovers, with a third sold off. The Joseph Rowntree research showed that redundancies feature relatively low down on the list of reasons for job insecurity and ranked significantly behind mergers or takeovers as employee concerns (Burchell et al. 1999). Mergers and takeovers create uncertainty and anxiety across occupational groups throughout the corporations involved.

(2) Precarious employment is less a matter of estimated job risk and more about anxiety over the cost of losing jobs and welfare benefits. When people express a fear of redundancy within the next 12 months they are not necessarily suggesting the *likelihood* of job loss but its *consequence*. If, as in the United States, the loss of a job also means the loss of health benefits, the consequences can be significant. During a period that has seen the erosion of social protection systems and the rise of workfare, fears of job loss will be enhanced, especially if the associated benefit coverage extends to the family.

(3) Industrial restructuring combines with changes in the form and composition of employment, with differential impacts on public perceptions of security. The symbolic significance of job gains and losses is highly imbalanced, such that public attention is drawn unevenly to particular social developments and industrial changes. Media coverage of labour market transformation is highly discriminating, but not necessarily discerning, in what is deemed newsworthy, and it inculcates a selective memory and misperception of job losses and job gains. Employment changes in particular sectors are 'signifiers' for the economy or society as a whole and speak to a labour market experience far beyond their sector boundaries. Thus 'traditional industries' in decline have latterly become associated with stable employment, while new service industries in the ascendant are linked, in many accounts, with the flexible labour market and temporary, part-time and casual employment. Despite the fact that long-term job loss is confined to a few sectors, employing 5% of the workforce in Europe and 20% in the United States, the loss of stable employment is perceived to be widespread throughout the labour force.

At the other end of the spectrum, job gains in particular industries such as Distribution and Hotels, Restaurants and Catering come to symbolize the casualization of employment that sustains job insecurity. While the workforce in most industries has aged, public attention is focused instead on one or two sectors that have large representations of young workers that symbolize the 'McDonaldization' of service sector employment. However the juvenescence of the workforce in Distribution, Hotels, Catering and Restaurants has risen for very specific reasons and runs counter to demographic trends in all other sectors.

(4) Particular forms of employment have a visibility and public profile that emphasizes not only the weakening of bonds with employers but individualization and the fragmentation of work arrangements. The growth of temporary help agencies is a case in point. Yet these account for a very small constituency, literally 1% of the workforce in Europe and the United States. Part-time employment is seen in many instances as 'half a job' and a source of marginalization within the workforce. The European evidence strongly suggests that part-time employment can enhance labour market attachment.

These are some specific explanations for the paradox of job stability and employment insecurity but there are wider institutional and ideological explanations that situate employment insecurity in the broader context of globalization and welfare state retrenchment, and explain precariousness as a mode of domination in contemporary capitalism.

8

Job Insecurity, Precarious Employment and Manufactured Uncertainty

The new forms of engagement between worker and employer that suggest relational change are characterized by greater insecurity and precariousness. It is therefore important to consider the extent to which job insecurity is suggestive of a shift towards new capitalist employment arrangements or, more prosaically, a deterioration of working conditions, a loss of employment protection and work intensification. In order to explore these issues it is necessary to consider job stability, job insecurity and precariousness. Since the mid 1990s American labour economists have emphasized the difference between job stability and job insecurity. Job stability refers to the length of tenure, while research on job insecurity often refers to 'a fear of redundancy' of varying degrees or, less emotively, 'an expectation' or 'the probability' of job loss in the short to medium term. The phenomenon under the spotlight goes by the name '*job* insecurity' and not 'employment insecurity', at least not in the English-speaking world. In the former case insecurity is a property of the job that s/he holds, whose characteristics determine its durability. However the discussion inevitably refers back to the job holders and their employability and their work prospects should they be laid off, which might suggest that employment or labour market insecurity is a more appropriate term. Indicators of job insecurity, on closer inspection, extend very quickly from an assessment of the security of the job to a wider set of perceptions about employer performance and profitability, the strength of employment protection legislation, general market conditions and employment alternatives. Thus job insecurity connotes a wider set of meanings than can be usefully captured in a narrow definition of estimated job risk. In fact the appropriateness of the term is matter of debate.

In many accounts job security is a subjective belief, quantified at the level of individual opinion, which can then be aggregated to indicate a general sense of public confidence or anxiety, or of optimism or pessimism. If it is subjective the question is posed as to whether it is real or psychosomatic, and whether this even matters. Some people have phobias which bear no relation to any statistical incidence of the dangers that create the anxiety. The fear of flying is a classic case of a very real fear that stubbornly defies all homilies about the safety record of aeroplanes. True, the number of mid-air collisions seems rarer than a lottery jackpot pay out, and most people have not crash landed into snow covered mountains, but this is scant comfort for the white knuckled passenger whose mildly sedated heart leaps with every bump of turbulence. One response is to say that job insecurity, like the fear of flying, is real regardless of the statistical incidence of job loss or plane crashes. However, further conundrums await this line of thought. Why does the fear of redundancy in many instances seem unrelated to the incidence of job loss and the level of unemployment? Why do anxieties about corporate relocation and jobs migrating to cheap labour countries seem so disproportionate compared with the immobility of capital and its destination of choice in the rich markets of the developed economies?

Job Insecurity – The View From Mars

If the proverbial Martian, recently landed on earth, examined the statistics of increasing long-term employment in North America and Europe it would be left scratching its head(s) as to why job insecurity had attained such a prominence in public discussion. If the same Martian were to ask Earthlings how they know that job insecurity is an authentic experience, an obvious response is to point to opinion poll evidence and also to media references to job insecurity. A much cited study by the OECD describes media coverage of job insecurity in the European Union (EU) and America which had risen significantly since the 1980s. It reported that media references to insecurity in the G7 countries have risen threefold between 1982 and 1997 (OECD 1997). Francis Green's examination of the rise and fall of job insecurity shows that press references to job insecurity in UK nationals and in *The New York Times* and *Boston Globe*, rose dramatically between 1990 and 1996, when it peaked, and then fell between 1996 and 2000. These studies of media references might suggest that job insecurity was a phenomenon of the 1990s and a media creation. Such a view is not wholly unreasonable, since the role of the media in sustaining the sense of job insecurity is not insignificant, but the suggestion that job insecurity has largely abated does not ring true.

It is necessary to consider the role of the media as it raises questions about the representation of job insecurity, and also the gap between media coverage of job insecurity and supporting labour market evidence. This gap between the statistical evidence of job stability and the media representation of job insecurity has been the subject of American debates (Neumark 2000), but has been largely bypassed in European discussion. One explanation for this is that interest in job stability among labour market researchers in America has been greater than in Europe, while media coverage of job security in the US media has had a higher profile than in the European press. In the United States this intense media speculation culminated in the appearance in 1996 of a series of seven articles in The New York Times on 'The Downsizing of America', which had an impact on public discussion without counterpart in Europe. The mood and substance of the reports reveal much about the depiction of job instability in the US.

The first article in the series is introduced with a brief biography of a bank loan officer whose story sets the tone for the 'national heartache' that had befallen America. This bank loan officer who, for two decades enjoyed a $1,000 a week salary, was told on returning from holiday that he no longer had a job, whereupon his wife left him and his children shunned him. He slid to the bottom step of the economic ladder, pumped gas in a station owned by a former bank customer, became a guinea pig in a drug test, and ended up dispensing brochures at a tourist centre. This is not the stuff of John Steinbeck novels or Woody Guthrie folk songs. This is *The New York Times* talking to an anxious Middle America. A strong theme in *The New York Times* narrative is the message that the casualties of the new economy are those who previously experienced the security of permanent employment and the fruits of a good income. The consequence of losing one's job is not simply a question of belt tightening, but a profound personal tragedy. On the face of it *The New York Times* is simply coming up with a new slant, putting a human face on lifeless statistics, but this case study also reveals the class content of the message they seek to impart. No one is safe, especially not the prosperous educated middle classes who had taken such comfort and security for granted. The report moves on from biography to offer a smattering of statistics, which give the narrative a sense of rigour and authority. Anecdotal and statistical evidence combine to indicate the prevalence of the job insecurity and to convey the personal costs of job loss.

> *Peek into the living rooms of America and see how many are touched:*
> * *Nearly three quarters of all households have had a close encounter with layoffs since 1980 according to a new poll by The New York Times. In one third of all households, a family member has lost a job, and nearly 40% more know a relative or friend or neighbour who was laid off.*
> * *One in 10 adults – or about 19 million people, a number matching the adult population of New York and New Jersey combined – acknowledged that a lost job in their household had precipitated a major crisis in their lives according to the Times Poll . . .*
> * *In a reversal from the early eighties, workers with at least some college education make up the majority of those whose jobs were eliminated, outnumbering those with no more than high school education. And better paid workers – those earning at least $50,000 – account for twice the share of the lost jobs than they did in the 1980s.* (Uchitelle and Kleinfield 1996)

In this series of articles *The New York Times* clearly wants to convey a social ill of almost biblical proportions. The journalists are not describing the world of expectation and possibility, the paper tells of the *actuality* of job loss that, it claims, has been experienced at first hand by three quarters of American households. The argument is spurious and the interpretation fanciful. To say that, amongst the three quarters of households who had close quarter experience of layoffs, 40% know someone who has been laid off, lacks credibility at a number of levels. In the first instance it is very difficult to imagine any household that did *not* know a friend, neighbour or relative who had been laid off in the previous 20 years, and so the figure of 40% who do seems improbable. Journalistic licence has been stretched to the limit for the sake of a 'good story'. Moreover, to suggest that 10% of American adults had lost their jobs and consequently experienced a major crisis (presumably of the kind experienced by the bankworker who was abandoned by his wife and shunned by his kids) is quite implausible. If this is added to the (unstated) proportion of the American workforce who lost their jobs without experiencing a major personal crisis, the journalists must imagine job separation on a truly epidemic scale.

The social costs of job loss can be humanized to represent the grim realities of some workers lives, but it should be done judiciously. The journalists in this case, however, are playing with figures in such a sensational manner that milks personal tragedy for the sake of newspaper sales. The claims are based in large part on the evidence of a poll by *The New York Times*, but this raises another credibility issue. Why would *The New York Times* conduct a poll to provide new evidence when there is a mass of high quality data from pre-existing statistical and documentary sources which has been analysed by legions of labour market experts? If one considers that expert opinion, based on rigorous survey analysis, in almost every case is at odds with the picture presented by the paper, the question almost answers itself.

The excesses of *The New York Times* apart, the particular impact of the recession of 1989–91 is an important context for the discussion. This was the first recession to extend significantly outside of manufacturing and mining into the service industries, and to affect non-manual occupations. The experience of employment insecurity for manual workers in the production industries has been a feature of life since the beginning of industrial capitalism, as witnessed by Friedrich Engels' writings on the conditions of the working class in Manchester in the middle of the nineteenth century. In the recession of 1989–91 casualties were sustained in white collar jobs that previously might have seemed untouchable. A much broader sense of anxiety about employment prospects spread across occupational groups, which instilled a more general mood of pessimism in the workforce. As mentioned previously, after the recession a second feature of the 1990s was the rise in mergers and acquisitions, which are forms of corporate restructuring that can create great uncertainty within a company. This can generate company-wide job insecurity even though the number of jobs lost in any subsequent rationalization might be relatively small. Both factors are important elements in considering the rise of job insecurity.

The Distribution and Costs of American Job Losses

The distribution and costs of job losses have a higher prominence in American debate compared to Europe. The tenor of public discussion suggested that the experience of layoffs has changed from a temporary inconvenience during slack times to a 'permanent irrevocable goodbye' from the firm. It has often been said that the better educated groups within the workforce are no longer protected when the axe of company closure falls, and that, unlike the experience of the 1970s and 1980s, subsequent jobs are lower paid or part-time or temporary. Henry Farber offers the most authoritative research on the topic, based on his analysis of the Displaced Workers Surveys (DWS), which are supplements to the Current Population Survey organized by the

Bureau of Labor Statistics. The DWS data cover workers who have experienced an involuntary job loss in the preceding three years (earlier DWS data cover job loss over a five year period). Farber's research provides the source material for many others analyses of job losses in the United States (see Osterman 2001 and Michel et al. 2002) and also helps test the media claims that job stability of older and better educated workers has declined.

In the first instance it should be noted that the recession of 1989–91 in the United States was different from its predecessors in terms of the industrial and occupational distribution of job losses (Gardner 1995). In common with the experience of other advanced economies, such as the United Kingdom, the recession of 1989–91 extended beyond manufacturing into the service industries and from manual to non-manual jobs. Secondly the rate of job loss did *not* recover with the economic expansion of the early 1990s, such that when the unemployment rate fell, job losses either grew or, depending on the interpretation of the survey material, at least remained stable. These are important findings and help explain persistent job insecurity when labour market conditions improve. The decline of job security during periods of falling unemployment is less mysterious if the discussion considers that layoffs and closures will still make headlines even if the number out of work subsides.

Other elements of the changing composition of lost jobs refer to age and education. Earlier work (Farber 1993) looked at the experience of job displacement in the period 1982 to 1991, and suggested that there were 'slightly elevated' rates of job loss for older and more educated workers in the early 1990s compared to the early 1980s, which may have provided grist to the journalist's mill. However, his overall view is that job loss rates for younger and less educated workers are substantially higher than those for older and more educated workers. The more recent work covers the period 1981 to 2001 and looks at the rates of job loss for four education categories ranging from high school drop outs to those who have had at least sixteen years of education and correlates with reasons for job loss. The general line of argument is the same, the less educated have significantly higher chances of involuntary job loss, but the more recent work correlates education and reason for job displacement. Among workers with at least sixteen years of education, the fraction reporting a job loss due to a position or shift abolished increased from 1.5% in 1981–3 to 3.2% in 1993–5 falling to 2.2% in 1997–9. This is consistent with reports of substantial job losses among white collar employees in some large organizations in the early and mid 1990s. In terms of age, the rate of displacement is significantly higher in the 20–29 age group than in the older age groups, and the reasons for job loss relate more to cyclical rather than structural factors. In parallel with the more educated workers, job displacement among older workers, although lower, is more related to the reorganization of companies and the abolition of positions or shifts.

The employment significance of involuntary job loss reveals important differences between the 1980s and 1990s. The post-displacement employment rates are cyclical but were generally *higher* in the 1980s compared to the 1990s, suggesting that although the rates of job loss were higher than expected in the early 1990s, the economic costs diminished during the decade. The employment rates after displacement were considered in terms of age, education and tenure. Post-displacement employment was found to be positively correlated with educational attainment. In relation to age, post-displacement does not vary by age until job losses affect the oldest age groups. Some 28.8% of job losers aged 55 years and older leave the labour force compared to 12.3% of those less than 55 years, reflecting a move into retirement after involuntary job loss. Relatedly, post-displacement employment correlates positively with job tenure, except for very long tenure, which is associated with retirement.

In terms of the earnings impact of job displacement Farber introduces two elements in the earnings impact of involuntary job loss. There is the difference in earning pre- and post-displacement at the time of survey and a second element which captures foregone earnings loss due to real wage growth had the job survived. Surprisingly the earnings loss after displacement declined in the 1990s compared with the 1980s. In other words the drop in income associated with accepting the new job offer decreased, which is counter to the many public perceptions of the earnings impact of enforced job changing. However, when the loss of foregone earnings is factored into the analysis the difference between job losers and non-losers increases. Thus even though college educated workers have a lower risk of job loss and have a high probability of regaining reemployment should they lose their jobs the total loss of earnings is substantial. This is important evidence, although Farber also acknowledges the research of Kletzer, Neal and Parent that distinguishes between those who find new employment in different industries and those retained in similar firms. 'Industry switchers' suffer a greater loss of earnings after displacement than those who are reemployed in the same sector, suggesting the transferability of industry specific capital in which workers 'earn a return' on their work experience and skills.

Job Insecurity in the United Kingdom

The distribution and consequence of job loss raise important considerations which cannot be dismissed as a product of journalistic hyperbole. Much of the survey evidence of job insecurity in the UK presents a fairly consistent picture of a significant fear of redundancy, which appears disproportionate to the level of unemployment and the rate of job loss. Data on the fears of redundancy provided by MORI show that, during the 1990s, between 28% and 53% of the workforce were 'very or fairly concerned' about being made redundant in the next twelve months (MORI 1997). The Economic and Social Research Council (ESRC) skills survey of 1997 reported that 23% of employees thought that they might lose their job. An important study commissioned by The Joseph Rowntree Foundation survey reported that 26% of their study expressed a similar fear of redundancy (Burchell et al. 1999). Thus between one quarter and a half of the workforce expressed a fear of redundancy during a period of economic recovery and when the rate of redundancy was less than 1%. This is significantly higher than the fear of job loss recorded in employee surveys in the United States, which was in the 10% to 15% range (Schmidt 2000).

The Joseph Rowntree researchers maintained the critical distinction between job stability and employee insecurity and recast the discussion of insecurity to encompass a wider set of anxieties and fears than those generated by actual job losses. The scope of insecurity was widened to consider the greater exposure of employees to market forces, the impact of the intensification of the labour process and a loss of status and control at work. The researchers probed employees' fears of redundancy to reveal a set of anxieties that are increasingly disconnected from the likelihood of job loss. Thus, when people feared redundancy, they expressed anxiety about the consequences of unemployment rather than an assessment of the probability of dismissal or lay off.

> Hence, even when people are confident about keeping their job, they can still worry about the prospect of losing it, and particularly so when they find it hard to sustain such a loss. (Burchell et al. 1999)

Further, they distinguish between insecurity which is 'workplace dependent' and that which is independent of the workplace. The latter is related to personal circumstances such as age, transferability of skills and responsibility for dependants, all of which shape perceptions of the consequences of job loss. The factors that are workplace dependent derive from market conditions, sectoral or corporate restructuring through mergers and acquisitions, and the employees' working environment. Interestingly the Joseph Rowntree research showed that redundancies feature relatively low down on the list of reasons for job insecurity and ranked significantly behind mergers or takeovers as employee concerns (Burchell et al. 1999). Mergers and takeovers create uncertainty and anxiety across occupational groups throughout the corporations involved. Indeed the Joseph Rowntree study suggested that professionals were among the most insecure groups in their study (see also Felstead 1998). MORI opinion polls show that redundancy fears are widespread across social classes from 29% in manual groups to the relatively high expression of insecurity in managerial and professional groups 21% (MFS 1999).

In a helpful summary of 'The Insecurity Thesis', Heery and Salmon (1998) define insecurity along three dimensions: (1) as a property of jobs; (2) as a property of the environment in which jobs exist; and (3) as a property of the subjective experience of workers in terms of cognitive and affective attitudes towards security. The analysis considered here would place the discussion of insecurity in terms of the environmental factors, such as the costs associated with job loss, diminished social protection systems, particularly in the form of state welfare provision, and a perceived loss of trades union bargaining capacity. However, the single most important environmental factor is the qualitatively greater exposure of the workforce to market forces during the last fifteen years and a growing awareness of its instability. The 'manufactured uncertainty' that accompanies the introduction of market forces in the public sector is of far greater import than the impact of technological change or job obsolescence, and strongly suggests that employment insecurity is not unintended in the minds of the public sector modernizers.

Precarious Employment in Canada

The concept of precarious employment has been developed to provide a Canadian perspective on job insecurity. In recent time these debates have been led by Leah Vosko and colleagues who have based the idea of precarious employment on the departure from the norm of standard employment and the growth of forms of employment characterized by dimensions of labour market insecurity such as temporary employment and solo employment. The standard employment

norm is an 'ideal type' construction of the way things were characterized by full-time continuous employment where the employee has one
employer, works on the employer's premises under his or her direct
supervision, normally in a unionized sector with access to social
benefits that complete the social wage (Vosko 2004). The standard
employment relationship was at first primarily limited to male blue
collar workers and subsequently spread to male white collar workers.
'It engendered and sustained social norms and regulatory mechanisms organized around employee status and full-time permanent
work' (Vosko 2004).

Vosko has examined the emergent forms of work that depart from
this norm and links them with the increased involvement of women in
the workforce, strongly emphasizing the gendered dimensions of precarious employment. Her concept of precarious employment builds
on the work of Gerry and Janine Rogers whose research identified four
dimensions of precarious work: (1) The degree of certainty of continuing employment and risk of job loss; (2) Control over the labour
process; (3) The degree of regulatory protection; and (4) Income
level.

Researchers from the United States and the UK might find the
inclusion of control over the labour process and income level stretches
the concept beyond the normal indicators of precariousness. If these
dimensions are included what is the basis of excluding lack of
promotion prospects or job satisfaction amongst the dimensions of
precarious employment? However, Vosko's particular interests in precariousness lie in regulatory protection, the development of new
employment patterns and their impact on women. A basic feature of
the non-standard employment is the regulatory framework that grants
'relatively unfettered power to the employer to terminate'. Regardless
of tenure or the prospect of extended tenure, the absence of regulatory protection, which one assumes to be legal protection, is central
to the rise of precarious employment.

Vosko's encouragement to consider the broader employment
framework helpfully extends debate into the coverage of welfare benefits and entitlement. Employment benefits seem to have a surprisingly low profile in the debate about job security in the United States
and it is probably wise to include in this discussion the effects of the
potential loss of benefits or the rising costs of participating in health
insurance programmes. However there are three challenges to
Vosko's position. In the first instance such ideal type construction of
the standard employment relationship, even if licence is given for
some degree of generalization, requires a degree of qualification that

might be unreasonable. It conveys an image of the 1950s and 1960s that has to some extent airbrushed out the non-standard employment relationships of the time. The role of migrant labour and the hiring of guest workers in Northern European Countries was a core component of the manufacturing workforce of the time, whose inferior status finds no place in the retrospective on offer. There is an implicit assumption that secure employment was the preserve of the manual worker, which spread to male white collar workers. Yet the civil and public service bureaucracies that expanded in the post-war era seem to offer the ideal image of 'time serving' career workers, whose job longevity had been enhanced by retirement provisions. Indeed, the fortunes of heavy industries in the post-war period might not offer the support for the idealized model that Vosko imagines. In many instances restructuring in the mining industry has been a process that has taken place over decades, with miners cast as 'industrial nomads' having to leave their homes to go in search of work. The third challenge from the empirical evidence presented here is that the new forms of work have, in many instances, increased the recruitment and retention of women in the labour force. It has led to labour market attachment and not disaffiliation. This does not feature in Vosko's analysis, which focuses on the diminution of employment protection without which employers are free to sack workers at will. However, most of the survey measures do not mention a fear of sacking but instead of redundancy and lay off. Employment protection offers workers relatively little safeguard against the threat of outsourcing, mergers and closures, which appear on the face of it to dominate their concerns.

Précarité de l'emploi – Precarious Employment in France

In his comparative analysis of precarious employment in Europe Jean-Claude Barbier provides a useful genealogy of the term 'précarité de l'emploi' in French intellectual life. He points out that précarité first entered French academic discourse in connection with poverty rather than employment. He notes that familles précaires (precarious families) were vulnerable to any sort of incidents, in which precariousness was linked to 'points of disruption'. Moreover he notes that the precarious families of the time were not the normal recipients of social assistance, but were lower middle class. Later precariousness extended to the question of employment status which was covered by statutory rights and those which were not given employment status such as the jobs offered to young people on public employment pro-grammes. In the early 1990s Barbier noted that Paugam distinguished between precarious jobs and precarious work which is low quality, badly paid and of little value to the firm. Finally Barbier describes a further extension of the term to the idea of précarization – the process by which society as a whole is becoming more and more precarious and basically destabilized (Barbier 2004).

Pierre Bourdieu was the highest profile French intellectual most commonly associated with précarité. In his writings for *Contre Feux* he sees précarité as a

> *new mode of domination in public life . . . based on the creation of a gener-alized and permanent state of insecurity aimed at forcing workers into submisssion, into the acceptance of exploitation. To characterize this mode of domination . . . a speaker here proposed the very expressive concept of flex-ploitation. The word evokes the rational management of insecurity . . . what is presented as an economic system . . . is in reality a political system which can only be set up with the active or passive complicity of the official political powers.*

Insecurity, as understood by Bourdieu, acts directly on those it touches and indirectly on all the others through the fears it arouses. Corporate globalization methodically exploits insecurity-inducing strategies. By encouraging the delocalization of capital workers in high wage unionized companies compete with low wage workers on the other side of the world, but the impact spreads throughout society.

Yet Bourdieu is not entirely blameless in his acceptance of the short-termism in economic engagement or work commitment, and his portrayal of 'delocalized' multinational corporations who have dis-engaged from the nation state. These are incontrovertible social facts taken as read. Yet part of the strength of this mode of domination resides in the uncritical acceptance of capital mobility and the 'self-evident' decline of job stability. Précarité is therefore a very significant development of the concept of job insecurity and is particularly useful in describing a generalized condition of contemporary society and he is entirely accurate to identify the political and ideological content of the insecurity-inducing strategies. However, this needs to be chal-lenged rather than reluctantly accepted as some outcome of the new work order. Precariousness as a mode of domination assumes, as a social fact, the hypermobility of capital, the fragmentation of the labour market and the casualization of employment. There is a debate in the making but the only challengers appear to be those labelled as sceptics.

Where the Left Can Go Wrong

One of the more controversial aspects of the present work is the view that many left wing commentators can make their own contribution to this mode of domination. Perhaps out of sympathy for the downtrodden masses, or because of some smokestack nostalgia for the good old days when workers had 'real' jobs and could bargain with their bosses, many radical commentators have accepted and reproduce the tenets of an argument that is at best profoundly pessimistic, or at worst consciously undermining of labour's position in contemporary capitalism. The pessimism of Hardt and Negri's assessment of the impotence of organized labour is based on the uncritical acceptance and indeed recycling of the new capitalist discourse of immaterial labour. Thus neoliberal discourse finds curiously distorted echoes in the portrayal of flows of disembedded capital, and of a transience and temporariness in employment. Both accounts accept that the balance of power has shifted irreversibly in favour of capital, that global market forces demand constant restructuring and that there are inevitable casualties in this process. The difference being that the left are sympathetic to the plight of those whose lives are blighted by job loss, contingent or temporary employment, poverty and insecurity. The left also adds to its concern for the casualties of restructuring by suggesting that many, if not most new jobs, are essentially 'McJobs', of low quality, low paid and lacking in prospects, and to acknowledge any other scenario would be somehow right wing or unsympathetic. Such generalization is debilitating and undermines rather than raises confidence on the part of labour. If, as seems likely, uncertainty and anxiety about job losses are engendered in the routine exchanges between employers and workers, then it ill behoves those sympathetic to labour to amplify the sense of insecurity by exaggerating the sense of transience and temporariness in the labour market. It would be a remarkable own goal if the left championed a cause in such a way as to amplify any feeling of insecurity. A left wing mindset that sees only temporariness and contingency in new employment patterns is blind to the basic proposition that *capital needs labour*. Despite all the rhetoric of foreign competition and threats to relocate and outsource, employers generally prioritize the recruitment and retention of labour. Otherwise it would be difficult to explain the international evidence of job stability and rising long-term employment.

9
Conclusion

The research presented in this account was prompted by the realization of the gap between widespread perceptions of job insecurity and the actuality of employment stability. If at the end of the day, all that has been achieved is some measurement of this gulf between perception and statistical reality and an acknowledgement that the general mood of impermanence is overstated, it might be viewed as a modest success. However, as the research progressed the task shifted, in some sense, from the mismatch between statistical measurement and public discernment, to a desire to understand the emergence of the gap itself. Interest broadened when it became clearer that this gap was not confined to questions of job security and tenure, but to a wider set of perceptional mismatches in relation to demography, corporate mobility and technological change. Secondly, in several cases the gap could not simply be described as an exaggeration or overstatement of reality because economic trends were seen to be moving in the opposite direction to public understanding. As was pointed out in the Introduction and Chapter 1, job insecurity came into prominence as a global theme when general labour market conditions improved in the 1990s. Additionally in relation to demographic change public concern appeared, at one point, preoccupied with runaway population growth, but within a very brief period, the mood music was of very different tone, concerned with falling birth rates, ageing societies and population decline. Taking up the theme from Colin Hay the challenge was to describe and explain the relationship between material reality and discursive reality.

It is argued here that new capitalism rests upon a specific mode of representation of socio-economic development. The ideological platform on which new capitalism is based is described here as an extended form of dematerialization. An abstract or ethereal world view is presented – all motion no matter – preoccupied with flows of capital and flows of communication, knowledge and technology. The transformativity of social forces rests on the extent to which they are seen as disembedded, autonomous and disembodied. This is a mode of representation that eschews the 'static' world of structures and organizations for the dynamic turbulence of processes which imbue social relations and identities with a sense of fragility and impermanence. Social relations, we are told, are constructed in and through global flows of images, the circulation of capital, and networks of interactivity which generate new patterns of engagement. This is a narrative of societal development that systematically overstates and exogenizes social change. In this dematerialized world of disembedded, autonomous processes, economic forces are externalized beyond institutional control, giving rise to a 'new spirit of capitalism' in which markets appear all the more mysterious and irrational. The only practical response we are told is 'to go with the flow' of change, to be smart, flexible and adaptive.

The task presented was to rematerialize social development, to reveal 'the machine in the ghost' and redress the balance between motion and matter, between process and structure. It was necessary to examine the emergence of this mode of representation, for what has transpired is not some spontaneous shift in public sensibility but an ideological shift that had substantive agency. It is suggested here that new capitalism is a confluence of narratives, which merges a neo-liberal managerial discourse and a post-industrial social science, which has been influenced by postmodern epistemology and post-Marxist perspectives on societal restructuring. The narrativity of new capitalism depends on the articulation and transmission of ideas across different milieux and enjoys a currency across the political spectrum which gives it significant ideological power.

What is New and What is Not New about Contemporary Capitalism?

Taking the negative aspect of this question it is important to examine the three elements of the case for societal change, namely: (1) transformative forces in the guise of technological change and globalization; (2) the labour market as the mechanism or medium through which social processes are transmitted; and (3) new patterns of engagement between employers and workers that constitute broader social relations. Taking each in turn, the case for a new mode of development based on a new technological paradigm, which Castells has called informationalism, was found wanting. The idea of a new dynamic in society based on a step change in the pace and extent of innovation relies on the autonomization of technological development as self-sustaining naturalized processes which run on their own momentum and logic. Such perspectives inevitably overstate the transformativity of technological change.

New employment relations are said to evolve from a more tenuous connection between workers and employers that emerges with globalization. The looser attachment between capital and labour is seen as a consequence of the increased capital mobility and the growing importance of transnational corporations. In Chapter 3 the mobility and transnationality of capital were subjected to scrutiny and produced the most significant indictment of new capitalism. In short the transnationality and mobility of multinational corporations seem of far lower order than is assumed in most contemporary accounts. Even the more circumspect versions of corporate globalization, that acknowledge a concentration of capital in the advanced economies, argue that global capital movement tends towards deconcentration and dispersal. However, the new economy boom reversed any such trend and restored the concentration of capital within the core regions of the world and its further confinement to a handful of countries. At the time of writing, the latest annual report on world investment produced by UNCTAD showed that in 2005, the UK accounted for 18% of total inward movement of FDI in the world, and with the addition of the United States, France, the Netherlands and Canada represented three quarters of all inward FDI movements to the advanced economies. Meanwhile, at the other end of the economic spectrum, the fifty poorest countries in the world accounted for 0.8% of global FDI movement. Such extraordinary unevenness in the distribution of FDI challenges the idea of planetary movements of capital and imbues ideas of globalization with a profound irony. Indeed the transnationality of TNCs reveals non-financial capital as enduringly attached to the domestic economy. UNCTAD has provided an indicator of transnationality based on the balance between the ratio of foreign to domestic assets, sales and employment and, on average, since the early 1990s, shows that the 100 largest multinational corporations have a transnationality index of approximately 50%, showing that the domestic economy is as important as the international markets of the largest TNCs. Further evidence considered in Chapter 3 examined the foreign and domestic activities of American multinationals since the 1970s and showed that the balance between domestic and foreign operations has hardly changed over three decades. Taken together, the transformativity of technological change and capital mobility seems remarkably exaggerated in contemporary accounts.

Furthermore globalization as external force compelling the denationalization of economic and political life has to be challenged. The processes and mechanisms of globalization have a strong national dimension. In the first instance the operations of transnational corporations are largely embedded in their domestic economies, secondly key states provide the principal target for investment flows, and thirdly strong states or alliances of states 'institute' the global market. Therefore there are strong synergies between the domestic and global economies which challenge the idea of globalization as an exogenous force compelling domestic policy adaptation. Neoliberalism has rendered denationalization as privatization, liberalization and state withdrawal from social protection, but this is predicated on an understanding of the global as exotic. The economic evidence, when closely scrutinized, provides the opposition to neoliberalism with strong grounds for contesting the denationalization of political and economic life.

The labour market was considered in Chapter 4 as the possible medium through which societal processes are transmitted. It was suggested that, when both productive and reproductive requirements are acknowledged, the labour market acts as both conductor of and insulator against change. An appreciation of the dual function of the labour market allows a more comprehensive theoretical framework, which overcomes the productionist bias in most analysis of employment change. The labour market should not be seen as the repository of institutional changes emanating from production, since only a minority of the workforce is taken up with the immediate productive requirements. Moreover, for all the hype around the new economy it is education, health and social service which have made the largest contribution to jobs creation. European evidence in particular shows that health and social services accounted for half of all additional jobs created between 1992 and 2002. This broader framework for labour market theorizing is much better suited to explaining adjustment in employment patterns and compositional change. Dual labour market theory, with its preoccupations with primary and secondary labour markets and core and periphery groups, makes the critical mistake of lumping together part-time, temporary and casual employment patterns and is blind to genuinely new developments such as the rise of the student labour market. Accordingly contemporary labour market outcomes do not constitute qualitative shifts in employment relations that can support societal transformation. Evidence of job instability and impermanence are found wanting and, interestingly, 'atypical' employment patterns, such as the part-time employment of women are seen as enhancing labour market attachment rather than disaffiliation. Consequently, by theorizing the labour market in its own right, and by examining the commodification of labour power in the foundation and development of the wage system, the labour market is revealed as a 'deep structure' that is particularly resistant to change.

What is new in contemporary capitalism can be inscribed under the banner of neoliberalism. There are important changes within the ruling class that express a reconfiguration between financial and non-financial capital and a new division of functions between the ownership and control of capital. Following Harvey, Dumenil and Levy, and Brenner the present account stresses the importance of financialization and changes in corporate leadership. Previously, capitalist expansion depended on the separation between ownership and managerial control, but more recent changes see a realignment of interests between shareholders and corporate leaders, through changes in systems in remuneration. Brenner shows that between 1995 and 1999, the value of stock options granted to US executives increased from $26.5 billion to $110 billion, representing one fifth of non-financial corporate profits, net of interest. In 1992 he points out that CEOs held 2% of the equity of US corporations, today they own 12%: 'One of the most spectacular acts of appropriation in the history of capitalism'.

More widely neoliberalism gives rise to a more intensely ideological form of capitalism. Corporate elites and governments have invested heavily in the promotion of ideas, that are not simply pro-business, but contribute to a world view of market forces as unpredictable and uncontrollable yet naturalized expressions of human interaction. The experience of the 1990s was tellingly captured in Shiller's notion of 'irrational exuberance' in which companies that had not produced one cent of profit were valued by Wall Street in millions of dollars. Eventually dot.com became dot.bom but the speculative frenzy that produced the subsequent telecoms crash was an even greater example of market madness. Every time mention is made of the new economy and the knowledge economy it is worth remembering that these were the buzz words the speculators used to justify massive investments in millions of miles of fibre optic cable that now lie largely underused in local networks and on the sea bed.

Neoliberalism redraws sector boundaries between finance, production and services, and between public and private agencies. The evolving role of the state continuously reconfigures the division between public and private sectors in relation to the finance and delivery of welfare. American contributors in particular stress that government finance can take a variety of forms from hard budget revenue support to soft budget tax concessions. Private insurance and occupational benefits systems rely heavily on soft budget support, which in addition to employee 'cost sharing', maintain employer benefit schemes even in the face of enormous increases in costs. This redrawing of boundaries adds complexity to the analysis, but it is important that a larger trans-sectoral picture is maintained so that a one sided view of retrenchment and state withdrawal can be balanced by welfare expansion and recommodification.

Contrived Competition and Manufactured Uncertainty

In the course of the present discussion it becomes apparent that the level of capital mobility and international trade cannot, in itself, sustain the raft of polices that had been developed in its name. Nor can welfare state restructuring, aimed at privatization and fiscal austerity, be licensed by the competition for foreign investment, since FDI flows are increasingly directed to the advanced economies with rich markets, educated workforces and good infrastructure. In retrospect it was one of the triumphs of neoliberalism that social policy makers came to accept that welfare standards and public provision should be trimmed in recognition of the limitations of state capacity in a globalized world. If anything, given the motives and direction of capital flows, such competition as there is should be successfully engaged by governments with little inclination to take part in any 'race to the bottom'. However, as was seen in the discussion of NAFTA in Canada and the US, even though the level of imports and exports are relatively low, free trade agreements have become 'the external conditioning framework' for policy development across public and private sectors. Similarly, and particularly in the United States, given the relatively low levels of trade and the (im)mobility propensity of American capital, the widespread fears of import penetration, capital flight and jobs migration seem entirely disproportionate. It appears that employers, unions and policy makers are accepting and articulating a contrived competition with overseas suppliers and with low wage economies.

This has intensified recently with the arrival of China on the global scene. The spectre of Chinese competition has come to haunt the

American economy in recent years to the apparent consternation of suppliers, manufacturers and contract negotiators. BusinessWeek has produced a special report on 'The China Price' which it claimed were 'the scariest words in US industry' and concluded that 'a massive shift is underway' as 'nearly every manufacturer is vulnerable' and 'forced to cut prices by at least 30% or lose customers' (BusinessWeek 2004). As in the nature of spectres, however, this is not real competition in the sense the American purchasers are not actually comparing separate quotes from Chinese and American suppliers. Rather this is an imaginary benchmarking, against an assumed competitor, as if they were able to compete with domestic providers. In this case competition is therefore based on speculation, the potentiality and not the actuality of business rivalry. This gap between actual and artificial competition is made all the greater when the significance of import penetration is overemphasized and the threat of corporate relocation goes unchecked. Contrived competition in the private sector and other forms of manufactured uncertainty in the public sector are two sides of the same coin which helps to explain the conundrum of the coexistence of job insecurity and employment stability.

Left Harmonies in the Neoliberal Chorus?

One of the most difficult conclusions to address relates to the contribution that radical or left voices make to the general zeitgeist of instability, precariousness and powerlessness. This operates at different levels and in different milieux. Intellectually the set of changes described by neoliberal managerial discourse is infused with post-industrial social science and elevates discussion from institutional restructuring to societal transformation. Left wing commentators have greatly overstated trends towards temporariness in economic life and have 'mainstreamed' minority experience at the margins of the labour market. Left wing accounts often seem nostalgic for the good old days when people, usually men, held down real jobs in traditional industries and seem eager to characterize employment in new service industries as McJobs. This is not to say that researchers should not expose sweat shop industries and low paid jobs, but job insecurity is an issue that should be handled judiciously, taking care not to add to the general mood of precariousness.

It is perhaps best to highlight this problem by referring back to the discussion in Chapter 3 of the AFL-CIO campaign against outsourcing jobs, for it is difficult to imagine a more misplaced campaign on the part of American labour. As Brofenbrenner has pointed out American employers systematically exaggerate the threat of corporate relocation and raise fears of the jobs migration to push through productivity gains and force contract concessions from the workforce. Yet in the first five years of the new millennium, when manufacturing employment fell precipitously, losing 17% of the workforce in the collateral damage from the telecoms crash, the AFL-CIO launched its campaign against 'Exporting America'. This campaign consists of the union promoting awareness of the extreme risks of jobs being shipped overseas from the United States. Rather than attempt to address the move of jobs to 'non-union states' in the south of the country, the AFI-CIO campaign targets the threat from low wage economies. This is especially incongruous, not only has the US been a net beneficiary of FDI in manufacturing over a twenty year period that has seen the loss of four million jobs, but also the more recent job losses attributed to offshoring coincided with the precipitous decline in FDI in the early years of the new millennium. When the unions could have campaigned against corporate America's waste of investment and the loss of jobs in industry due to over production, they seem more concerned with foreign competition. Thus a perverse logic prevails when trades unions recognize that employers use the threat of capital relocation as a bargaining tool, but seem to prepare the ground for them in stressing the vulnerability of the American workforce to cheap foreign labour.

To understand new capitalism, at the end of the day, is to understand an ideological offensive, a mode of domination, as Bourdieu suggests, that seeks to create uncertainty and anxiety and fear on the side of labour in order to guarantee its compliance. Accordingly, sympathetic commentators should recognize the risk of self-inflicted weaknesses created by the overstatement of capital mobility, job instability and powerlessness. A very different bargaining environment might pertain if unions accepted that capital is relatively immobile, and not inclined to relocate overseas in search of cheap labour. In addition to reducing the threat of withdrawal, if bargainers recognized the high value that companies actually place on labour retention, as witnessed by the persistence of job stability and the widespread increase in long-term employment, a more favourable environment for negotiation would arise. The fact that this does not occur suggests that the weaknesses on the side of labour are not structural but ideological.

References

AFL-CIO (accessed 2007). Exporting America; corporate myths about shipping jobs overseas. http://www.aflcio.org/issues/jobseconomy/exportingamerica/

Aglietta, M. (1980). *A Theory of Capitalist Regulation*. London, Verso.

Akers, J. (2005). Vigilantes at the border: the new war on immigrants, *International Socialist Review*, Issue 43.

Albritton, R., Itoh, M., Westra, R. and Zuege, A., eds (2001). *Phases of Capitalist Development: Booms Crises and Globalizations*. London, Palgrave.

Allen, S., Clark, R., and Scheiber, S. (2000). Has job stability vanished in large corporations? In Neumark, D. (ed.), *On the Job: Is Long-term Employment a Thing of the Past?* New York, Russell Sage Foundation.

Amin A. (1994). *Post-Fordism: A Reader*. Oxford, Blackwell.

Atkinson, J. and Gregory, D. (1986). A flexible future: Britain's dual labour market force. *Marxism Today*, April, 12–17.

Atkinson, J. (1987). Flexibility or fragmentation? The United Kingdom in the 1980s. *Labour and Society*, vol. 12, no. 1.

Auer. P. and Cazes, S. (2000). The resilience of the long-term employment relationship; evidence from the industrialised countries. *International Labour Review*, vol. 139, no. 4.

Auer, P., Cazes, S. and Spiezia, V. (2001). Stable or unstable jobs? Has job stability decreased in industrialised countries? Employment and employment strategy. *International Labour Organization*, Paper no. 26.

Bach, S. (2004). Overseas recruitment of health workers sparks controversy. European Industrial Relations Observatory. http://www.eiro.eurofound.ie/2004/07/feature/uk0407107f.html

Bairoch, P. (1996). Globalization myths and realities: one century of external trade and foreign investment. In Boyer and Drache (eds), *States against Markets*. New York, Routledge, pp. 84–114.

Baker, D. (2005). Bush's numbers racket; why social security privatization is a phony solution to a phony problem, the American prospect.

http://www.prospect.org/web/page.ww?section=root&name=ViewPrint&a rticleId=9028

Barber, B. (1977). Absolutization of the Market. In Dworkin, G., Bernant, G. and Brown, P. (eds), *Markets and Morals*. Washington DC, Hemisphere, pp. 15–31.

Barbier, J-C. (2004). A comparative analysis of employment precariousness in Europe. www.ceerecherche.fr/fr/fiches_chercheurs/texte_pdf/barbier/BarbierEmpPrecFeb2004.pdf.

Bardhan, A.D. and Kroll, C. (2003). The New Wave of Outsourcing. Fischer Center for Real Estate and Urban Economics. University of California, Berkeley.

Barr, N. (2002). Reforming pensions: myths, truths, and policy choices. *International Social Security Review*, vol. 55, no. 1, 3–35.

Bauman, Z. (2001). *The Individualized Society*. Cambridge, Polity Press.

Beck, U. (1992). *Risk Society*. London, Sage.

—— (2000). *The Brave New World of Work*. Cambridge, Polity Press.

Beck, U., Giddens, A. and Lash S. (1994). *Reflexive Modernisation: Politics, Tradition and Aesthetics in the Modern Social Order*. Cambridge, Polity Press.

Bell, D. (1974). *The Coming of Post-industrial Society*. London, Heinmann.

Biviano, M. and Makarechi, F. (2002). Globalization and the Physician Workforce in United States. Paper presented to the Sixth International Medical Workforce Conference, Ottawa Canada, April 25. ftp://ftp.hrsa.gov/bhpr/nationalcenter/gpw.pdf

Blackburn, R. and Mann, M. (1979). *The Working Class in the Labour Market*. London, MacMillan.

Blanchflower, D. (2000). Globalization and the Labor Market. Dartmouth College and NBER. http://govinfo.library.unt.edu/tdrc/research/fedtc4thdraft.pdf

Block, F. (1990). *Postindustrial Possibilities; A Critique of Economic Discourse*. Berkeley, University of California Press.

Blum, A. (ed.) (1981). *International Handbook of Industrial Relations, Contemporary Developments and Research*. London, Aldwich.

Boltanski, L. and Chiapello, E. (2007). *The New Spirit of Capitalism*. London, Verso.

Bonoli, G. and Taylor-Gooby, P. (2000). *European Welfare Futures: Towards a Theory of Retrenchment*. Cambridge, Polity Press.

Boulding, K. (1964). *The Meaning of the Twentieth Century: The Great Transformation*, New York, Harper.

Bourdieu P. (1998). *Contre feux*. Paris, pp. 95–9.

—— (1998). *Acts of Resistance: Against the New Myths of Our Time*. Cambridge, Polity Press.

Boyett, J. and Conn, H. (1991). *Workplace 2000, The Revolution Reshaping American Business*. New York, Penguin.

Bradley, H., Erickson, M., Stephenson, C. and Williams, S. (2000). *Myths at Work*. Cambridge, Polity Press.

Brandes, S. (1976). *American Welfare Capitalism 1880–1940*. Chicago, University of Chicago.

Brenner, R. (1998). The economics of global turbulence. *New Left Review*, no. 229, May/June.

—— (2003). Towards the precipice. *London Review of Books*, vol. 25, no. 3, 6 February.

—— (2004). New boom or new bubble: the trajectory of the US economy. *New Left Review*, vol. 25, 59–100.

Bressand, A. and Nicolaidis, K. (1990). Regional integration in a networked world economy. In Wallace, W. (ed), *The Dynamics of European Integration*. London, Royal Institute of International Affairs.

Bridges, W. (1996). *How to Prosper in a Workplace Without Jobs*. London, Nicholas Brealey.

Bronfenbrenner, K. (2000). Uneasy terrain: the impact of capital mobility on workers, wages and union organizing, trade deficit review commission. September.
http://govinfo.library.unt.edu/tdrc/research/bronfenbrenner.pdf

Burchell, B. J. et al. (1999). Job Insecurity and Work Intensification; Flexibility and The Changing Boundaries of Work. York, Joseph Rowntree Foundation.

Burgess, S. and Rees, H. (1998). A disaggregate analysis of the evolution of job tenure in Britain, 1975–1993. *British Journal of Industrial Relations*, 629–57.

Burnham, J. (1941). *Managerial Revolution*. Bloomington and London, Indiana University Press.

Burrows, R. and Loader, B. (1994). *Towards a Post-Fordist Welfare State*. London, Routledge.

BusinessWeek (2004). The China price: a special report. 6 December.

Cairncross, F. (1997). *The Death of Distance*. London, Orion Business Books.

Campbell, B. (2001). False promise: Canada in the free trade era. In NAFTA at Seven, its impact on workers in all three countries. *Briefing Paper*. Economic Policy Institute,Washington.

Campbell, B., Jackson, A., Larudee, M. and Gutierrez Haces, T. (1999). Labour market effects under CUFTA/NAFTA. *International Labour Organization, Employment and Training Papers*, no. 29. http://www.ilo.org/public/english/employment/strat/publ/etp 29.htm

Canny, A. (2002). Flexible labour? The growth of the student labour market in the UK. *Journal of Education and Work*, vol. 15, no. 3, 277–301.

Capelli, P. (2001). Assessing the decline of internal labor markets. In Berg and Kalleberg A. (eds), *Sourcebook of Labour Markets Evolving Structures and Processes*. New York, Plenum Press, pp. 207–45.

Carré, F., Ferber, M., Golden, L. and Herzenberg, S.(2000). Non-standard work: the nature and challenges of changing employment arrangements. *Industrial Relations Research Association*. ILR Press, Cornell University Press.

Castells, M. (1996). *The Rise of the Network Society*. Oxford, Blackwell.

Cerny, P. (1997). Paradoxes of the competition state: the dynamics of political globalization. *Government and Opposition*, vol. 32, no. 2, 251–74.

Christensen, R., Fronstin, P., Polzer, K. and Werntz, R. (2002). Employer attitudes and practices affecting health benefits and the uninsured. EBRI Issue Brief, no. 250, October. *Employee Benefit Research Institute*.

Clark, C. (1957). *Conditions of Economic Progress*. London, MacMillan.

Coase, R. (1988). *The Firm, the Market and the Law*. Chicago, University of Chicago Press.

Cohen, S., DeLong, J. and Zysman, J. (2001). Tools for thought: what is new and important about the 'e-conomy'. Berkeley, Berkeley Roundtable on the International Economy.

Concialdi, P. (2006). Demography, the cost of pensions and the move to pension funds. *Review of Political Economy*, vol. 18, no. 3, 301–15.

Congressional Budget Office (2003). The effects of NAFTA on U.S. – Mexican trade and GDP. http://www.cbo.gov/showdoc.cfm?index= 4247&sequence=0&from=0#anchor

Coyle, D. (1998). Jobs in a weightless world. *Economic Report*, vol. 12, no. 5. London, Employment Policy Institute.

—— (1999). *The Weightless World*. MIT Press.

—— (2001). *Paradoxes of Prosperity: Why the New Capitalism Benefits All*. New York, Texere.

Dahrendorf, R. (1959). *Class and Class Conflict in an Industrial Society*. Stanford, Stanford University Press.

Dent, C. (1998). *The European Economy: The Global Context*. London, Routledge.

Department of Health (2004). Medical and Dental Workforce Census. http://www.publications.doh.gov.uk/STATS/mdwforce.htm

Dicken, P. (1998). *Global Shift: Transforming the World Economy*. London, Paul Chapman.

DiMaggio, P. (1990). Cultural aspects of economic action and organization. In Friedland, R. and Robertson, A. (eds). *Beyond the Marketplace*. New York, Aldine de Gruyter.

DiMaggio, P. and Zukin, S. (1990) (eds). *The Structures of Capital; The Social Organization of The Economy*. Cambridge, Cambridge University Press.

Doeringer, P. and Piore, M. (1971). *Low Pay Labour Market Dualism and Internal Labour Markets*. Lexington D.C., Heath.

Doogan, K. (1992b). Flexible labour? Employment and training in new service industries: the case of retailing. SAUS Working Paper 105.

—— (1997). The marketisation of services and the fragmentation of labour markets. *The International Journal of Urban and Regional Research*, vol. 21, no. 2, 286–302.

—— (1998). The impact of European integration on labour market institutions. *International Planning Studies*, vol. 3, no. 1, 57–73.

—— (2001). Insecurity and long-term employment. *Work Employment and Society*, vol. 15, no. 3, 419–41.

—— (2005a). Job insecurity and long-term employment in Europe. In Szell, G., Bosling, C-H. and Hartkemeyer, J. (eds). *Labour Globalization and the New Economy*. Frankfurt am Main, Peter Lang, pp. 83–106.

—— (2005b). Long-term employment and the restructuring of the labour market in Europe. *Time and Society*, vol. 14, no. 1, 65–87.

Drucker, P. (1969). *The Age of Discontinuity*. London, Heinmann.

Duménil, G. and Levy, D. (2004). *Capital Resurgent: Roots of the Neoliberal Revolution*. Cambridge, Harvard University Press.

Dunleavy, P. (1994). The globalization of public services production: can government be the 'best in the world?' *Public Policy and Administration*. Summer, 36–63.

Dunleavy, P. and O'Leary, B. (1987). *Theories of the State: The Politics of Liberal Democracy*. Basingstoke, Macmillan.

EBRI (2005). The impact of the erosion of retiree health benefits on workers and retirees. http://www.ebri.org/publications/ib/index.cfm?fa=ibDisp&content_id=3497

Eisenstadt, S.N. (ed.) (1972). *Post-Traditional Societies*. New York, W. W. Norton.

Elliot, L. and Atkinson, D. (1998). *The Age of Insecurity*. London, Verso.

Engel, C. (1999). Health services industry: still a job machine? *Monthly Labor Review*, March, 3–14.

Esping-Andersen, G. (1990). *Three Worlds of Welfare Capitalism*. Cambridge, Polity Press.

—— (ed.) (1994). *Stratification and Mobility in Post-Industrial Society*. London, Sage.

Esteves-Abe, M., Iversen, T. and Soskice, D. (2001). Social protection and the formation of skills: a reinterpretation of the welfare state. In Hall, P. and Soskice, D. (eds), *Varieties of Capitalism: The Institutional Foundations of Comparative Advantage*. Oxford, Oxford University Press.

Etzioni, A. (1968) *The Active Society: A Theory of Societal and Political Processes*. New York, Free Press.

European Commission (1993). White Paper on growth, competitiveness, and employment: the challenges and ways forward into the 21st century. *COM* (93), 700 final. Brussels, 5 December 1993. http://europa.eu.int/en/record/white/c93700/contents.html

European Industrial Relations Observatory (1998). Migration and Industrial Relations. http://www.eiro.eurofound.eu.int/2003/03/study/tn0303105s.html

Eurostat (2002). The Social Situation in Europe 2002. http://europa.eu.int/comm/employment_social/news/2002/jun/inbrief_en.pdf

Evans P. (1997). The eclipse of the state? Reflections on stateness in an era of globalization. *World Politics* 50 (1), 62–87.

Evenett, S. (2003). The cross border mergers and acquisition wave of the late 1990s. Working Paper 9655. National Bureau of Economic Research. http://www.nber.org/papers/w9955

Fairbrother, P. and Rainnie, A. (2006). The state we are in (and against) In Fairbrother, P. and Rainnie, A. (eds), *Globalization, State and Labour*. London, Routledge.

Fallick, B. (1999). Part-time work and industry growth. Bureau of Labour Statistics. *Monthly Labor Review*, 22–9.

Farber, H. (1993). The incidence and costs of job loss: 1982–1991. Brookings papers on economic activity. *Microeconomics* 1, 73–119.

—— (2003). Job loss in the United States 1981–2001. *National Bureau of Economic Research*. Working Paper 9707. http://www.nber.org/papers/w9707

Faux, J. (2006). *The Global Class War, How America's Bipartisan Elite Lost Our Future and What it will take to Win It Back*. Hoboken, Wiley.

Federal Reserve Board (1997). Testimony of the Chairman Alan Greenspan. 21 January. http:// www.federalreserve.govboarddocs/ testimony/1997/19970121.htm

—— (1999). Testimony of chairman Alan Greenspan. Monetary policy and the economic outlook. 17 June. http://www.bog.frb.fed.us/boarddocs/testimony/1999/19990617.htm

Felstead, A., Burchell, B. and Green, F. Insecurity at work. *New Economy*, vol. 5, no. 3, 180–4.

Felstead, A., Jewson, N., Phizaclea, A. and Waters, S. (2002). The option to work at home: another privilege for favoured few? *New Technology, Work and Employment* 17(3), 204–23.

Felstead, A. and Jewson, N. (1999). *Global Trends in Flexible Labour*. London, MacMillan.

Fevre, R. (2007). Employment insecurity and social theory: the power of nightmares. *Work Employment and Society*, vol. 21(3), 517–535.

Fine, B. and Leopold, E. (1993). *The World of Consumption*. London, Routledge.

Food Security Learning Centre (2005). The growth of agribusiness and the market for farm labor. http://www.worldhungeryear.org/fslc/faqs/ria_010.asp?section=11&click=1

Frank, T. (2002). *One Market Under God*. London, Vintage.

Freedman, A. (1985). The new look in wage policy and employee relations. Conference board report, no. 685. New York, Conference Board.

Freeman, R. (2002) The labour market in the new economy. Working Paper 9254. http://www.nber.org/papers/w9254

Fronstin, P. (2005). Employment-based Health Benefits, Trends in Access and Coverage. EBRI Issue Brief, no. 284. Employee Benefit Research Institute.

Furman, J. (2005). How the individual accounts would work. Center on budget and policy priorities. http://www.cbpp.org/2–3–05socsec2.htm

Galbraith, J. (2003).What is the American budget really about? Soft budgets and Keyesian devolution. Public policy brief. *New York Levy Economics Institute*, no. 72. http://www.levy.org

Gardner, J. (1995). Worker displacement: a decade of change. *Monthly Labour Review*, 118, 45–57.

Genschel, P. (2004). Globalization and the welfare state: a retrospective. *Journal of European Public Policy* 11(4), 613–36.

George, V. and Wilding, P. (2002). *Globalization and Human Welfare*. London, Palgrave.

Gereffi, G. and Korzeniewicz, M. (eds) (1994). *Commodity Chains and Global Capitalism*. Westport, Praeger.

Giddens, A. (1994). Living in a post-traditional society. In Beck, U., Giddens, A., Lash, S. (eds), *Reflexive Modernization*, Cambridge, Polity Press.

—— (1998).*The Third Way* Cambridge, Polity Press.

—— (2002). *Runaway World: How Globalization is Reshaping our Lives*. London, Profile Books.

Gilder, G. (1990). *Microcosm, The Quantum Revolution in Economics and Technology*. New York, Touchstone Books.

—— (2002). *Telecosm, the World After Bandwidth Abundance*. New York, Touchstone.

Gordon, R. (2002). Technology and Economic Performance in the American Economy. NBER Working Papers 8771, National Bureau of Economic Research.

Gorz, A. (1982). *Farewell to the Working Class: An Essay on Post-Industrial Socialism*. London, Pluto Press.

Graebner, W. (1980). *A History of Retirement: The Meaning and Function of an American Institution 1885–1978*. New Haven, Yale University Press.

Granovetter, M. (1985) Economic action and social structure, the problem of embeddedness. *American Journal of Sociology*, 91, 481–510.

Green, F. (2005). *Demanding Work. The Paradox of Job Quality in the Affluent Economy*. New Jersey, Princeton University Press.

Groschen, E. and Levine, D. (1998). The rise and decline of US internal labor markets. *Federal Research Papers*, no. 9819.

Hakim, C. (1990). Core and periphery in employers' workforce strategies: evidence from the 1987 ELUS Survey. *Work Employment and Society*, vol. 4, no. 2, 157–88.

—— (1998) *Social Change and Innovation in the Labour Market*. Oxford, Oxford University Press.

Hammer, M. and Champy, J. (1993). Reengineering the Corporation: A Manifesto for Business Revolution. London, Brealey.

Handy, C. (1994). *The Empty Raincoat*. London, Hutchinson.

—— (2001) *The Elephant and the Flea*. London, Arrow.

Hanson, G., Mataloni, R. and Slaughter, M. (2005). Vertical production networks in multinational firms. *The Review of Economics and Statistics*, vol. 87, no. 4, 664–78.

Harman, C. (1991). The state and capitalism today. *International Socialism Journal*, 51.

Hardt, M. and Negri, A. (2005). *Multitude*. London, Penguin.

Harris, J. and Todaro, M. (1970). Migration, Unemployment and Development: A Two-Sector Analysis. American Economic Review, 60 pp. 126–142.

Harris, N. (2003). *The Return of Cosmopolitan Capital: Globalization, the State and War*. London, IB Taurus.

—— (2004). All praise war. *International Socialism Journal*, vol. 102, 143–52.

Harrison, B. (1994). *Lean and Mean: The Changing Landscape of Corporate Power in the Age of Flexibility*. New York, Basic Books.

Harvey, D. (1989). *The Condition of Postmodernity*. Oxford, Blackwell.

—— (2005). *A Brief History of Neoliberalism*. Oxford, Oxford University Press.

Hay, C. and Marsh, D. (2000). *Demystifying Globalization*. London, MacMillan.

Hay, C. and Rosamond, B. (2002). Globalization, European integration and the discursive construction of economic imperatives. *Journal of European Public Policy*, April, 147–67.

Hay, C., Watson, M. and Wincott, D. (1999). Globalization, European integration and the persistence of european social models. Working paper, 3/39. http://www.one-europe.ac.uk/pdf/w3.PDF

Heery, E. and Salmon, J. (eds) (1999). *The Insecure Workforce*. London, Routledge.

Held, D., McGrew, A., Goldblatt, D. and Perraton, J. (1999). *Global Transformations, Politics, Economics and Culture*. Cambridge, Polity Press.

Hemerijck, A. (2002). The self-transformation of the European social model(s). In Esping-Andersen, G., Gallie, D., Hemerijck, A. and Myles, J. (eds), *Why We Need a New Welfare State*. Oxford, Oxford University Press, pp. 173–213.

Henderson, J., Dicken, P., Hess, M., Coe, N. and Wai-Chung Yeung, H. (2002). Global production networks and the analysis of economic development. *Review of International Political Economy* 9, 436–64.

Henwood, D. (2003). *After the New Economy*. New York, The New Press.

Hiles, D. (1992). Health services: the real jobs machine, *Monthly Labor Review*, November, vol. 115, no. 11. 3–16.

Hipple, S. (1998). Contingent work: results from the second survey. *Monthly Labor Review*, November, vol. 121, no. 11. 22–35.

—— (2001). Contingent work in the late 1990s. *Monthly Labor Review*, March, 3–27.

Hirst, P. and Thompson, G. (1996). *Globalization in Question*. Cambridge, Polity Press.

Hobsbawn, E. (1977). *The Age of Revolution*. London, Abacus.

Hirst, P. and Zeitlin, J. (1991). Flexible specialisation versus post-Fordism, theory evidence and policy implications. *Economy and Society* 21(1), 1–56.

Hofman, W. and Steijn, A. (2003). Students or lower skilled workers? Displacement at the bottom of the labour market. *Higher Education*, vol. 45, 127–46.

Holzman, R. (2000). The World Bank approach to pension reform. *International Social Security Review*, vol. 53, no. 1, 11–34.

Hoskins, D. (2002). Thinking about ageing issues. *International Social Security Review*, vol. 55, no. 1, 13–20.

Howard, C. (2007). *The Welfare State Nobody Knows*. Princeton, Princeton University Press.

HRSA (2002). Projected supply, demand and shortages of registered nurses 2002–2020. Bureau of Health Professionals. http://www.ahca.org/research/rnsupply_demand.pdf

—— (2003). Changing demographics and the implications for physicians, nurses, and other health workers. Bureau of Health Professionals. http://bhpr.hrsa.gov/healthworkforce/reports/default.htm

Hufbauer, G., and Schott, J. (1993). *NAFTA. An Asssessement*. Washington DC, Institute for International Economics (Revised ed. 1996).

—— (2005). *NAFTA Revisited: Achievements and Challenges*. Washington DC, Institute for International Economics.

Hutson, S. and Cheung, W-Y (1992). Saturday jobs: sixth formers in the labour market and in the family. In Marsh, C. and Arber, S., *Families and Households: Divisions and Change*, Basingstoke, MacMillan, 45–62.

Hutton, W. (1998). *The Stakeholding Society*. Cambridge, Polity Press.

—— (2002). *The World We're In*. London, Little Brown.

Incomes Data Services (1999). IDS Report, no. 776, January.

Jones (1986) Fast food and throw away jobs. *The Listener*, 29 May.

Kahn, H. and Weiner, A. (1967). *The Year 2000*. New York, MacMillan.

Kaiser Family Foundation (2005). Employer Health Benefits Annual Survey. http://www.kff.org/insurance/7315/sections/upload/7316.pdf

Kalleberg, A. (2000). Nonstandard employment relations: part-time, temporary, and contract work. *Annual Review of Sociology* 26, 341–65.

Keochlin, T. (2005). US multinational corporations, and the mobility of productive capital: a skeptical view. *Review of Radical Political Economy*, vol. 38, no. 3, 374–80.

Knowledge@Wharton (2006). Unlike death and taxes, pensions are no longer guaranteed. http://knowledge.wharton.upenn.edu/article/1375.cfm

Knuth, M. and Erlinghagen, M. (2002). In search of turbulence, labour mobility and job stability in Germany. Paper presented to the Third International Congress of the Work and Labour Network on the theme of globalization, the new economy and labour. Osnabruck, Germany, 22–5, May.

Korpi, W. and Palme, J. (2003). New politics and class politics in the context of austerity and globalization; welfare state regress in 18 countries, 1975–1995. *American Political Science Review*, vol. 97, no. 3, 425–46.

Krugman, P. (2005). Many unhappy returns. *New York Times*, 1 February.

Landefield, J. and Kozlow, R. (2003). Globalization and multinational companies: what are the questions and how well are we doing in answering them? *Statistical Journal of the United Nations Economic Commission for Europe*, vol. 20, no. 2, 111–20.

Landry, J. (2002). The Powell Manifesto: how a prominent lawyer's attack memo changed America. Media transparency. 20 August. http://www.mediatransparency.org/story.php?storyID=21

Lash, S. (1994). Reflexivity and its doubles. In Beck, U., Giddens, A. and Lash, S. (1994). *Reflexive Modernisation; Politics Tradition and Aesthetics in the Modern Social Order*. Cambridge, Polity Press.

Lash, S. and Urry, J.(1987). *The End of Organized Capitalism*. Cambridge, Polity Press.

—— (1994). *Economies of Signs and Space*. London, Sage.

Launov, A. (2004). An alternative approach to testing dual labour market theory. IZA Discussion Paper, no. 1289. http://www.iza.org/en/web content/publications/papers/viewAbstract?dp_id=1289

Leadbeater, C. (2000). *Living on Thin Air: The New Economy*. London, Penguin.

Le Grand, J. and Bartlett, W. (1993). *Quasi-Markets and Social Policy*. Basingstoke, Macmillan.

Levenson, A. (2000). Long run trends in part-time and temporary employment: towards an understanding. In Neumark, D. (ed.), *On the Job: Is Long-term Employment a Thing of the Past?* New York, Russell Sage Foundation.

Levitt, T. (1983). The globalization of markets. *Harvard Business Review* 101, May–June.

Lichtheim, G. (1963). *The New Europe: Today and Tommorrow*. New York, Praeger.

Lichtenstein, N. (2002). *State of the Union: A Century of American Labour*. Princeton, Princeton University Press.

Lipietz, A. (2001). The fortunes and misfortunes of post-Fordism. In Albritton, R., Itoh, M., Westra, R. and Zuege, A. (eds). *Phases of Capitalist Development: Booms Crises and Globalizations*. London, Palgrave.

Lucas, R. and Ralston, L. (1997). Youth gender and part-time employment: A preliminary appraisal of student employment. *Employee Relations* 19, 51–66.

Luttwak, E. (1999). *Turbo-Capitalism, Winners and Losers in the Global Economy*. London, Orion Books.

MacDonald, H. and Sjoberg, G. (1972). *Politics in the Post Welfare State; Responses to the New Individualism*. New York, Columbia University Press.

Machlup, F. (1962). *The Production and Distribution of Knowledge in the United States*, Princeton, Princeton University Press.

Marcuse, P. (2002). Depoliticizing globalization: from neo-Marxism to the network society of Manuel Castells. In Eade, J. and Mele, C. (eds), *Understanding the City: Contemporary and Future Prospects*. Oxford, Blackwell, pp. 131–58.

Marginson, P. and Sisson, K. (1994). The structure of transnational capital in Europe; the emerging Euro company and its implications for industrial relations. In Hyman, R. and Ferner, A. (eds), *New Frontiers in European Industrial Relations*. Oxford, Blackwell.

Marx, K. (1954). *Capital: A Critique of Political Economy, vol. 1*. London, Lawrence and Wishart.

—— (1973). *Grundrisse, Foundations of the Critique of Political Economy*. London, Penguin, p. 278.

Mataloni, R. (2005). US multinational companies, operations in 2003. *Survey of Current Business*, July, 9–29.

Mataloni, R. and Yorgason, D. (2006). Operations of US multinational companies preliminary results from the 2004 benchmark survey. *Survey of Current Business*, November.

May, C. (2002). *The Information Society: A Sceptical View*. Cambridge, Polity Press.

McNally, D. (1993). *Against the Market Political Economy, Market Socialism and the Marxist Critique*. London, Verso.

Meer, P. and Wielers, R. (2001). The increased labour market participation of Dutch students. *Work Employment and Society*, vol. 15(1), 55–71

Meyerson, H. (2005). Assault on social security, the American prospect. http://www.prospect.org/web/page.ww?section=root&name=ViewWeb&articleId=9141

Micklewright J., Rajah, N. and Smith, S. (1994). Labour and learning: part-time work and full-time education. *National Institute Economic Review* 148, 73–87.

Mishel, L., Bernstein, J. and Boushey, H. (2003). *The State of Working America*. Economic Policy Institute, Ithaca, ILR Press/Cornell University Press.

Mishra, R. (1990). *The Welfare State in Capitalist Society: Policies of Retrenchment and Maintenance in Europe North America and Australia*. Hemel Hempstead, Harvester Wheatsheaf.

Mares, I. (2001). Firms and the welfare state: when, why and how does social policy matter to employers, In Hall, P. and Soskice, D. (eds), *Varieties of Capitalism: The Institutional Foundations of Comparative Advantage*. Oxford, Oxford University Press.

Monbiot, G. (2000). *Captive State. The Corporate Takeover of Britain*. London, MacMillan.

Moody, K. (2007). *US Labor in Trouble and Transition*. London, Verso.

MORI (1997). Fear of redundancy chart. Omnibus. MORI Financial Services, August.

Mosisa, A. (2002). The role of foreign-born workers in the US economy. *Monthly Labor Review*, May, 3–12.

Moss, P., Salzman, H. and Tilly, C. (2000). Limits to market mediated employment: from deconstruction to reconstruction of internal labor markets. In Carré, F., Ferber, M., Golden, L. and Herzenberg S. (eds), *Nonstandard work: The Nature and Challenges of Changing Employment Arrangements*. Industrial Relations Research Association, ILR Press/Cornell University Press.

—— (2008). Under construction: the continuing evolution of job structures in call centres. *Industrial Relations*, vol. 47 (2), 173–208.

National Academy of Public Administration (2006). Off-shoring. How Big Is It? Report of the panel, October. http://www.napawash.org/pc_management_studies/offshoring/SecondOff-ShoringReport10-31-06.pdf

National Coalition on Health Care (2006). Health insurance cost. http://www.nchc.org/facts/cost.sthml

National Commission on Technology Automation and Economic Progress (1965). Report conclusions. Cited in Bell (1972), p. 195.

National Science Board (2003). The science and engineering workforce, realizing America's potential. http://www.nsf.gov/nsb/documents/2003 /nsb0369/start.htm

Neumark, D. (ed.). *On the Job: Is Long-term Employment a Thing of the Past?* New York, Russell Sage Foundation.

Neumark, D., Polsky, D. and Hansen, D. (2000). Has job stability declined yet? New evidence for the 1990s. In Neumark, D. (ed.), *On the Job: Is Long-term Employment a Thing of the Past?* New York, Russell Sage Foundation.

New York Times (2004). US no longer automatically gets best and brightest college students. 2 December.

North, D. (1977). Markets and other allocation systems in history, the challenge of Karl Polyani. *Journal of European Economic History*, vol. 6, 703–16.

Noteramus (1993). The abdication from national policy autonomy: why the macroeconomic policy regime has become so unfavourable to labor. *Politics and Society* 21(2), 133–67.

Oatley, T. (1999). How constraining is national mobility? The partisan hypothesis in an open economy. *American Journal of Political Science* 43(4), 1003–27.

OECD (1997). Is job insecurity on the increase in OECD countries? Employment Outlook, Paris, OECD.

—— (2004) Wage settings and institutions. Employment Outlook, Paris, OECD. http://www.oecd.org/document/62/0,2340,en_2649_201185 _31935102_1_1_1_1,00.html

—— (2004) Education at a Glance. http://www.oecd.org/document/ 7/0,2340,en_37455_33712135_1_1_1_37455,0 . . .

Ohmae, K. (1990). *The Borderless World, Power and Strategy in the Interlinked Economy.* London, Collins.

Oliner, S. and Sichel, D. (2000). The resurgence of growth in the late 1990s: is information technology the story? *Journal of Economic Perspectives* 14, 3–22.

O'Neil, M. (1996). *The Politics of European Integration: A Reader.* London, Routledge.

O'Reilly, J. and Fagan, C. (1998). *Part-Time Prospects: An International Comparison of Part-Time Work in Europe, North America and the Pacific Rim.* London, Routledge.

Osborne, D. and Gaebler, T. (1992). *Reinventing Government: How the Entrepreneurial Spirit is Transforming the Public Sector, from the Schoolhouse to the Statehouse, City Hall to the Pentagon.* Reading Mass., Addisson-Wesley.

Osterman, P. (2001). Flexibility and commitment in the United States labour market. Employment paper 2001/18. *International Labour Organization.* http://www.ilo.org.public/english/employment/strat/publ/epi01–18.html

Parker, M. and Jary, D. (1995). The McUniversity: organization, management and academic subjectivity. *Organization*, vol. 2(2), 319–38.

Parks, J. (2006). As employers cut back and even break pension promises, workers see their retirement security draining away. http://www.aflcio. org/aboutus/thisistheaflcio/publications/magazine/0205_pension_broken.cfm

Pearson H. (1977). *Editorial introduction to 'The Livelihood of Man' by Karl Polanyi*. New York, Academic Press.

Peck, J. (2001). *Workfare States*. New York, The Guildford Press.

Peck, J. and Theodore, N. (2001). Continent Chicago: restructuring the spaces of temporary labor. *International Journal of Urban and Regional Research*, vol. 25, 471–96.

Perkin, H. (1969). *The Origin of Modern English Society 1780 –1880*. Toronto, Toronty University Press.

Peters, T. (1987). *Thriving on Chaos: Handbook for a Management Revolution*. London, Macmillan.

—— (1992). *Liberation Management: Necessary Disorganization for the Nanosecond Nineties*. London, Macmillan.

—— (1997). *Circle Of Innovation: You Can't Shrink Your Way to Greatness*. London, Coronet.

Peters, T. and Waterman, R. (1982). *In Search of Excellence: Lessons from America's Best-Run Companies*. New York, Warner Books.

Pierson C. (1996). *The Modern State*. London, Routledge,

Pierson, P. (1994). *Dismantling the Welfare State? Reagan, Thatcher, and the Politics of Retrenchment*. Cambridge, Cambridge University Press.

Polanyi, K. (1957). *The Great Transformation*. Boston, Beacon Press.

Polivka, A., Cohany, S. and Hipple, S. (2000). Definition, composition, and economic consequences of the nonstandard workforce. In Carré, F., Ferber, M., Golden, L. and Herzenberg S. (eds), *Nonstandard work: The Nature and Challenges of Changing Employment Arrangements*, Industrial Relations Research Association. ILR Press/Cornell University Press.

Pollert, A. (ed.) (1991). *Farewell to Flexibility?* Oxford, Blackwell.

Presley, J. and Clery, S. (2001). Middle income undergraduates: where they enroll and how they pay for their education. National Centre for Education Statistics. http://nces.ed.gov/pubsearch/pubsinfo.asp?pubid=2001155

Public Citizen (2004). The ten year track record of the North American free trade agreement. US workers' jobs, wages, and economic security. http:// www.citizen.org/documents/NAFTA_10_jobs.pdf

Quay, D. (1996). Growth and dematerialization: why non-stick frying pans have lost the edge. http://econ.lse.ac.uk/~dquah/p/9610gDMTZ.pdf

Reich, R. (1992). *The Work of Nations*. New York, Vintage Books.

Rhodes, M. and Mény, Y. (eds) (1998). *The Future of European Welfare; A New Social Contract?* London, MacMillan.

Rifkind, J. (1995). *The End of Work*. New York, Tarcher Putnam.

Ritzer, G. (1993). *The McDonaldization of Society*. Thousand Oaks, CA, Pine Forge.

Rodrik, D. (1996). Why do more open economies have bigger governments? NBER working papers, no. 5537. National Bureau of Economic Research.

Sabel, C. (1994). Flexible specialisation and the re-emergence of regional economics. In Hirst, P. and Zeitlin, J. (eds), *Reversing Industrial Decline? Industrial Structure and Policy in Britain and her Competitors*. Oxford, Berg.

Sachs, J. and Warner, A. (1995). Economic Reform and the process of global integration. *Brookings Papers on Economic Activity*, vol. 1, 1–118.

Savage, M. (2000). *Class Analysis and Social Transformation*. Buckingham, Open University Press.

Saville, J. (1994). *The Consolidation of the Capitalist State 1800–1850*. London, Pluto Press.

Scharpf, F. (1998). Negative and positive integration in the political economy of European welfare states. In Rhodes, M. and Mény, Y. (eds), *The Future of European Welfare; A New Social Contract?* London, MacMillan.

Schmidt, S. (2000). Job security beliefs in the general social survey: evidence on long run trends and comparability with other surveys. In Neumark, D. (ed.), *On the Job: Is Long-term Employment a Thing of the Past?* New York, Russell Sage Foundation.

Schmidt, V. (2006). *Democracy in Europe, the EU and National Politics*. Oxford, Oxford University Press.

Schor, J. (1993). *The Overworked American: The Unexpected Decline of Leisure in America*. New York, Basic Books.

Scott, R. (2003). The high price of free trade. EPI briefing paper, no. 147. http://www.epinet.org/content.cfm/briefingpapers_bp147

Senge, P. (1990). *The Fifth Discipline: The Art and Practice of the Learning Organization*. London, Century Business.

Sennett, R. (1998). *The Corrosion of Character; The Personal Consequence of Work in the New Capitalism*. W. Norton, New York.

—— (2006). *The Culture of the New Capitalism*. New Haven, Yale University Press.

Shiller, R. (2000). *Irrational Exuberance*. Princeton, Princeton University Press.

Shin, D-M (2000). Economic policy and social policy: policy linkages in an era of globalization. *International Journal of Social Welfare* 9(1), 17–30.

Sigg, R. (2002) The challenge of ageing for social security. *International Social Security Review*, vol. 55, no. 1, 3–9.

Sklair, L. (2002). *Globalization Capitalism and its Alternatives*. Oxford, Oxford University Press.

Smelser, N. and Sweberg, R. (1994). *The Handbook of Economic Sociology*. Princeton, Princeton University Press.

Standing, G. (1999). *Global Labour Flexibility: Seeking Distributive Justice*. London, MacMillan.

Stoker, G. (1989). Restructuring local government for a post-Fordist society: the Thatcherite project? In Stewart, J. and Stoker, G. (eds), *The Future of Local Government*. Basingstoke, Palgrave Macmillan, 141–71.

Stopford, J. and Strange, S. (2002). *Rival States, Rival Firms; Competition for World Market Shares*. Cambridge, Cambridge University Press.

Streek, W. (1995). From market building to state building? Some reflections on the political economy of European social policy. In Liebfried, S. and

Pierson, P. (eds), *Fragmented Social Policy: The European Union's Social Dimension in Comparative Perspective.* Washington DC, Brookings Institution, 389–41.

Sullivan, C. (2002). What is in a name? Definitions and conceptualisations of homeworking. *New Technology, Work and Employment* 17(3), 158–64.

Swank, D. (2002). *Global Capital, Political Institutions, and Policy Change in Developed Welfare States.* Cambridge, Cambridge University Press.

—— (2005). Globalization, domestic politics and welfare state retrenchment in capitalist democracies. *Social Policy and Society*, 4(2), 183–95.

Thelen, K. (2004). *How Institutions Evolve: The Political Economy of Skills in Germany, Britain the United States and Japan.* Cambridge, Cambridge University Press.

Thompson, E. P. (1980). *The Making of the English Working Class.* London, Victor Gollancz.

Thrift, N. (2005). *Knowing Capitalism.* London, Sage.

Tilly, C. (1994). Capitalist work and labour markets. In Smelser, N. J. and Swedberg, R. (eds), *The Handbook of Economic Sociology.* Princeton, NJ, Princeton University Press, pp. 283–312.

—— (1996). *Half a Job: Bad and Goods Jobs in a Changing Labour Market.* Philadelphia, Templeton University Press.

Timmins, N. (1996). *The Five Giants: A Biography of the Welfare State.* London, Fontana Press.

Tipple, S. (1999). Worker displacement in the mid 1990s. *Monthly Labor Review*, July. http://www.bls.gov/opub/mlr/1999/07/art2abs.htm

Toffler, A. (1970). *Future Shock.* London, The Bodley Head.

Touraine, A. (1971). *The Post-industrial Society.* New York, Random House.

Tripplet, J. (1999). Economic statistics, the new economy, and the productivity slowdown. Business Economics, April, 13–17. www.brookings.org/es/research/productivity/Trip 4_99.PDF

Uchitelle, L. (2006). *The Disposable American.* New York, Knopf.

Uchitelle, L. and Kleinfield, N. R. (1996). On the Battlefields of Business. *The New York Times*, 3 March.

UNCTAD (1994). World investment report. Transnational corporations, employment and the workplace. United Nations Conference on Trade and Development. WIR 94 www.unctad.org

—— (2001) World investment report. Promoting linkages. United Nations Conference on Trade and Development. WIR01. www.unctad.org

—— (2004) World investment report. The shift services. United Nations Conference on Trade and Development. WIR04. www.unctad.org

—— (2006) World investment report. FDI from developing and transition economies: implications for development. WIR06. www.unctad.org

—— (2007) World investment report. Transnational corporations, extractive industries and development. WIR07. www.unctad.org

United States Chamber of Commerce (2004). Globalization and technology. July. http://www.uschamber.com/government/issues/technology/globalizationandtechnology.htm

Van Ark, B., Inklaar, R., McGukin, R. and Timmer, M. (2003). The employment effects of the 'new economy'. A comparison of the European Union
and the United States. *National Institute Economic Review*, no. 184, 86–98.

Vosko, L. (2000). *Temporary Work: The Gendered Rise of a Precarious
Employment Relationship*. Toronto, University of Toronto Press.

—— (2004). Confronting the norm: gender and the international regulation
of precarious work. Research paper. Law Commission of Canada.
http://www.lcc.gc.ca/research_project/er/tvw/resources/vosko_confronting
-en.asp

Vosko, L., Zukewich, N. and Crawford, C. (2003). Precarious jobs: A new
typology of employment. *Perspectives*, vol. 4, no. 10, 16–26.

Walters, I. (1994). Tempting fate. Reason Magazine. http://www.
reason.com.contrib/show/649.xml

Watson, M. (1999). Globalization and the development of the British political economy. In Marsh, D. et al., *Post War British Politics in Perspective*.
Cambridge, Polity Press.

Weisbrot, M. and Baker, D. (2005). Social security 'reform': a solution in
search of a problem, centre for economic and policy research.
http://www.cepr.net/columns/baker_weisbrot/mark_weisbrot_dean_baker
_1_23_05.htm

Weiss, L. (1998). *The Myth of the Powerless State, Governing the Economy in a
Global Era*. Cambridge, Polity Press.

Wheen, F. (2004). *How Mumbo Jumbo Conquered the World: A Short History
of Modern Delusions*. London, Fourth Estate.

Wiatrowski, W. (2004). Medical and retirement plan coverage: exploring the
decline in recent years. *Monthly Labor Review*, August, 29–36.

Wilmott, H. (1995). Managing the academics: commodification and control
in the development of university education in the U.K. *Human Relations*,
vol. 48, no. 9, 993–1027.

Winner, L. (1977). *Autonomous Technology*. Cambridge, MIT Press.

World Economic Forum (2005). The economic implications of ageing.
http://www.genpolicy.com/initiatives/economic_implications_of_age_agen
da.html

Wray, L. R. (2006). Social security in an aging society. *Review of Political
Economy*, vol. 18, no. 3, 391–411.

WTO (2004). Regional trade agreements: facts and figures. http://www.
wto.org/english/tratop_e/region_e/regfac_e.htm

Yeates, N. (2001). *Globalization and Social Policy*. London, Sage.

Zysman, J. (1996). The myths of a 'global' economy: enduring national and
emerging regional realities. *New Political Economy*, vol. 1 (2), 157–84.

Zysman, J. and Newman, J. (2004). How revolutionary is the revolution: will
there be a political economy of the digital era? Working paper 161. Berkeley
Roundtable on the International Economy (BRIE). http://brie.berkeley.
edu/research/workingpapers.htm

Index